Web Analytics Strategies for Information Professionals

S0-AAD-250

ALA TechSource purchases fund advocacy, awareness, and accreditation programs for library professionals worldwide.

Web Analytics Strategies for Information Professionals

A LITA Guide

Tabatha Farney
and
Nina McHale

ALA TechSource

An imprint of the American Library Association

CHICAGO   2013

© 2013 by the American Library Association. Any claim of copyright is subject to applicable limitations and exceptions, such as rights of fair use and library copying pursuant to Sections 107 and 108 of the U.S. Copyright Act. No copyright is claimed for content in the public domain, such as works of the U.S. government.

Printed in the United States of America

17 16 15 14 13   5 4 3 2 1

Extensive effort has gone into ensuring the reliability of the information in this book; however, the publisher makes no warranty, express or implied, with respect to the material contained herein.

ISBNs: 978-1-55570-897-9 (paper); 978-1-55570-954-9 (PDF); 978-1-55570-955-6 (ePub); 978-1-55570-956-3 (Kindle). For more information on digital formats, visit the ALA Store at alastore.ala.org and select eEditions.

Library of Congress Cataloging-in-Publication Data

Farney, Tabatha.
    Web analytics strategies for information professionals : a LITA guide / Tabatha Farney and Nina McHale.
        pages   cm. — (LITA guide)
    Includes bibliographical references and index.
    ISBN 978-1-55570-897-9 (alk. paper)
    1. Library Web sites—Management. 2. Library Web sites—Statistical methods. 3. Web usage mining. 4. Library statistics. I. McHale, Nina. II. Library and Information Technology Association (U.S.) III. Title.
    Z674.75.W67F37 2013
    025.17'4—dc23   2012044515

Book design in Berkeley and Avenir. Cover image © roopert/Shutterstock. Inc.

♾ This paper meets the requirements of ANSI/NISO Z39.48-1992 (Permanence of Paper).

Contents

Preface   vii

■ PART 1 ■
Introduction to Web Analytics in Libraries
Tabatha Farney and Nina McHale

1 Understanding Web Analytics for Libraries   3

2 Talking the Talk: Web Analytics Terms
   and Definitions   15

3 Selecting and Evaluating a Web Analytics Tool   31

4 Creating Customized Web Analytics Reports
   for Libraries   51

5 Action-Oriented Analytics: Turning Data
   into Decisions   79

6 Communicating Website Usage within
   Your Library   95

7 Mobile Analytics in Libraries   115

■ PART 2 ■
Using Web Analytics in Libraries Case Studies

8 The Right Tools for the Job: Using Analytics
   to Drive Design   131
   Joelle Pitts and Tara L. Coleman

9 Using Web Analytics Tools to Revise a Humanities
   Library Website   147
   Harriett E. Green, Jordan Ruud, and Andrew Walsh

10 Web Analytics Applied to Online Catalog Usage at
   the University of Denver   167
   Christopher C. Brown

11 Optimizing Open-Source Web Analytics Tools for
   Increased Security of WordPress and Drupal   183
   Junior Tidal

APPENDIXES

   A Glossary of Web Analytics Terms and Concepts   203
   B Web Analytics Tool Profiles   207
   C Bibliography and Suggested Resources   211

About the Authors and Chapter Contributors   213
Index   217

Preface

As libraries continue to forge ahead into the brave new digital world, tracking usage in our digital spaces is becoming increasingly important. Library staff have long kept statistics of usage of physical resources, such as gate counts, reference and circulations transactions, and shelving and reshelving statistics. Many a paper tally sheet has been used to compile a report for administration to provide a day-to-day snapshot of how users interact with library resources and services. The same holds true in the digital realm, and for the same reasons: at assessment time, managers need to account for resources allocated, and directors need big-picture information to share with their superiors and stakeholders to justify continued funding and support for library resources and services. Knowing which online resources, whether locally created or licensed from vendors, are highly used—and which are not—can help project managers and administrators make important decisions about precious resources, especially staff time and training.

The web analytics guru Avinash Kaushik likens the analysis of web statistics to the reading of tea leaves: it's not a precise science, but one can detect and track general patterns that are informative and enlightening. Kaushik (2010) provides an overview of web analytics and lays out the framework for commercial organizations to effectively analyze their web statistics. This LITA guide differs from Kaushik's contributions, however, in that it focuses on web analytics in the library world. Understanding "customer" behavior is critical in the world of online commerce, but the same holds true in library web environments. Other nonprofit-based organizations can also refer to this book, as it focuses on using web analytics for noncommerce websites. Additionally, since this book focuses on libraries that seldom have budgets for commercial web analytics tools that businesses can afford, we focus primarily on free or low-cost tools like Google Analytics, Piwik, and

AWStats. Although we also discuss other tools, we use these three in the majority of examples.

Once a web analytics tool of choice is in place, a library can collect and harness the data. Web analytics data can reveal how website users find and use a website, basic technological information about the user, what content is being consumed, and trends in user behaviors. Additionally, library staff can craft website related goals and use website statistics to measure the effectiveness of their websites against their goals. All of this data is collected and analyzed automatically, without ever disturbing the website user.

Web statistics aren't just for web librarians and developers; they can inform libraries of online resource usage, peak times of library use, and how website users are actually interacting with the site. These data should interest all areas of the library: technical services can verify which resources visitors use and how they find them, public services can learn which content visitors need, and administrators can better understand the impact of the library's online services. *Web Analytics Strategies for Information Professionals* emphasizes the importance not only of collecting and analyzing website use data but also of reporting, sharing, and acting on those data within the library. This book takes readers through a step-by-step process of understanding and using web analytics for libraries with examples of how libraries can turn data into actions.

ORGANIZATION

Chapter 1, "Understanding Web Analytics for Libraries," introduces the general concept of web analytics. A detailed look at how libraries can use analytics follows, as well as some pro tips for beginners. Next is a look at which data are actually captured by statistics-gathering web analytics tools, and how individual data points can be used to create bigger pictures of web use. Analytics is not without its unique set of challenges, however, so the first chapter concludes with the caveats and a description of shortcomings in analytics tools and practices.

Chapter 2, "Talking the Talk: Web Analytics Terms and Definitions," demystifies the terminology commonly used by web analytics tools, singling out which are particularly of interest to libraries and information centers. This chapter explains basic concepts, such as visits, visitors, traffic sources and referrers, landing and exit pages, and bounce rate, in addition to more advanced web analytics concepts, like conversion and key performance indicators. Web analytics tools provide detailed information on who comes to the site, where they have come from, how long they stay, and where they go while they are on the site.

In chapter 3, "Selecting and Evaluating a Web Analytics Tool," we take a closer look at available analytics tools. Google Analytics is wildly popular in library circles—and it is the most likely to integrate with a catalog, content management system, or other online tool—but it is by no means the only option. There are several commercial and open-source offerings from which to choose; some of them are hosted by the vendor, and others are installed locally on the web server. As with any software products, the features and reporting differ widely as well. The chapter also offers an overview of planning for statistics-tracking software, with tips on planning usage, budgeting for tools and staff time to implement, getting support, and testing.

Chapter 4, "Creating Customized Web Analytics Reports for Libraries," introduces core concepts in web analytics to help libraries go beyond using standard data reports. In this chapter, you'll learn how to efficiently segment data to analyze specific user groups and create customizable reports tailored to your library's needs. The chapter discusses several highly useful reports and demonstrates how libraries can use them.

After gaining an understanding of the basic and advanced web analytics concepts, it is time to learn how to turn data into actions. Chapter 5, "Action-Oriented Analytics: Turning Data into Decisions," discusses the process of benchmarking data so that libraries can better measure improvement to a website. It also provides examples of web analytics strategies that incorporate data to measure website goals and how to use the data for various purposes, ranging from measuring the effectiveness of a marketing campaign to assisting in a website redesign process.

There are a variety of uses of web analytics data, and those uses should not be restricted to just the web services area in the library. Chapter 6, "Communicating Website Usage within Your Library," outlines potential audiences for different segments of website use data and, more important, how that data can be shared effectively and efficiently within an organization. This chapter discusses the best practices for sharing the data and the data-export methods that are available to simplify this process.

Chapter 7, "Mobile Analytics in Libraries," discusses mobile analytics, or the use of web analytics to monitor both mobile users and mobile web presences. Even if your library does not currently offer a mobile version of its website, it is important to track how mobile users are interacting with it. Tracking mobile use comes with a few technical caveats, which this chapter covers. How much of your traffic is mobile? What content do your mobile users access? Collecting this type of data can make a case for mobile development. If you do have a mobile site, what are its goals, and how can you use web analytics to ensure that the mobile site is achieving them?

Finally, the case studies presented in chapter 8–11 bring together all these new web analytics terms and concepts. Chapters 8 and 9 provide two different case studies—the first from the University of Illinois at Urbana-Champaign and the second from Kansas State University—demonstrating how libraries can use the data during the website redesign process. Chapter 10 compares the usage of two library catalog platforms at the University of Denver. Chapter 11 examines how open-source web analytics tools can help libraries monitor security issues in Drupal and WordPress, and how this was put into practice at New York City College of Technology (City University of New York). These real-world success stories illustrate web analytics in action and the value that they add in assessing online resources and services in libraries.

This LITA guide concludes with three handy appendixes. Appendix A, "Glossary of Web Analytics Terms and Concepts," is a handy reference to the jargon of analytics. Appendix B is a comparative shopping list of the analytics tools discussed in the pages of this guide to help you jump-start your analytics practice. Appendix C is a bibliography and list of further reading for those readers wishing to delve even deeper. Finally, "About the Authors and Chapter Contributors" provides a bit more information about all the analytics experts in the library world who have brought you this guide.

It is our hope that with this guide, librarians and library staff will become as comfortable tracking, interpreting, and reporting web statistics as they have been previously with pencil and paper. Turning these data into decisions and actions will help library staff stay informed about how their websites are being used and promote the development of responsive, user-centric websites.

REFERENCES

Kaushik, Avinash. 2010. *Web Analytics 2.0: The Art of Online Accountability and Science of Customer Centricity*. Indianapolis, IN: Wiley.

PART 1

Introduction
to Web Analytics
in Libraries

Tabatha Farney and Nina McHale

Chapter One

Understanding Web Analytics for Libraries

L ibraries love to collect use data. We track the use of the physical library by keeping gate counts, recording the number of transactions at the reference desk or other service points and counting how many times a book is checked out. It is, therefore, only natural to also monitor traffic on the library's digital presences, including its main website, online catalog, electronic resources, blogs, and virtual services. The best way to do this is to implement a web analytics tool that can unobtrusively gather use data automatically from each of the library's web presences. Since the creation of the World Wide Web, people have been interested in gathering website use data (Kaushik 2007). Today, setting up a web analytics tool to track a website takes mere minutes, but the data the tool provides are invaluable to libraries. This chapter introduces the concept of web analytics and how libraries can leverage web analytics data. We provide advice to those who are new to web analytics and conclude the chapter with a discussion of what web analytics can provide and what it cannot. After reading this chapter, you will start to understand how libraries can benefit from monitoring their website use data.

DEFINING WEB ANALYTICS

Web analytics is more than just monitoring use data on a website. According to the Web Analytics Association (2008, 3), "Web Analytics is the measurement, collection, analysis and reporting of Internet data for the purposes of understanding and optimizing Web usage." To simplify, web analytics is the process of gathering and interpreting the virtual traffic on a website to learn how users interact with a site. By understanding user interactions, libraries can improve their websites to better serve their users' needs. Web analytics empowers libraries to go beyond collecting data for the sake of collecting data and to turn those data into actions.

The concept of web analytics is often confused with web analytics tools, such as Google Analytics, Piwik, and AWStats, to name a few. These tools assist in analyzing and filtering website use data into intelligible reports. There is a great variety of web analytics tools available, and each one differs in how it reports use data; we discuss this more in chapter 3. Although selecting the right web analytics tool for your library is important, it is ultimately a human who decides which data are essential and how those data should be used. That is the true practice of web analytics. You do not even need a web analytics tool to analyze your website use data, but it will help you save a great deal of time in synthesizing your data.

So how does a web analytics tool collect and organize a website's use data? It depends on the web analytics tool used. In general, web analytics tools use

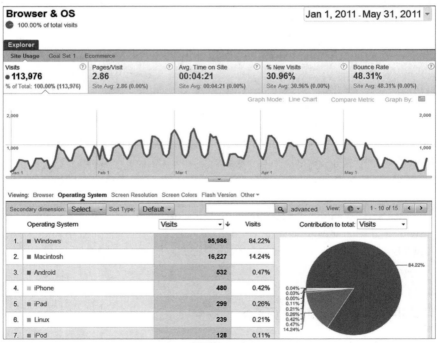

FIGURE 1.1
Browser and OS Technology Report, Google Analytics,
Kraemer Family Library, University of Colorado Colorado Springs

two methods for gathering data: web server log analysis or a tracking code, such as JavaScript tags. Although they collect use data differently, both record when a person's Internet browser "hits," or requests a file from, a website. A file request includes loading a web page in a browser or opening a picture or file on a computer. A web analytics tool does more than just record the hit; it instantly captures data about that hit, including the name of the file accessed and a date and time stamp of when the action occurred, along with data about the machine or device that downloaded the file, including its browser type, operating system, screen resolutions, and more. That data are then collected and made accessible into reports (see figure 1.1) for further analysis.

Web Server Log Analysis or Tracking Code?

A web server automatically records interactions on a website into log files that are stored on the server. Web server log analysis is software that must be installed on the same web server that houses the website that is being tracked. The software synthesizes the log files from the website, which are mere text files, as demonstrated in figure 1.2, into use reports.

```
109.206.179.218 - - [11/Sep/2011:07:26:41 -0500] "GET / HTTP/1.1" 302 - "http://www.google.com" "Mozilla/5.0 (Windows; U; Windows NT
6.1; ru; rv:1.9.2.3) Gecko/20100401 Firefox/3.6.3"46.109.196.167 - - [11/Sep/2011:08:07:22 -0500] "GET /libnotes/ HTTP/1.0" 200 38366
"http://uccslib.org/libnotes/" "Mozilla/4.0 (compatible; MSIE 5.5; Windows NT 5.0; T312461)"46.109.196.167 - - [11/Sep/2011:08:07:23
-0500] "GET /libnotes/wp-content/uploads/2011/08/board.jpg HTTP/1.0" 200 193790 "http://uccslib.org/libnotes/wp-
content/uploads/2011/08/board.jpg" "Mozilla/4.0 (compatible; MSIE 5.5; Windows NT 5.0; T312461)"67.195.114.219 - -
[11/Sep/2011:09:09:04 -0500] "GET /libnotes/category/news/ HTTP/1.0" 200 13182 "-" "Mozilla/5.0 (compatible; Yahoo! Slurp;
http://help.yahoo.com/help/us/ysearch/slurp)"]
```

FIGURE 1.2
Log Files, Kraemer Family Library, University
of Colorado Colorado Springs

Tracking code is snippets of code that must be inserted on every single web page you want your web analytics tool to track. The most popular tracking codes currently in use by web analytics tools involve JavaScript tags or scripts that set a cookie on a user's web browser. Web analytics tools that use this method will generate the tracking code (see figure 1.3) for you, which you will then need to manually add to your website. JavaScript tags can be placed either at the beginning of the web page in the head-tag section (<head>) or close to the bottom of the page right before closing the body tag (</body>). However, the location of the tracking code, especially JavaScript, has an impact on how data are collected and the time it takes for a web page to load, so typically we recommend placing the code as close

(cont.)

```
<script type="text/javascript">

var _gaq = _gaq || [];
_gaq.push(['_setAccount', 'UA-2728892-3']);
_gaq.push(['_trackPageview']);

(function() {
  var ga = document.createElement('script'); ga.type = 'text/javascript'; ga.async = true;
  ga.src = ('https:' == document.location.protocol ? 'https://ssl' : 'http://www') + '.google-analytics.com/ga.js';
  var s = document.getElementsByTagName('script')[0]; s.parentNode.insertBefore(ga, s);
})();

</script>
```

FIGURE 1.3

**Tracking Code, Google Analytics, Kraemer Family Library,
University of Colorado Colorado Springs**

to the bottom of the body section as possible (Carlos 2006). That said, it is best to first check your web analytics tool's documentation to see where it suggests that the tracking code be placed. Libraries that use a template to manage their websites can easily add the tracking code to just the template file, which will then automatically insert the web analytics tool on every web page to which that template is applied. Major web content management systems, such as Drupal and WordPress, also make it easy to integrate statistics tracking since they are template driven. If your website does not use a template, you will have to add the tracking code to each individual web page on your website to track the entire site. This may prove too daunting on a large legacy site that consists of individual HTML pages, but even installing tracking code on just the home page and other key pages can still offer valuable, if incomplete, data, on how your site is used. Log file analysis may offer a more complete solution in this scenario.

So which is best for tracking your website use data: web server log analysis or tracking code? As Avinash Kaushik (2010, 139) finds, it "is like comparing apples and watermelons." Because log analysis and tracking code are two different methods of collecting and measuring website use data, they will not produce the same results; therefore, it is difficult to compare them directly, yet both are completely acceptable methods for tracking website use data.

USING WEB ANALYTICS IN LIBRARIES

Web analytics is a huge industry. There are entire companies dedicated to helping organizations use their website use data effectively. Commercial web analytics tools, such as Webtrends, Omniture, and ClickTale, are used by businesses to track website use and can easily range in price from hundreds to thousands of dollars per month. Because most libraries do not have the luxury of being able to afford such all-encompassing tools or to hire a web analytics consultant to help interpret use data, we have intentionally focused on inexpensive or free web analytics tools that are more accessible to libraries. Yet web staffing and access to technology can vary greatly from library to library. Large libraries may have an entire department (and staff) dedicated to maintaining their web presences and web servers, whereas smaller libraries may have only one person who edits the website, who may or may not be permitted to access the web server's logs. Some libraries may even be in a completely hosted environment where they can only edit content and basic design elements but cannot access the web server or even the actual back-end code of the website. To access web analytics, libraries must either have direct access to the server logs of the web server that houses their website or be able to edit—or, at the very least, request that another person edit—the code of the web page to add the custom web analytics tool's tracking code to the website.

Many libraries have access to web analytics but do not use it to its full potential. In fact, your library may already be using some basic web analytics process to produce annual reports to show the volume of traffic a website has received. For example, each year the Association of Research Libraries asks research libraries to report the total of "virtual visits" to their library's website as part of its supplementary statistics request (Bland and Kyrillidou 2009). Many public library boards expect monthly reports of web usage, as well. Any type of library may already be creating internal annual reports that reflect website usage; however, this use of web analytics is merely a virtual gate count of a library's website and does not even begin to tap the potential for what web analytics can do for library websites. We also find that some libraries are using web analytics in innovative ways; if your library is one of them, kudos! We showcase several examples of these in chapters 8–11.

GETTING STARTED WITH WEB ANALYTICS

Our advice to those new to web analytics is in the words of Arthur C. Clarke: "DON'T PANIC." Learning about web analytics is comparable to learning about any new subfield related to library and information science: there is always new jargon to acquire. To make it more complicated, each web analytics tool may have its own set of definitions to understand.

Beyond the terminology, it is essential to understand that web analytics is only as useful as the amount of planning put into it. Many libraries suffer from the "set it and forget it" mentality, in which they implement a web analytics tool on their website and then do little with the data collected. Web analytics is a dynamic process. As your data needs change, you may have to modify what use data you analyze and report. We encourage web analytics newcomers to integrate the review of web analytics reports into their regular routines. That said, avoid reading through all the massive web analytics reports; not every single piece of data recorded is going to be useful. You must decide which data are of use or interest to your library; as noted, this will likely change over time. Identify the data that matter and when they matter. For example, whenever a significant edit is made to a web page, pay particular attention to the use data on that specific page to see how your users are reacting to it. Your job responsibilities will determine which web analytics reports you will want to review regularly (meaning at least every two to four weeks). Taking a few minutes out of your schedule to go through your web analytics data will help you stay informed on—among other things—what content is being used (or not used) on your website, which will help you make improved content decisions.

You should understand all the options your web analytics tool provides in order to maximize your ability to use your website use data effectively. Be prepared to take the time to experiment with your tool and consult its documentation. Research your web analytics tool and see what type of support is available for it. There are numerous web analytics blogs out there, but focus and read the ones that discuss your specific tool. Doing so will help show you the capability of your web analytics tool and will keep you informed of new features to use.

WHAT WEB ANALYTICS TOOLS ACTUALLY REPORT

So, what information can you glean from analyzing your website usage? As you will learn, each web analytics tool creates reports differently; however, each tool should include the basic web analytics reports. These reports inform you of the following:

- how visitors find your website
- how much the visitors are interacting with your website
- which content your visitors use or do not use
- which type of web browsers and computers the visitors use to access your website

These are typically referred to as standard reports, and they are only the tip of the web analytics iceberg. Some web analytics tools have a custom reporting ability along with other capabilities that will boost your library's ability to use its web use data more effectively.

Besides their reporting functionality, web analytics tools are designed to store website use data. Once implemented, the tool automatically collects and manages the data gathered from your website. If you have been running a web analytics tool on your website for more than three years, then that tool should contain the three years' worth of data for you to sift through—unless for some reason you decide to delete the use data or log files. We generally do not recommend deleting your website use data, and some hosted web analytics tools may not give you the option to delete your own data. The benefit of storing your website use data is that your tool will give you the option to look at all that data at once or to break it down into specific date ranges. Most tools allow you to at least look at data for an individual day, month, or year, and others permit you to look at your data more granularly through the use of customizable date ranges. This makes creating that annual report a breeze, but it also opens up the possibility for you to compare your website use over different time periods. For example, you can monitor use trends, such as an increase or decrease of use, over time. This is useful for tracking different versions of a web page or website because it allows you to compare use data on the old and new versions of a page to see whether a new design had the intended effect. We discuss this process more in chapter 5.

LIMITATIONS IN WEB ANALYTICS

Web analytics is an extremely powerful practice and can reveal a lot about how visitors use a website; however, it is not a precise measurement, nor can it answer all of your potential questions involving website use. By understanding the limitations of web analytics—and of your web analytics tool—you are better prepared to use the strategies and tools to their fullest potential.

Inexact Measurement in Web Analytics

To start, web analytics is not the exact measurement of your website's use. You could use two web analytics tools to track the same website and get different results in each. What's going on? Many factors have an impact on the accuracy of data collection and reporting in web analytics tools. Again, the type of tool, whether it is server-side tracking through web log analytics or click-side tracking through the implementation of tracking code or cookies, will have an impact on your data results. Also, how that tool is implemented will affect the data accuracy, as demonstrated earlier in the discussion of where to add the tracking code on a web page. Yet even if you use two different web analytics tools that both use the same tracking method and are implemented in the same way, each tool will still report contrary results, because each web analytics tool tracks website use *differently*. No matter what web analytics tool you choose, there will likely be inaccuracies in the data. Do not let this impede your web analytics use; rather, take the time to understand how your specific web analytics tool collects data and which factors affect the accuracy of that data. There may be best practices for implementing your web analytics tool to maximize its data accuracy.

Tracking Groups of Users

A popular question libraries have when it comes to web analytics is, "Can I track specific groups of users?" It depends. Yes, web analytics can assist in tracking specific groups of users, but with limitations. Basically, the power to track a specific group of users depends on whether your web analytics tool provides you with the necessary data to segment, or separate, user groups. If you want to track how a specific age group or class, such as teenagers, uses your website, you will find that doing so is beyond the scope of most web analytics tools because they do not track information about the age of users. You could implement a web analytics tool on a specific website designed for your teen users, but your web analytics tool still could not report how many teenagers used the site, since it does not track that level of detail.

However, once you are familiar with the data that your web analytics tool tracks, you will find that is possible to track some user groups. For example, most web analytics tools can separate your mobile device users from your regular users because those tools collect data about the users' operating systems. A mobile device has a different operating system than a typical computer, so it easy to see who is on a computer running a Mac operating system (OS X) versus who is on an iPad or iPhone (iOS). Even if the necessary information is tracked, segmenting your user groups is not always easy. Many web analytics tools track the geographic location of users; however, tracking a group of users based on geographic location—for instance, users inside the physical library compared to users outside the library— is complicated and not always possible. Most web analytics tools track users' geographic location by their Internet protocol (IP) address, which is not a perfect measurement for various reasons (see chapter 2). So, keep in mind that tracking users by groups is possible, but it is not always accurate.

Tracking Individuals

At this point you may be asking, "If I can track some groups of users, can I track individual users?" The main problem with this question is that we define users as individual people in the library world. In the web analytics world, users are called "visitors," and a visitor is defined as a computer or device accessing the website, not the individual person. This means that a person who accesses your website from a computer in the library and also accesses your website on a smart phone is counted as two different visitors, because the web analytics tool registers two different devices. Conversely, visitors might also be underreported when they use computers in a computing lab or commons: if ten people use one commons computer, they are recorded as a single user. Even in the case when a person always uses the same computer or device to access your website, your web analytics tool may not be able to recognize that user as the same person because of a potential lack of persistence in IP address assignments and web browser cookies. So, although it is technically possible to monitor a specific IP address's interactions on a website, your web analytics tool cannot confirm that it is the same person controlling the machine, or even the same computer is using that IP address, since IP addresses, for the most part, are not static. This makes tracking individual users problematic in most web analytics tools.

11

User Motivation

Last, web analytics shows how your users are interacting with a website, but it is difficult, if not outright impossible, to divine the motivation behind their actions. Web analytics is purely a quantitative measurement. To get additional qualitative data, such as user feedback, you will need to do regular usability testing of the website. The good news is that web analytics and usability testing complement each other. A web analytics report may reveal a potential problem on a website, but it may not be clear what is causing the problem. This is the time to do some basic usability tests. Need assistance in designing your usability studies? There is another LITA guide dedicated to usability testing in libraries titled *Making Library Websites Usable* and written by Thomas Lehman and Terry Nikkel (2008).

PRIVACY CONCERNS AND WEB ANALYTICS

Given our profession's dedication to protecting our users' privacy, it is important to understand how web analytics tools collect personal information. In a world where libraries adamantly delete a patron's borrowing history to protect that person's privacy, libraries need to be aware of the privacy issues that web analytics may raise. Web analytics tools have the ability to track a computer's IP address, and this is particularly sensitive because that address can be used to identify the network, Internet service provider (ISP), and approximate geographic location of that computer. There are websites like IP Location Finder (www.iplocationfinder.com), shown in figure 1.4, that are designed to look up information about individual IP

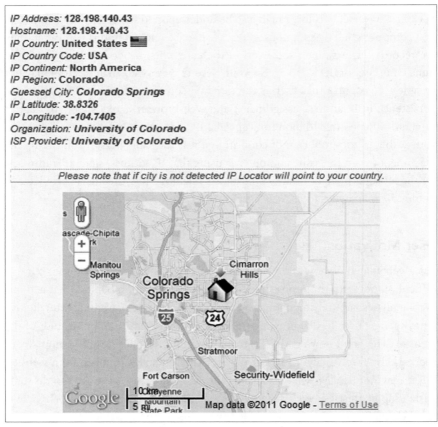

FIGURE 1.4
IP Location Finder and Visual IP Locator,
University of Colorado Colorado Springs

addresses. With web analytics, you can track to see how an individual IP address, which could be used to locate a specific machine, is using a website. Sounds a bit invasive, right? Take comfort that many hosted web analytics tools, such as Google Analytics, have privacy policies that state that direct access to IP addresses is not permitted (www.google.com/analytics/learn/privacy.html). Libraries that use web server log analysis tools, such as AWStats, can access a full list of IP addresses that visit a website, so organizations running these tools need to decide how they want to handle that data. No matter which web analytics data you have access to, Kate Marek (2011) suggests that libraries that actively use web analytics should create a privacy policy for their website outlining which data are collected and how they will be used. This policy should include visible and clear "opt-out" procedures for users who do not what to contribute their use data.

Suggestions for Handling IP Addresses

As you will read in chapter 2, IP addresses are assigned and managed by an Internet service provider that may or may not use persistent IP addresses on individual machines. Regardless, libraries must be sensitive to privacy matters when handling IP data. Libraries with direct access to IP addresses through their web analytics reports need to do the following:

Make sure that data are secured on a web server or where they are hosted. If you have questions about the security of your web analytics tool or reports, consult your systems administrators.

Remove the IP addresses if are you exporting your web analytics reports off the web server. Many web analytics tools allow you to export reports into Microsoft Excel or the other programs that make it easier to share this information with library administrators or others who do not have access to the web analytics tools. If you export a report with IP addresses in, remove just the IP addresses if possible and keep all the other information. The actual IP address numbers mean little to most people and would not detract from most reports.

State that the website collects use data, including IP addresses, in your privacy policy. Be open with your users about what an IP address is and what it can and cannot reveal.

Libraries that do not have direct access to IP data should still state in their privacy policy that a third-party web analytics tool collects IP addresses and link to that web analytics tool's privacy policy.

CONCLUSION

Web analytics can serve many needs in libraries, ranging from producing annual reports based on website use data for library administrators to helping library web-content creators and web managers make website revisions based on the use data. However, it is essential to understand that committing to web analytics is more than just implementing a web analytics tool. Good practice of web analytics analysis requires regular human input and action. Libraries can use web analytics to find out how users are interacting with a website, but those data serve no purpose unless libraries act on that knowledge.

REFERENCES

Bland, Les, and Martha Kyrillidou, eds. 2009. *ARL Supplementary Statistics 2007–2008*. Washington, DC: Association of Research Libraries. www.arl.org/bm~doc/sup08.pdf.

Carlos, Sean. 2006. "Web Analytics Embedded JavaScript Page Tracking Code: Place at the Top or Bottom of the Page?" *Antezeta Web Marketing*. http://antezeta.com/news/javascript-embedded-page-tracking-position.

Kaushik, Avinash. 2007. *Web Analytics: An Hour a Day*. Indianapolis, IN: Sybex.

———. 2010. *Web Analytics 2.0: The Art of Online Accountability and Science of Customer Centricity*. Indianapolis, IN: Wiley.

Lehman, Tom, and Terry Nikkel. 2008. *Making Library Web Sites Usable: A LITA Guide*. New York: Neal-Schuman.

Marek, Kate. 2011. "Web Analytics Overview." *Using Web Analytics in the Library*. Chicago: ALA TechSource.

Web Analytics Association. 2008. "Web Analytics Definitions." www.webanalyticsassociation.org/resource/resmgr/PDF_standards/WebAnalyticsDefinitions.pdf.

Chapter Two

Talking the Talk
Web Analytics Terms and Definitions

The library world is full of jargon. Does an average non–library worker know what RDA, OPAC, or even the phrase "reference interview" actually mean? Probably not. Web analytics comes with its own set of jargon, too, but many of the terms sound misleadingly commonplace, such as a *bounce*—which has nothing to do with a ball. In the web analytics world, the Digital Analytics Association, formerly known as the Web Analytics Association, has created a standard definitions document, but not every web analytics tool conforms to it. So, you may find some discrepancies between the terminology that we use here and the terminology that your tool uses. Yet most web analytics tools include a help section that also defines the terms they use. You will find that many of the definitions we use are still the same in a majority of the web analytics tools available. With that in mind, this chapter aims to clarify the basic analytics terms and concepts. Additionally, it highlights standard web analytics metrics and reports that are of particular interest in library web environments. All the terms and concepts introduced here are also included in appendix A, "Glossary of Web Analytics Terms and Concepts," for quick reference.

METRICS AND REPORTS

We have already casually used the terms *metrics* and *reports*, but we have not taken the time to define them. A metric is exactly what it implies: a unit of measurement,

Pageviews	Unique Pageviews	Avg. Time on Page	Bounce Rate	% Exit
475,905	**346,825**	**00:01:38**	**58.94%**	**36.67%**
% of Total: 100.00% (475,905)	% of Total: 100.00% (346,825)	Site Avg: 00:01:38 (0.00%)	Site Avg: 58.94% (0.00%)	Site Avg: 36.67% (0.00%)

Primary Dimension: Page   Page Title   Other ▾

Plot Rows   Secondary dimension ▾   Sort Type: Default ▾   🔍 advanced   ▦ ◉ Ξ ᴝ Ⅲ

Page		Pageviews ↓	Unique Pageviews	Avg. Time on Page	Bounce Rate	% Exit
☐ 1. /ald/	🔗	200,472	151,949	00:02:38	59.27%	53.54%
☐ 2. /ald/aldsearch	🔗	65,809	25,629	00:00:55	59.54%	15.17%
☐ 3. /ald/books	🔗	14,746	10,544	00:01:07	32.17%	25.50%
☐ 4. /ald/locations-and-hours	🔗	12,135	9,526	00:01:56	64.31%	53.84%
☐ 5. /ald/downloads	🔗	11,890	9,285	00:00:11	21.26%	2.54%
☐ 6. /ald/movies	🔗	9,066	6,147	00:00:53	44.20%	16.17%
☐ 7. /ald/ebooks	🔗	7,871	6,209	00:04:09	58.33%	60.21%
☐ 8. /ald/content/freegal	🔗	5,563	3,344	00:05:39	57.71%	49.67%
☐ 9. /ald/programs-and-classes	🔗	5,333	3,639	00:02:20	50.57%	45.42%
☐ 10. /ald/research-and-databases	🔗	5,196	3,606	00:00:28	12.35%	6.10%

FIGURE 2.1
Pages Report, Google Analytics, Arapahoe Library District,
Englewood, Colorado

such as page view. Avinash Kaushik (2010) explains that a metric can be either a count, a totaled number such as page views, or a ratio, a figure that is one number divided by another number, such as the bounce rate.

A web analytics report is a combination of metrics into one document. Most web analytics tools come with standard reports, which are generic reports that contain commonly used metrics. For example, a standard content report contains the page views metric along with other metrics that complement these data (see figure 2.1). Even more desirable are custom reports, which allow libraries to create individualized reports containing the metrics they wish to compare and monitor. Custom reports are extremely useful and are discussed in depth in chapter 4.

VISITS AND PAGE VIEWS

"Visits" is an essential metric. Visits are, simply, interactions on a website from an individual browser over a specified period of time. Different web analytics tools may refer to a visit as a session or visitor, but essentially the terms imply the same thing: someone accessed a website and interacted with it. Visits should not be confused with page views, which report the instances that a visitor accesses a single web page or online document. Page views are great for identifying the content a library user is actually using, and visits are better for quantifying the number of sessions on a website. The visits metric is roughly analogous to gate count in the physical library realm, whereas the page views metric would record each inter-action a person had once in the library.

Many libraries have an annual report that tracks website usage, and it is easy to pull information from the visits metric to satisfy this requirement. It is best to use visits to track overall website usage since a visit encompasses all pages a visitor interacted with in one sitting. When it comes to reports, you will find that the metric of visits or page views is commonly included. In fact, a "top content report" is a standard web analytics report that relies heavily on page views.

Top Content Reports

Top content reports use page views to reveal which individual pages in a site are the most popular. In library environments, it is common for the top page to be the home page, followed by a database A–Z web page(s) or similar resource listing, with a "long tail" trailing off beyond those two points. This report is useful to show what parts of your website are actually being used. For content creators, this report identifies the web pages that should be closely monitored to ensure that they are routinely updated. Libraries should also consider the web pages that do not appear on this report. Web pages with very low usage should be evaluated to determine whether they are even necessary on the website. We weed or deselect from our physical library collections, so why not prune our websites as well to keep them fresh? If an underutilized web page is important to keep, then libraries may want to improve the content or its placement on the site to increase its usage. If the content is largely useful for internal staff, consider moving it to an intranet or other internal space.

Duration of Visit

Duration of visit, usually expressed in minutes and seconds, records the amount of time a visitor is on a website or on an individual web page. This metric is often used to report visitor engagement; if a person is on the site longer, he or she must be engaged and doing something with it. Unfortunately, web analytics tools have no method for determining whether users are truly active on your website during this time or whether they just landed on one of your pages and walked away from the computer. Additionally, the metric duration of visit is usually an averaged figure that calculates the total time a website is being used and then divides it by the number of visits. The average time on site data is not an exact measure, as it is difficult in most cases to record the precise time a visitor leaves a website. According to Google Analytics (2012), "It is not possible to calculate how much time the visitors spent on the last page in the session, because there is no data available to Analytics that indicates when the visitor left." With this in mind, the duration of visit metric is still important because it provides some insight about how long users are interacting with your website.

So, what is the recommended average duration of visit that library websites should aim for? There is no single answer, as each library website and its respective users are different. Many feel that visitor time on a library website, which averages between two and five minutes, is disappointingly short; however, consider that a high percentage of visitors come to library sites looking for research, such as journal articles, and as soon as they click a link to EBSCO, JSTOR, or other vendor product (including the online catalog), they are leaving the library's website, and the duration of their visit on it is over. Once in a commercial database, visitors are tracked using tools provided by the vendors or other statistical products specific to databases, and not your web analytics tool. As many library websites prominently place their database links on their websites in a portal model, visitors can quickly access them. Hence, it is important to understand that longer user visits are not an indication of a higher-quality site, and the duration of visit data can be put in context when reviewing the data on exit pages—more on this below—which can be used to determine where users went when they left the library's site.

Depth of Visit

The metric depth of visit outlines the total number of web pages viewed in a visit. For example, you can see how many visits there were in which the user viewed only three web pages before navigating away from your website. Depth of visit should not be confused with the metric average pages per visit, which is calculated by taking the total number of web pages viewed and dividing that by total visits. This metric is typically used to measure the average number of pages per session visitors click through on a website. Although these metrics are slightly different, both do provide a measure for user engagement: the more web pages with which a person interacts typically implies more involvement in the website. Yet libraries may streamline their website's information architecture (organization of a website's pages) by placing heavily used web pages, like the database listings web pages or the links to the library catalog, prominently on the library's home page so that users have fewer pages to go through to get to the desired information. In this case, a lower depth of visit would be preferable. Similar to the duration of visit metric, depth of visit is more useful when creating a report that compares this data with exit pages or other metrics. You want to ensure that your users are exiting your website where you planned.

VISITORS

Analytic tools also reveal a great deal of information about the individual device or, in web analytics terminology, visitor to websites. To clarify, a visit is a session, and a visitor is the individual computer or device accessing the website. Most web analytic tools segment, or separate, this metric into all visitors and unique visitors. Unique visitors are counted only once, regardless of how many times they access your website in a specific period of time. To determine unique visitors, your web analytics tools track all your visitors by either tracking their IP address or installing a cookie on a visitor's computer the first time that person visits your site. Recall the library gate-count analogy used earlier; in this scenario, the gate would tag each visitor as he or she entered, so if a person left the library and then reentered later in that day, the gate would register the visit but not count that person again as another visitor—only as another visit. Since the metric of unique visitors uses cookies or IP addresses, it is not an exact measurement, which we discuss in the next section. However imperfect, this metric is useful for tracking how many individuals use a website. In web analytics, it is the ideal to identify those individual users and how they interact with your site. We talk about how to collect this information via data segmentation in chapter 4.

Visitors is a common web analytics metric used in a variety of web analytics reports. Specific standard reports that use visitors as the primary metric include the new and/or returning visitor, visitor technology, and geographic location reports. These reports help libraries identify user behaviors and abilities on their websites.

19

New versus Returning Visitors

Analytics tools also classify visitors as "new" or "returning," meaning, quite simply, whether they have been to your site before or not. Neither new nor returning is more important or necessarily better than the other; however, this metric is still useful for tracking trends in use. For example, a high percentage of new visits indicates that a site is having a great deal of traffic driven to it, which is a positive.

A high rate of returning visitors also indicates that library users are loyal and frequently return to engage with web content, which is also desirable.

In libraries, determining returning versus new visitors can be problematic, as new and returning visitors are not easy to discern all the time. If your library analyzes raw data from web server logs or uses a web log analysis tool, you track your visitors' IP addresses to confirm whether they are new or returning visitors. Basically, you or your tool monitors the entire list to see whether an IP address is repeated during a selected period. Since AWStats, a web log analysis tool, does not offer a new or returning visitor report, libraries using this tool will need to do additional, manual analysis to get to those data. The problem with tracking by IP addresses is that IP addresses do not always imply a single computer; ISPs may assign IP addresses randomly on the basis of demand. If you have a computer lab in your library, many labs share a range of IP addresses and appoint a given IP (via Dynamic Host Configuration Protocol, or DHCP) whenever someone logs on to the machine and accesses the Internet. The same goes for home computers; your Internet provider at home likely does the same. Additionally, even if your computer lab does use static IP addresses, your users are not always confined to the same computer. Although the computers may be on the same network, a person's Internet preferences and history may not transfer between the computers. Therefore, a student could be on a computer in the library using the library's website for the first time, but if that student logs off that computer and goes to another computer to access the library's website again, he or she would still be a new visitor because it is the first time that browser accessed the library's website.

The same issue applies to the hosted web analytics tools that rely on JavaScript tags to track users. These tools place a cookie in the visitor's Internet browser to monitor whether they are a new or returning visitor. Since that cookie is applied to the Internet browser on that particular computer, the cookie most likely will not transfer over to another computer, even though the user is on the same network, and the cookie will definitely not transfer to a computer off the network. Also, visitors can opt to block cookies from being installed or can constantly clear their cookies with a few simple browser settings.

The message here is not that tracking new or returning visitors is impossible, but rather that it is an inexact measurement. There really is not an efficient workaround for this issue without invading a user's privacy. Rather, it is important to understand factors that could have a negative impact on the accuracy of this number in order to use it wisely. Although the metrics of new or returning visitors are not perfect, they are still best method of measuring who is new to your website and who is among your returning, if not frequent, users. This helps measure how your site engages users because it demonstrates that they are willing to come back on different occasions to use your site.

Visitor Technology

Web analytics tools record useful data about visitor technology, ranging from details about the user's web browser to the type of operating system that the computer uses. This information is critical to web designers and developers, as it indicates which browsers and operating systems ought to be supported. Even people who are not web managers should be aware of the visitor technology data gathered in web analytics to understand which data are available to them. The following list covers the basic visitor technology web statistics found in most web analytics tools; however, not all tools are comprehensive in reporting visitor technologies, so remember to check your tool's documentation to determine what it offers:

21

- **Browser type**—The web browser the visitor used to access the website. While there are a few popular browsers you can expect to see in these reports (e.g., Internet Explorer, Firefox, Chrome, Safari, Opera), you will also see mobile-device-specific browsers, such as the Android browser, and possibly gaming consoles like the Sony PlayStation 3, which has its own browser to search the Internet. Most web analytics tools also provide data about which version of the browser is being used, so do not be surprised to see your visitors use a wide variety of browser versions, for example, ranging from Internet Explorer 6 to Internet Explorer 9.

- **Operating system**—The operating system is the software that manages a device and its applications. By "device," we mean computers, cell phones, tablets, video game consoles, and more. Most of your use will likely come from computers, cell phones, and mobile devices. Just like the browser type, most web analytics tools log the operating system type and its specific version.

- **Screen resolution**—The screen resolution is reported in pixels; 1280 × 768 implies that the screen is set to display 1280 pixels in width and 768 pixels in height. For the non–web designer, these numbers may not mean much; however, these numbers are important because they tell the size of the screen being used to access the site. If a majority of your users view your website through small screens, like 320 × 480 or less, then content creators may want to reconsider the ways in which content displays for optimal use across devices. Although we could elaborate about using this information for additional usability testing, we instead refer you again to *Making Library Web Sites Usable: A LITA Guide* (Lehman and Nikkel 2008).

Flash support and Java support—Both of these metrics inform you of whether your users' browsers support Flash or JavaScript functionalities. Obviously, if your library's website has Flash components, you need to ensure that a majority of the visits to your site are able to display the Flash content. The same goes for Java support. Your users can easily turn off support for Java via their browser settings. Give it a try with your library's website. How does your site look without Java enabled? Is it functional? Even if you are not a web designer or developer, you can see the website from your users' technical perspective, which can help you improve the overall user experience.

Interestingly, some web analytics tools have options to segment usage data from mobile users separately from visits coming from a browser on a computer. Google Analytics has two separate reports dedicated to mobile devices. Although not all web analytics tools create separate mobile visits reports, most will list mobile devices data in the other aspects of the visitor technology report. Chapter 7 discusses the importance—and some of the pitfalls—of tracking usage from mobile devices for libraries.

Geographic Location

Geographic location information about visitors is determined by IP addresses. Map overlay reports, such as those generated by Google Analytics (figure 2.2), give an eye-popping visual representation of where library site visitors originate. However, because of the privacy concerns discussed at the end of chapter 1, most web analytics tools do not divulge specific IP information for specific visitors. Generally speaking, library sites will have a regional cluster of users in the city where the library is located; however, it is not uncommon to find international visitors to a library's site, which could be accounted for by regular users traveling internationally. Think of a public library user on a cruise downloading another e-book or a college student studying abroad.

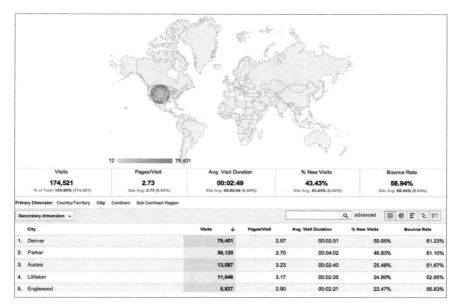

City	Visits ↓	Pages/Visit	Avg. Visit Duration	% New Visits	Bounce Rate
1. Denver	78,401	2.57	00:02:31	50.65%	61.23%
2. Parker	38,120	2.70	00:04:02	46.83%	61.10%
3. Aurora	13,587	3.23	00:02:40	25.48%	51.67%
4. Littleton	11,946	3.17	00:02:35	24.80%	52.95%
5. Englewood	8,927	2.90	00:02:21	22.47%	56.83%

FIGURE 2-2
Google Analytics "Map Overlay" Report by City,
Arapahoe Library District, Englewood, Colorado

Although geographic location is important, it is generally limited in granularity to the country and city levels, which makes it difficult to determine information important to libraries, such as whether users are accessing the library's website on campus or off campus, in the case of an academic library. Are users off campus but in the same city as the campus? Thankfully, some web analytics tools, such as Google Analytics, that do not supply IP addresses will let you filter or remove IP addresses from your data sets that you do not wish to track. This allows you to track only website use outside your library by excluding the IP range used within the library. There are directions to create filters in Google Analytics (version 5) in the help section (www.google.com/support/analyticshelp/bin/answer.py?hl=en&answer =1034840&topic=1034830). Check out your web analytics tool's documentation or directly contact your tool's provider to see whether it offers a similar functionality.

An additional complication in analyzing geographic information is that ISPs typically own large ranges of IP addresses, so although a visitor may reside in one city, the IP address used by that visitor may be registered to another city in which the ISP does business. You can identify the ISPs known to do this and filter them from your web statistics, or you can live with the results, knowing that while they are not perfect, they still offer some insight into your users' geographic locations.

ENTRY AND EXIT PAGES

The library's website is often not a user's first—or last—stop when it comes to locating information. Entry and exit pages show how users move through the Internet, arriving at and then departing from library sites. Most web analytics tools will allow you to see your entry or landing pages, which are the web pages through which a majority of your visitors enter your site. In a perfect world, from a librarian's perspective, all users would first start at a library home page and then navigate their way through the site; however, it quickly becomes obvious that users come to library websites from a variety of entry points and do not move through sites in the prescribed paths we would prefer. The reports on entry pages are typically organized by their use, so the more times users enter your site on that page, the higher the page's rank in the report. While the report includes all of a site's entry pages, we recommend that library web managers focus on the top ten to twenty entry pages to find out which pages are driving users to your site. After identifying your top entry pages, get comfortable with reviewing additional metrics (especially the referring source and bounce rate, which we cover next) from those individual web pages to learn more why users are finding those pages. Additionally, web pages that do not rank high as entry pages can be identified and their content improved to attract more entries.

Just as visitors enter your website, they will eventually have to leave it at some point. An exit page is the last web page a user views before navigating away to another website or closing their browser. Common top exit pages for library websites are web pages containing links to other resources, such as vendor-hosted databases, a catalog, or any outbound link that navigates the user away from the library's website. Exit pages alone should not be a point of concern, unless you find that your top exit pages are ones that you did not anticipate. If that is the case, review the content on that page and consider usability testing to identify the issue.

REFERRERS

Another common metric, referrers, shows how your visitors became your visitors. Referrers indicate how users are finding the site, where they are linking from, what page they land on, and where they specifically link to once they arrive. Referrers are separated into three categories: "direct traffic," "referral traffic," and "search traffic." Figure 2.3 illustrates the Google Analytics traffic sources report, which contains data on three types of traffic.

Direct traffic implies that visitors came to the website either by typing the exact URL into their browser's address bar or by setting your website as their browser's home page. Libraries that have their library website serve as the home page on their lab or commons computers will notice a high direct-traffic rate in their web statistics each time a browser is opened.

Referral traffic is traffic that arrives on your site via links on another website. Common referring sites for a library's web space can be web pages from parent institutions. Examples in an academic setting might include the college or university's site, or learning management tools such as Blackboard. For public libraries, common referrers include the library's online catalog and other electronic resources, including the e-book platform OverDrive and social networking sites like Facebook and Twitter. It is still important to monitor your referral traffic, as you may be surprised who is linking to your site. Identifying which of the pages in your site the referrers link to may shed light on how the top entry web pages on your site were driven up in the results.

Search traffic reports when a visitor is directed to your website from any search engine, ranging from the market-dominating Google search engine to a small local

25

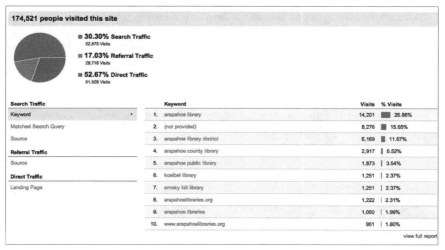

FIGURE 2.3
Traffic Sources Overview Report, Google Analytics,
Arapahoe Library District, Englewood, Colorado

search engine used on your institution's website. The keywords metric is a subset of the search-traffic data that allows you see the search terms visitors entered into a search engine to find a site. Keyword reports provide insight into how library users perceive the library and can be used to improve search engine optimization. As figure 2.4 shows, this report often includes multiple misspellings or variations of your library's name, the names of branches and locations if applicable, as well as staff member names (if you include a staff directory on your site). The number of keywords, even only a month's worth, can easily number in the thousands.

	Keyword	Visits ↓	Pages/Visit	Avg. Visit Duration	% New Visits	Bounce Rate
☐ 1.	arapahoe library	14,201	3.37	00:02:52	21.99%	49.04%
☐ 2.	(not provided)	8,276	3.54	00:02:50	31.27%	43.90%
☐ 3.	arapahoe library district	6,169	3.61	00:03:06	24.62%	46.05%
☐ 4.	arapahoe county library	2,917	3.99	00:03:15	33.90%	37.30%
☐ 5.	arapahoe public library	1,673	3.52	00:02:37	29.36%	45.49%
☐ 6.	koelbel library	1,251	3.80	00:02:48	26.30%	44.52%
☐ 7.	smoky hill library	1,251	3.63	00:02:33	32.85%	46.92%
☐ 8.	arapahoelibraries.org	1,222	2.94	00:02:36	22.59%	56.30%
☐ 9.	arapahoe libraries	1,050	3.74	00:04:14	17.90%	47.14%
☐ 10.	www.arapahoelibraries.org	951	3.70	00:02:49	21.14%	51.95%

Show rows: 10 ⌄ Go to: 1 1 - 10 of 4386 < >

FIGURE 2.4
Sample Keywords Report, Arapahoe Library District, Englewood, Colorado

Additional Resources for Web Analytics Definitions

There are many sources of definitions for web analytics terminology, including the following:

- The Digital Analytics Association (www.digitalanalyticsassociation.org) provides a downloadable PDF of its web analytics definition at the site www.webanalyticsassociation.org/resource/resmgr/PDF_standards/WebAnalyticsDefinitionsVol1.pdf.

- Google Analytics Help Pages (www.google.com/support/analytics/) provides various documentation on the reports, metrics, and dimensions used .

- The blog *Occam's Razor*, by analytics expert Avinash Kaushik, frequently features information about term definitions (www.kaushik .net/avinash/web-analytics-101-definitions-goals-metrics-kpis -dimensions-targets/).

BOUNCE RATE

Bounce rate is a complicated, but extremely useful, metric. The bounce rate is determined by the percentage of visitors who "bounced" from, or left, the site after viewing only a single page or who stayed on your site for only a short period. If we measured a bounce rate in the physical library, it would be like a patron coming into the library and then turning right around and walking out. It is unclear what motivated that person to act in that manner, but it could indicate a problem with the user-friendliness of your website's design if there is a high occurrence of bounces. Generally speaking, a lower bounce rate is better; Avinash Kaushik (2007) recommends a target bounce rate of 35 percent or less.

Several factors may also influence your bounce rate in a library setting. If your web analytics tool does not automatically track outbound links, as is the case with Google Analytics, this may increase the number of bounces. For example, if a user opens your website's home page and clicks on a library catalog link that navigates to the library catalog website, then Google Analytics would count that as a bounce—if your library did not configure it to track outbound links. This is because Google Analytics is not able to measure interactions off the website it is tracking. Additionally, libraries with computers in labs or commons settings that set the library's home page as the default in web browsers will have a higher bounce rate because patrons may bounce away from the home page to go directly to a web mail site, a news site, or any other site they need on that library computer. It is important to understand how your web analytics tool measures bounces and which factors influence it, to better understand how visitors are interacting (or not interacting) with your website.

ADVANCED WEB ANALYTICS TERMS: GOALS AND KEY PERFORMANCE INDICATORS

Now that you have a basic understanding of the data you will find using web analytics, it is time to make sense of those data and put them to work for you! A standard web analytics report contains so much data that it can be either overwhelming or a waste of time to decipher all the data that you really did not need to know. To help focus your data, you can create goals (more commonly known as conversions) and key performance indicators to monitor just the data that interest you.

Goals and Conversions

The concept of goals in web analytics is murky because many web analytics tools have "goal"-creating features that are truly only designed to help to create conversions, which are not necessarily goals in the planning sense. Conversions are the number of times a desired result was achieved. For a library, a desired result may be to get library users to a web page containing the list of all of the library's databases. In this case, the conversion would be the total visits to that database page. A more useful metric is the conversion rate, which takes the total number of conversions and divides it by the total number of visits or unique visitors. The conversion rate puts that number into context, so libraries can identify, out of all their users, how many are performing the desired action. The concepts of goal-setting features and conversion rates are further discussed in chapter 5.

Key Performance Indicators

Key performance indicators (KPIs) is a huge buzzword in the business sector, and it has been creeping into the library world as well. On his blog *Occam's Razor*, Avinash Kaushik (2008) defines KPIs as "measures that help you understand how you are doing against your objectives." By "objectives," Kaushik means your overall website objectives or goals, or what your website was actually designed to do. Any person interested in using KPIs in web analytics must be familiar with the web presence's purpose and goals, or at least identified goals, they want to measure. There is not a standard set of KPIs because goals vary depending on the purpose of the web presence. A library blog with the intent of informing library users of new services will have different KPIs than a library website, which may have multiple goals or objectives, such as directing users to library resources, providing research help, containing information about the library, and so on. However, by understanding the basic web analytics metrics and identifying the goals to be measured, there are core metrics to help you evaluate your KPIs. Again, conversion rates are the best metric for measuring KPIs, as they are customizable and allow you to quickly measure a goal. Other recommended metrics include page depth or visit duration to measure user engagement with a website—these metrics are so popular that you will often find them associated with goal reporting.

CONCLUSION

Although the practice of web analytics does not involve precise measurement of website use data (since it based on whatever data the web server and cookies capture), it does provide insight into website users and how are they interacting with your site. Also, as highlighted throughout this chapter, it is important to familiarize yourself with terminology commonly used by the different web analytics tools. We have covered the very basic metrics, including visits, page views, and visitors, and the more advanced concepts of goals, conversions, and KPIs. Remember that each web analytics tool will measure website usage differently, and your chosen tool's documentation should not only define your metrics but also describe how they are measured. Now that you understand the typical web analytics metrics available in most web analytics tools, you are ready to learn how to create advanced reports that are useful to you, your library, and all of its stakeholders.

REFERENCES

Google Analytics. 2012. "Time on Site, Avg." http://support.google.com/analytics/bin/answer.py?hl=en&ctx=share&answer=1006253.

Kaushik, Avinash. 2007. "Standard Metrics Revisited: #3: Bounce Rate." April 6. *Occam's Razor*. www.kaushik.net/avinash/standard-metrics-revisited-3-bounce-rate/.

————. 2008. "Web Six Web Metrics/Key Performance Indicators to Die For." September 16. *Occam's Razor*. www.kaushik.net/avinash/rules-choosing-web-analytics-key-performance-indicators/.

————. 2010. "Web Analytics 101: Definitions: Goals, Metrics, KPIs, Dimensions, Targets." April 19. *Occam's Razor*. www.kaushik.net/avinash/web-analytics-101-definitions-goals-metrics-kpis-dimensions-targets/.

Lehman, Tom, and Terry Nikkel. 2008. *Making Library Web Sites Usable: A LITA Guide*. New York: Neal-Schuman.

Chapter Three

Selecting and Evaluating a Web Analytics Tool

Before selecting a web analytics tool, libraries must fully understand their analytics needs and how an analytics tool will satisfy them. If you choose the wrong tool, your library will have to suffer either not getting the required data or repeating the process of evaluating and selecting another web analytics tool. Either way, time, effort, and data are lost. Even if your library already has a tool implemented, it is still necessary to evaluate that tool to ensure that it is meeting your library's statistical needs. There are so many tools currently available that it can be overwhelming for libraries to choose the best tool for them. To effectively evaluate a web analytics tool, libraries must first understand the wide range of tools available, consider their organization's web analytics needs, and test the tools before making any final decisions.

There is not one perfect web analytics tool for libraries. If there were, this chapter would not be necessary. Therefore, this chapter presents foundational concepts for comparing the different web analytics tools on the basis of their features and options. Web analytics tools are constantly changing, which requires libraries to do their own testing when they consider implementing a new tool rather than solely relying on reviews. We discuss how libraries can identify their web analytics needs so they know which features to look for in a tool. This chapter concludes with tips on testing the tools and questions to ask during the selection process.

UNDERSTANDING THE OPTIONS

The first step in evaluating any web analytics tool is to know which options are available to libraries. All web analytics are different; even if the tools sound and look similar, you will find that each tool has a different way that it tracks, collects, and reports data. By understanding these options, libraries can better choose the web analytics tool that works for them.

Costs

Not all web analytics tools are free; they can range in price from free to very expensive (read: easily in the thousands of dollars for a subscription). In our experience, most libraries cannot afford expensive web analytics tools, so this book focuses on the more affordable tools or ones that offer a free or low-cost service alternative. Tools that are not free typically have a subscription model, in which organizations pay a monthly or annual subscription fee to access the tool. Subscription models can be based on a flat fee per month (or some other defined period), the number of clicks or visits the tool tracks, or whatever fee model the tool's vendor uses. Additionally, there are tools that have optional, fee-based services for support and maintenance of the tool or assistance in analyzing the data. These services could be worthwhile for libraries that do not have the staff to perform these necessary tasks.

Even if a web analytics tool has a "free" price tag, that does not mean there are no costs associated with it. There will always be a cost associated with the time and people involved with implementing and maintaining the tool, in addition to the actual time spent analyzing and reporting the data. Although this may not be written into a budget, a library's investment in a web analytics tool is real, and again this underscores why libraries should take the time to select the right tool for their organization to receive the best value for their investment.

Data Tracking and Storage Options

This chapter is designed to present you with the different options so you can choose the correct tool for your library, not to tell you which tracking and storage options are the best. Nakatani and Chuang (2011) recommend that organizations compare tools on the basis of their tracking methods, data storage options, ability to track mobile and nonmobile devices, and the time lag between data collection and reporting. These are the more technical elements in a web analytics tool, and they affect how the data are collected and accessed.

Tracking Methods

There are several ways a web analytics tool can track website use data; however, for the scope of this book, we focus on page tagging, web server logs, and web beacons. Chapters 1 and 2 introduced the page-tagging method, which relies on a tracking code (typically JavaScript) being added to every single web page that the tool is to track. This tracking code can place a cookie on the visitor's browser to improve the tracking process. Currently, this is a widely used method for tracking website usage with major tools, such as Google Analytics. The main disadvantage to this method is that it cannot track visitors who disable their JavaScript functionality or devices, like some older mobile browsers that do not use JavaScript.

Web server logs are perhaps the most traditional way to track website use data. As mentioned in chapter 1, a web server records any and all requests (click-throughs or downloads) made to a website into log files that are stored on the server. The log records the name of the page being accessed, basic visitor information such as IP address and device or browser type, and date and time stamps for the action. Making sense of these logs requires a web server log analysis tool, such as AWStats (http://awstats.sourceforge.net) or Deep Log Analyzer (www.deep-software.com), which is installed on the web server. Server logs are excellent for tracking 404 ("page not found") errors or other technical problems with the site. Yet the data they provide are basic compared to those of the page-tagging methods, because more robust information is available from a cookie than from log files.

The last method to discuss is web beacons, which are objects embedded in each web page (and even email!) that is tracked. These objects are typically small, transparent images (GIF or PNG) that load in an HTML image tag. As with the tagging tools, web beacon products will provide a snippet of code, which includes a link to the invisible image, to embed in your website. When a visitor accesses the web page, the image is loaded on that user's browser and sends a message to the web analytics tool containing the data the tool was configured to track. Just like JavaScript, browsers can be set to block images from downloading—so it still is not a perfect tracking method. Web beacons are very popular for tools that focus on tracking mobile-device users, since some mobile devices find it easier to load a small invisible image than JavaScript.

Mobile versus Nonmobile Tracking Ability

As libraries trend toward developing mobile versions and applications of their web presences, there is a greater need to track those mobile device users. Even if your library does not have a mobile presence, you should still be monitoring those mobile users to determine when to start developing a mobile site or monitoring the content that those mobile users are using. Most comprehensive web analytics tools, such as Google Analytics or Piwik, have the ability to track mobile devices, but mobile tracking in them is limited because of their use of JavaScript tags or cookies. As Tony Bryne (2009) points out, mobile-device web browsers are notorious for not accepting JavaScript or cookies. Essentially, if your web analytics tool tracks only via this method, you are missing an unknown portion of your mobile users whose devices cannot be tracked using this method. Your options are to use a server log analysis tool or a different web analytics tool that uses web beacons. There are quite a few web analytics tools available that specifically track mobile websites or applications; a majority of these tools use the web beacon option.

Chapter 7 further discusses and demonstrates the importance of mobile web analytics. For now, it is important to be aware of how a tool tracks mobile visitors when you are selecting or evaluating your web analytics tool. Libraries need to know whether their tool is representing a majority of their mobile users or just a fraction, because this information could have an impact on future decisions to develop a mobile website or application, which requires a great deal of resources, whether in staff time or contractor dollars.

Data Storage

Web analytics tools are either hosted by the tool's provider or installed on a local server. This affects not only how you will access your web analytics tool but also how your site's data are stored. Your web analytics data will be either stored on an outside server or retained on a local web server.

The benefit of storing the data on a nonlibrary web server is that some libraries may not have direct access to a server, which makes this the only option. Storing data on a nonlibrary server means less work for the library, but some may cringe over the fact that potentially sensitive data, such as IP addresses, may be hosted on a different server by a company that may not share the same privacy values as your library. Existing technology policies may even forbid the use of third-party data storage. There are also fears over persistent access to the data. These are all legitimate concerns, but many web analytics tools, including the ever-popular Google Analytics, provide this option only for accessing and storing the data. If your library opts to go with a hosted service, you must find a web analytics provider you trust to house data. It is also highly recommended that the library read the web analytics tool provider's privacy policy and understand its implications for its website's users, to ensure that the provider's policy does not contradict any existing library policies.

There are many tools that can be installed and configured on a local server, such as Piwik and Open Web Analytics. If the tool is installed locally, then the data will also be local, which means that the library retains full control over its website use data. The trade-off is that the library must have the staff with the technological expertise and time to dedicate to installing and maintaining the tool over an extended period, as well as providing storage space for analytics data and reports.

Google Analytics Core Reporting API

Vendors that provide hosted web analytics solutions typically store—and completely control—data. However, this is not always the case. Some hosted web analytics tools offer extensive export options that allow library web staff to copy and store their site use data locally. An excellent example is Google Analytics Core Reporting API (http://code.google.com/apis/analytics/docs/gdata/home.html), which can regularly export the data to a local server. This requires some extra programming on the part of the library, but it may be worth the effort. Although Google controls the data on its servers, libraries have an option of backing up their data locally.

Real-Time and Delayed Reporting

In the web analytics world, data are delivered two ways: in real time or with a delay. Many web analytics tools tout their ability to provide data in real-time, which provides up-to-the-minute website monitoring capability. What are your users doing right now? In Google Analytics' real-time report (currently in beta at the time of writing), shown in figure 3.1, you can literally watch users enter your site, navigate to different pages, and leave your site. While it is interesting to watch, and potentially astounding for your coworkers, it is not exactly easy to analyze these data because multiple users come and go simultaneously, in a matter of minutes, leaving you little time to gain any insights into those visits. This is especially the case on a high-traffic site for a very large user population—think of a large public library district with hundreds of thousands of patrons. However, real-time reporting can be useful for identifying server errors or other website problems as

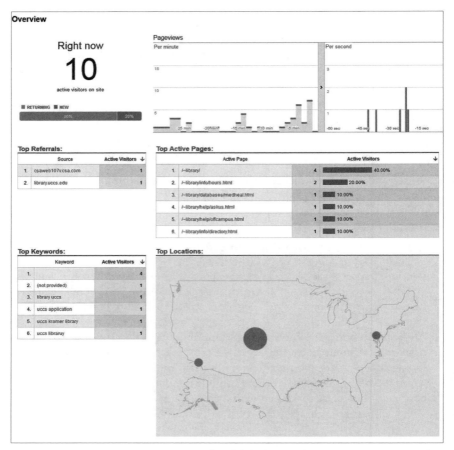

FIGURE 3.1
Real-Time Report, Google Analytics, Kraemer Family Library,
University of Colorado Colorado Springs

they happen. For example, if your web analytics tool provides custom alerts for spikes in visits to the "404 error" page on your site, you can instantly know that there is an error on the site that needs to be fixed.

Not all tools report in real time; some have a slight delay or lag between when the data are collected and when they appear in a report. This delay will vary across web analytics tools, but waiting a day for results to appear is not uncommon. A slight delay in a web analytics tool's reporting ability is not a huge drawback, but knowing when up-to-date data are or will become available is important.

Comparing Data, Reports, and Features

Understanding the technical side of how a web analytics tool functions is just as important as comparing the reports and features that a tool provides. You need to understand which data the tool does and does not collect, the types of standard and custom reports it provides, and what special features it offers.

Data Collection

In general, libraries should be aware of what data their web analytics tool tracks and does not track—whether it is part of a data-sampling method implemented or the tool's inability to track certain types of data.

Data Sampling

Some tools have different methods for sampling the data. Data sampling is the process of collecting and analyzing a subset of the site use data rather than entire data set. The subset is still large enough to provide similar results as the full data set, but since there are fewer data, it speeds up the tool's ability to analyze the data quickly (Kaushik 2010). Rather than record every single click or visit a website receives, a tool may record only every tenth visitor, or perhaps it collects all the data but analyzes only every tenth session. This varies by web analytics tool. This option is usually available either for heavily visited sites (millions of visits in short time span) because the massive amount of data takes time and computing power to process or as a cost-saving option from some commercial web analytics tools, again trying to save web server space or processing power.

Robots as Visitors

When we talk about visitors and unique visitors, we think of a human being behind the browser who is driving the interactions on a website; however, that is not always the case. Library sites are also crawled by search engine spiders and potential spammer bots—also called robot traffic—which access your site for various reasons, ranging from benign indexing content for a search engine to malicious attempts to hack your site. Either way, these nonhuman visitors may be integrated into your total counts of visits or unique visitors, depending on the web analytics tool. Adam Greco (2010) warns that if your tool includes these "garbage data" in its data collection and reports, it will inflate or skew your data on visits, unique visitors, and bounce rate, which has a negative impact on the reports produced. If your tool does track nonhuman visitors, it will also typically provide a separate

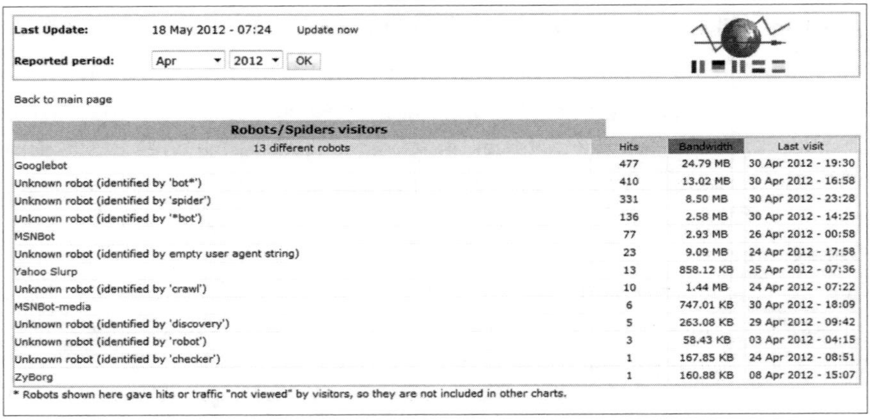

Last Update:	18 May 2012 - 07:24	Update now			
Reported period:	Apr ▼ 2012 ▼ OK				

Back to main page

Robots/Spiders visitors			
13 different robots	Hits	Bandwidth	Last visit
Googlebot	477	24.79 MB	30 Apr 2012 - 19:30
Unknown robot (identified by 'bot*')	410	13.02 MB	30 Apr 2012 - 16:58
Unknown robot (identified by 'spider')	331	8.50 MB	30 Apr 2012 - 23:28
Unknown robot (identified by '*bot')	136	2.58 MB	30 Apr 2012 - 14:25
MSNBot	77	2.93 MB	26 Apr 2012 - 00:58
Unknown robot (identified by empty user agent string)	23	9.09 MB	24 Apr 2012 - 17:58
Yahoo Slurp	13	858.12 KB	25 Apr 2012 - 07:36
Unknown robot (identified by 'crawl')	10	1.44 MB	24 Apr 2012 - 07:22
MSNBot-media	6	747.01 KB	30 Apr 2012 - 18:09
Unknown robot (identified by 'discovery')	5	263.08 KB	29 Apr 2012 - 09:42
Unknown robot (identified by 'robot')	3	58.43 KB	03 Apr 2012 - 04:15
Unknown robot (identified by 'checker')	1	167.85 KB	24 Apr 2012 - 08:51
ZyBorg	1	160.88 KB	08 Apr 2012 - 15:07

* Robots shown here gave hits or traffic "not viewed" by visitors, so they are not included in other charts.

FIGURE 3.2
Robots and Spider Visitor Report in AWStats, LibNotes, Kraemer Family
Library, University of Colorado Colorado Springs

report with this information. Figure 3.2 demonstrates a robots and spider visitor report generated in AWStats.

Many web analytics tools track and include robot traffic in their reports, but it is important to check the tool's documentation or ask the company whether those data are automatically included. If they are, ask for or find strategies for minimizing robot traffic. For example, Google Analytics includes robot traffic if the robot triggers the tracking JavaScript or cookies (http://support.google.com/analytics/bin/answer.py?hl=en&answer=1315708), but if you know the robot's name or IP address, you can create a filter or custom segment to block that traffic from being collected or reported. Since new robots are released regularly with new names or IP addresses, this is a constant process. Naturally, this requires more work on the library to stay current and customize its tool's configurations, but it creates a more accurate use data set.

Outbound Links

As discussed in chapter 2, outbound links are links that navigate website users from the current website off to a different site. While developers of e-commerce and other nonlibrary sites might not care so much about outbound links—often, the focus is on keeping visitors on a site until a conversion is attained—for libraries, this is particularly important. Our outbound links include links to catalogs, subscription databases, electronic reserves, e-book platforms, and any and all online resources for which the site is hosted on a separate domain or web server. Tracking these links is important because it shows that users are able to access these resources on the library's website and that the library's website is providing sufficient access to these resources, which often account for the lion's share of our increasingly strained budgets. Additionally, libraries want to select a tool that tracks most, if not all, of the interactions on the website (including clicks on those outbound links) in order to receive a comprehensive picture of how visitors use the site and how all the pieces of our web presences are fitting together.

Some tools, such as Piwik, automatically track outbound links; however, other tools, like Google Analytics, require further customizations to track this data (for more information about tracking outbound links in Google Analytics, see chapter 4), and some tools do not offer the option to track these data at all. If the tool does not track outbound links, then it typically reports whenever a visitor clicks on an outbound link as a bounce rather than an exit. This is an important distinction, because bounces imply a bad interaction in which a visitor came to the page and automatically ran away from it, whereas exits can be good if a person exits a site as designed—such as by clicking on an outbound link to a library catalog or database, which satisfies the purpose of the visit. When using tools that do not track outbound links, do not justify a high bounce rate as a positive indicator because you assume users must be clicking on those outbound links and triggering all those bounces. This is poor web analytics practice, because that unfounded assumption is based on the tool's bounce rate report alone. The library needs to determine where users are exiting versus bouncing—perhaps by implementing a secondary web analytics tool that tracks outbound links—or they run the risk of missing potential problems on the website.

Again, check the tool's documentation or work with the tool's provider to ensure that the tool can track outbound links—and if it cannot automatically track these data, determine which alternatives are available. With the numerous web analytics tools available to libraries, there really is no excuse for settling for a tool that does not track the data your library needs, especially for a report that is so important to typical library web presences.

Reporting the Data

Just like data collection, each web analytics tool has different reporting capabilities. Although all tools should have a set of standard web analytics reports, such as a top content report or browser or technology report, they may have different ways of expressing the data or additional features to help you analyze the data. Libraries

39

should understand the standard reports that come prebuilt in the tool; the options that exist for creating custom reports; and any other additional functionality, such as segmenting, creating custom variables, or goal or event tracking. The tool should provide desirable data and a way to analyze and report those data to your specifications. You will most likely need some type of semicustomizable and customizable report functionality, which is further discussed in the next chapter.

Support

Regardless of how much actual money your library invests in its web analytics tool, libraries should investigate the type of support that is available for that tool. Support is essential for understanding how to utilize the tool to its fullest potential and for troubleshooting when problems arise. Support can range from documentation created by the tool's provider to open community forums and working directly with the tool's company tech-support staff. For commercially hosted tools, libraries should at least have access to the tool's documentation that outlines which metrics are tracked and how that tool defines them. For open-source or locally installed tools, libraries should have that basic documentation, in addition to some type of support for upgrading and maintaining the tool in-house.

Regardless of the tool selected, always research what type of support is available for that tool before committing to it. Check the documentation or support venues (e.g., official documentation, sites, direct support via phone, chat), and research other forms of support on the open web (e.g., forums, blogs). For example, Google Analytics enjoys an enormous amount of support options. It offers an array of free help including its support and documentation site (http://support.google .com/analytics), an official blog that provides advice and alerts users of new tools (http://analytics.blogspot.com/), and a user forum (https://productforums.google. com/forum/#!forum/analytics). In searching the web, you will find additional support and information from Google Analytics users who post useful content to their own websites and blogs. If that is not enough support for your library, there are companies that specialize in helping organizations utilize Google Analytics for a price, and Google Analytics Premium, a fee-based service offered by Google, includes a support team (www.google.com/analytics/premium/). Be prepared to do some research into the different support options available.

Comprehensive versus Specialized Tools

Web analytics tools range from comprehensive tools designed to track an entire website's usage to specialized tools that track only certain types of web presences or data. Google Analytics, Piwik, and AWStats are just a few examples of comprehensive tools—they are designed to be implemented on an entire website and to gather a wide assortment of data to help interpret how users are accessing and using a site. Libraries must have at least one comprehensive tool to understand their website's usage, but some libraries may need or want an additional, specialized tool that provides data their tool may miss. Special web analytics tools are very diverse in features and capabilities; some may be completely separate tools in which a separate tracking tag needs to be added to every web page to be tracked; others are automatically generated reports incorporated in separate service or software. Here are examples of some specialized tools:

Crazy Egg (www.crazyegg.com)—A commercial web analytics tool that specializes in visualizing web analytics data in three different reports or views: site overlays, heat maps, and confetti views.

Facebook Insights (www.facebook.com/help/search/?q=insights)—This free report is automatically available to any administrator of a Facebook page, with no installation required. It includes metrics on number of posts, likes, reaches, and other useful data to determine the effectiveness of your Facebook presence. Facebook developers can further customize this report or implement a more comprehensive tool to track their library's page usage.

FeedBurner (www.feedburner.com)—A free service provided by Google to publish RSS feeds. Because FeedBurner publishes the RSS feed, it is also able to track use to that feed, such as reporting the total number of subscribers to the feed, click-throughs generated from the feed, and other use data.

Visual Website Optimizer (http://visualwebsiteoptimizer.com)—Another commercial tool that combines web analytics data and usability testing. This tool (or ones similar to it) can be invaluable during the development and testing phase of a website (re)design process.

In addition to these examples, chapter 11 further discusses specialized web analytics tools for WordPress and Drupal software, which continue to increase in popularity as web content management systems among library web developers.

Libraries that feel that they are not getting the complete picture of their website's usage may consider adding a specialized tool or tools to help gather and analyze the data they need. Avinash Kaushik (2007) calls this multiplicity, or using multiple tools and data sources to track the complete picture of website use for an organization. Libraries do not just have a single website to represent them on the web; they have a main website, an online library catalog, social media presences, and more. One web analytics tool is no longer sufficient to track all those data. In the process of selecting or evaluating a web analytics tool, develop a plan to have one comprehensive tool, and select any other tools necessary for specialized tracking. Libraries should be prepared to test how those tools' technology function together, specifically how well their data complement each other. Many of the case study chapters in the second half of this book provide insights into how multiple tools may be used in conjunction.

UNDERSTANDING YOUR LIBRARY'S WEB ANALYTICS NEEDS

Even before you begin shopping for a new web analytics tool or evaluating your current tool, you should understand your web analytics needs. We are implying here that libraries should determine the data or information the library wants to get from the tool *and* how much a library can "invest" in that tool, whether human or fiscal resources. Both are instrumental in selecting the right tool for the job.

Investing in a Web Analytics Tool

When it comes to investing in a tool, libraries need to evaluate the technology, and staff, that goes with a successful web analytics practice. It really is an investment because the library will need to allocate resources for analytics activities in order to see any significant return on that investment—in other words, libraries should choose a tool that will provide the necessary data yet will still be affordable to maintain and use.

Information technology resources will determine which types of web analytics tools are realistic for your library. Do you have your own servers and enough staff to maintain those servers? If not, then selecting a tool that must be locally hosted is likely a less desirable option. A library that does have access to servers and staff (whether directly or via a parent institution, such as a campus information technology (IT) department that supports an academic library's web environment) that can maintain the server and software can explore locally hosted and open-source web analytics tools. However, that library still needs to consider how sustainable it is to maintain the tool for an extended period. How often does the tool need to be upgraded or patched? If external support (i.e., campus or city IT) is required, can that support staff devote the time necessary for upkeep? Does the locally hosted tool bring a perceived benefit to the library that an off-site hosted tool cannot? These are all questions libraries that plan to host their own tool should ask.

Although technology is important for deciding whether you can or cannot support a tool, at the end of the day, a web analytics tool is just a tool. It assists libraries in analyzing website use data, but it is really library staff who sift through the data and pull out the relevant finds. The data analysis is the most time-consuming part of the entire web analytics process! When selecting a tool, ensure that the staff responsible for data analysis have the time and ability to learn the tool. Do not select an overly complicated tool that offers great features but that no one can use.

Also, consider the amount of time your library can dedicate to analyzing data. We suggest that libraries review their key data on a regular schedule (at least monthly) and after substantial changes are made to a website that could have an impact on usage. If you believe that your library does not have the time to regularly analyze use data, then look for a tool that contains an alert or notification feature and useful, easy-to-read reports that require minimum customization to get to the data needed. Although these features are useful in any web analytics tool, they are ideal for library staff who are short on time because they can be configured to automatically send analyzed reports directly to the people that need it. Libraries that can dedicate staff time to actually analyzing the data should look for tools that offer segmentation, custom reports, and a method for exporting the data. These features allow libraries to explore their own data in the tool or in a statistical analysis program, such as SPSS, R, or even spreadsheet software—the tool goes beyond just reporting the data to actually allow libraries to perform their own analysis of the data. This will lead to more useful insights and tailoring of the data to the library's needs.

Take Inventory of the Library's Web Presences

Web presences can be websites, social media presences, or other online "places" in which the library maintains the content. Web analytics tools are usually installed at the organizational level, so libraries need to understand the web presences they have in order to select the best comprehensive tool that works with most of those sites. The more tools a library has, the more effort is required for maintaining the tools and the more time it takes to analyze the data collected for different tools. Can the same tool be used on both the library's website and catalog, or will you need two separate, comprehensive tools? Libraries can save themselves time and effort by selecting a comprehensive tool that can be applied to multiple web presences.

Start by taking an inventory of all the library's web presences, their hosted locations if your library has different hosting options, and any web analytics tool already tracking the site. If you do not know this information already, consult your library's web services or system administration people. Table 3.1 illustrates the Kraemer Family Library's website inventory. The Kraemer Family Library is

TABLE 3.1
Website inventory for the Kraemer Family Library

Web presence	Hosted location	Special considerations	Comprehensive tool	Specialized (secondary) tools
Main website	University server	Static site with some jQuery	Google Analytics	Crazy Egg
RSS feed	University server	None	NA	FeedBurner (integrated into Google Analytics)
Library catalog	Library server	Tracking outbound links is difficult	NA	Internal statistics from catalog vendor
LibGuides	University server	Mixture of static and dynamic content.	Google Analytics	Internal statistics from LibGuides
Blog	Off-campus server	Uses WordPress.	Google Analytics	WordPress Stats (plug-in)
Facebook page	Company server (Facebook)	None	NA	Facebook Insights
Flickr page	Company server (Flickr)	Have a Flickr Pro account	NA	Internal statistics from Flickr
Undergraduate research journal	University server	Uses Open Journal System (OJS)	Google Analytics	Internal statistics from OJS
Link resolver	Company server (Serials Solutions)	Completely hosted by Serials Solutions	NA	NA
Online tutorials	University server	Static site with PHP for quizzes	Google Analytics	NA

an academic library that serves a university of more than eight thousand full-time students. This library has only one internal web server, which is dedicated to the library catalog; all other web presences are hosted either on a shared university web server or off campus on a commercial web server, which makes it important to record where the sites were hosted. Since there were multiple hosting locations, the library could not use a web server log analysis tool as its comprehensive tool because the web presences were not all on the same web server. Instead, the library opted for a tool that offered the page-tagging method, in this case Google Analytics, to track a majority of the web presences.

Notice that table 3.1 does not include internal websites such as its reference tracking tool or staff wiki. Since internal websites are typically more sensitive (meant for library staff only), the Kraemer Family Library did not want to track their usage in a third-party analytics vendor like Google Analytics because of security risks. Instead, the library uses data from a web log analyzer that is installed on the same web servers as the internal sites, so all data are stored on the same server.

Review the Data Needs
of the Individual Web Presences

Taking an inventory of web presences works well if you are selecting a web analytics tool at the organizational level; however, that practice focuses on the compatibility of a tool with the websites to be tracked. Libraries should also consider the type of data they want to receive from their tool. Evaluate each website separately, because each one should have its own purpose, set of goals, and possibly target audiences. Is that comprehensive web analytics tool missing some data or reports you need? If so, it is time to add secondary, specialized tools that can fill in that tool's gap.

When selecting a specialized tool for a website, you need to understand the type of data or report that your library wants and then research which tool options are available. For example, the Kraemer Family Library used Google Analytics solely for its main website but found that it was still difficult to test effectiveness of a web page redesign. The library wanted to clearly see how users were interacting with a top-level redesigned web page. It tried to use Google Analytics' in-page report but found that the report was inaccurate because it did not include outbound links, although the library had configured Google Analytics to track them as events or page views, and it could not differentiate the same link listed on the web page multiple times. The library opted to use Crazy Egg, a commercial web analytics tool that specializes in visualizing click data at the web page level. This allowed the library to supplement the data from the Google Analytics profile and satisfy a data need specific to the redesign process (Farney 2011).

45

TESTING THE TOOL

The testing phase of a web analytics tool is the most important phase, because it gives you an opportunity to find out whether the library and the tool are a good match. Kaushik (2010) recommends that an organization spend at least six weeks with the tool in a trial phase to have enough time to get a feel of how the tool works and to allow the tool to collect enough data to do some preliminary analysis. Most commercial web analytics tools offer free trial periods, and free tools allow you an unlimited trial period. Take the time during the trial period to test the ability of the tool and ask questions to ensure the tool's suitability.

Questions to Ask during the Testing Period

It is recommended that any organization develop a list of questions to ask during the tool's testing period. We included a list of generic questions that all libraries should ask themselves (or their web analytics tool's vendor). Feel free to customize this list on the basis of your own library's needs:

Which web presences does the tool track extremely well? Which web presences does the tool insufficiently track? It may be hard to find one web analytics tool to track all of your library web presences, but the more sites for which a tool can be used, the easier it will be for the library to maintain the tool and gain experience in analyzing the tool's data.

Does the tool track a majority of the interactions on the site? Can it track outbound links, events, or customized goals? The more interactions the tool can track, the better picture of website use you will receive. We discuss the usefulness of event tracking and goal tracking in the next chapter.

Do the tool's standard reports provide you with the data you need? Standard reports provide basic information about the user, user technology, and some user behavior. Some tools have very minimal standard reports, and others offer more fully featured options.

What is the tool's segmentation ability? As you will find out, segmentation is an important feature in web analytics that lets you pull out a selection of data for further analysis. It turns those boring, standard reports into useful, insightful reports.

What type of customized reports can the tool create? Customized reports give you the power to create your own reports that focus on the data you want to analyze.

What support is available if something breaks or if you need help understanding a report? Even if the tool does not break, you are bound to have questions about the tool at some point. Find out where you can ask those questions and what kind of responses you should expect so that you will not be left searching for help when you need it.

Where are the data stored and how can you access them? Again, this returns to the discussion of local versus hosted (i.e., third party) data. Wherever those data are located, consider the ease of access to the tool and its data. Also, consider who should have access to the data and ensure that they also can easily access the data. If the data are to be stored locally, where should they live?

Does the tool have an export functionality to help share that data outside the tool? The ability to export data is useful for sharing with others in the library who could use the data but do not necessarily want to go into the tool to find it. Additionally, if your library ever plans to switch to a different tool, you should devise a strategy to harvest and back up your data on a local server so you do not lose access to it.

For non-locally-hosted tools, what is the company's privacy policy, and how does it align (or depart from) your library's current privacy and technology policies? Privacy is an issue with tracking website usage, and although you may not be able to change your tool's privacy policy, you can inform your users as to which data are being collected and how they are being used by the library and the tool's vendor.

If you cannot answer these questions during the trial period, consult the tool's documentation, ask the local user community (if available) for support, or contact the tool's provider.

Comparing Multiple Tools

The first rule in comparing more than one web analytics tool is to be fair. Since web analytics tools track and report data differently, it is difficult to compare them on the basis of the data they return alone. If tool A reports that your library's website received twenty thousand visits in a month and tool B reports only fourteen thousand visits that same month, you should not make the case that one tool is more accurate than the other. Rather, you should read the documentation for both tools to understand how each one defines a visit—some include robots and web crawlers as visitors or count bounced visits in their total numbers—and to determine whether the distinction matters for your library. And perhaps this goes without saying, but don't simply choose tool A from this scenario because it returns the highest number of visitors to inflate your reports. The numbers you give may be misleading to the stakeholders to whom you are reporting your use data.

While we do not recommend directly comparing two web analytics tools' data, we do highly recommend comparing the types of metrics, reports, and features that the tool offers. Does one tool have a report that your library values more highly? Also, compare how the reports are formatted. Is there a tool that provides easier-to-interpret reports? Use the questions we suggested or the questions your library develops as a starting point for the actual comparison of the tools.

To keep your library from being tempted to compare the data, we suggest creating different trial periods for each tool. Each trial period should be for the same length of time, for consistency. This helps libraries focus on the elements that matter when selecting a tool, but it also keeps to a minimum the problems that can occur by having multiple web analytics tools tracking the same site at the same time. Having multiple JavaScript tracking codes on one web page can have an impact on the accuracy of the tools' ability to track visits.

CONCLUSION

Selecting a web analytics tool is an important part of the web analytics process. Even if your library has already selected a tool, you should plan to evaluate that tool to ensure that it is meeting the library's needs. Compare your current tool against new tools that are available, and be prepared to evaluate your web analytics tool(s) as your library launches new web presences.

Although evaluating a tool should be an annual process, we are not advocating that you to go out and change your web analytics tool whenever a new tool is released. Selecting, testing, and implementing a tool is a long process and should not be taken lightly. When your library is no longer seeing the return on investment it put into the tool, that is when it is time to start looking at other tool options or to consider adding a specialized tool to help make up for the comprehensive tool's functionality. However, when your library is ready to start the evaluation process, remember to review your web analytics options because each tool will be different, to consider your library's web analytics needs, and to provide time to test the tool to ensure that you can answer all the necessary questions before making the final selection. Last, remember that with all the web analytics tools available, libraries should have no excuse for settling for a tool that does not fit. Select a comprehensive tool and a few specialized tools to help your library's web analytics strategy succeed.

REFERENCES

Byrne, Tony. 2009. "Mobile and Video Tracking Challenge the Web Analytics Marketplace." *KM World* 18, no. 8: 6–25.

Farney, Tabatha A. 2011. "Click Analytics: Visualizing Web Site Use Data." *Information Technology and Libraries* 30, no. 3: 141–148.

Greco, Adam. 2010. "Minimize Robot Traffic." *Web Analytics Demystified.* http://adam .webanalyticsdemystified.com/2010/09/20/minimize-robot-traffic/.

Kaushik, Avinash. 2007. "Multiplicity: Succeed Awesomely at Web Analytics 2.0!" November 6. *Occam's Razor.* www.kaushik.net/avinash/multiplicity-succeed -awesomely-at-web-analytics-20/.

———. 2010. *Web Analytics 2.0: The Art of Online Accountability and Science of Customer Centricity.* Indianapolis, IN: Wiley.

Nakatani, Kazuo, and Ta-Tao Chuang. 2011. "A Web Analytics Tool Selection Method: An Analytical Hierarchy Process Approach." *Internet Research* 21, no. 2: 171–186.

Chapter Four

Creating Customized Web Analytics Reports for Libraries

S tandard reports are those generic data reports that are prebuilt into most web analytics tools. Each tool comes with its own standard reports, but all are designed to provide you with basic data that the tool's provider thinks you want. For example, the report on top entry pages is a typical standard report that identifies the specific pages through which visitors enter a site. This report is somewhat useful, but it does not reveal how those visitors found the site, what type of visitor typically enters at that entry page, or even where those visitors go once they enter the site. To put this in perspective, if you notice that one of your top entry pages has a high bounce rate, you would want to look at different data to see whether there is a connection. Are new visitors contributing to that bounce rate? Do visitors who enter via a search engine bounce more often? What keywords did those bounced visitors use to find your site? All of these questions can help identify who those visitors are and potentially why they are turning away from your site, but they cannot be answered from standard reports alone.

Enter semicustom and custom reports! These nifty reports allow libraries to select the metrics they want to analyze in order to drill down to the data they really need. Semicustom reports are regular standard reports that either display the data in a unique way beyond the traditional chart or provide the ability to segment the data. Custom reports are completely open, and they allow you to choose all the metrics to be analyzed in the report. Standard reports are useful for web analytics beginners, but this chapter is geared toward taking you beyond the basic concepts covered in chapter 2 and introducing the concepts and library-specific uses of semicustom and custom reports.

Before we can jump into more customized reporting options, you must have the basic understanding of standard metrics, since they are the foundation of semicustom and custom reports. We also introduce the major web analytics concepts of segmentation and filters. Next, we demonstrate several semicustom and custom reports and discuss which reports libraries should implement. By the

Understanding the Core Standard Metrics

Understanding the basic metrics is a necessity in advanced web analytics. They are used for segmentation, conversions, and custom reports. These are a few of the standard metrics that we have already covered but that you will rely on regularly and should feel comfortable using:

Visits (or unique visitors)—By itself, this metric is not incredibly useful, but it is the basic unit of measure for conversions and most custom reports.

New visitors and returning visitors—Both metrics are useful when it comes to segmenting your web analytics data because they let you compare how new visitors, who are potentially unfamiliar with your site, and returning visitors, who have used your site before, access and utilize the site.

Bounce rate—This impressive metric is used in many types of custom reports because it shows the visitors who refuse to even interact with your website.

Page views—The page views metric is used to help determine visitor engagement (see depth of visit) and to help quantify how often an individual web page is used.

Pages per visit and average time on site—Both metrics are commonly found in custom reports because they measure the visitors' use of or engagement with the site. Additionally, these metrics are typically included in goal (conversion) reporting.

Referring sources—These data are useful for segmenting reports by how users find you and to compare the different user groups of the site. Naturally, referring sources are also helpful when creating custom reports that focus on a website's findability.

You will find these metrics demonstrated throughout this book. If you need a refresher on any of these core metrics, head back to chapter 2 for a review.

end of this chapter, you will start to understand how to go beyond the basic data sets to use the more customized options your web analytics tool offers in order to focus on the data you and your library need.

SEGMENTING WEBSITE USE DATA

A main problem with analyzing website use data is that those data generalize all of your website's users into one category: "visits." However, libraries have a variety of audiences, each with its own unique needs and search behaviors. For a public library, the primary intended audience is the surrounding community it serves. How can that library tell whether its website is meeting user needs? By segmenting the generalized data set so that the library can analyze just the data from that user group. Segmentation is the process of creating subsets of data from a report based on selected portions (or segments) of data, such as user characteristics or behaviors. When you apply a segment to a report, you exclude the data you do not want to see so you can focus on the data that matter. The public library interested in analyzing use data from local community members can segment various data reports to reveal use data from users in a specific geographic area.

Applying Segments to Standard Reports

Segments can make those standard web analytics reports useful. Figure 4.1 demonstrates Google Analytics' landing page report. This is already a useful report because it shows the website's most popular entry pages in conjunction with other great standard metrics that should sound very familiar, including visits, pages per visit, average time on site, percentage of new visits (new visitors), and bounce rate. While impressive, it does not describe the type of visitors that are bouncing away from your site.

Adding two basic segments, new visitors and returning visitors, to the landing page report (figure 4.2) shows which type of visitor traffic is bouncing more. The library's home page reports that new visitors spend more time on the website and look at more pages but that the returning visitors had a lower bounce rate. This indicates that new visitors navigated the site more, maybe getting lost or just exploring, than the returning visitors. The difference between the bounce rates reflects that the returning visitors were more likely to continue navigating through the website after landing on the home page. If this library has a goal to lower the

53

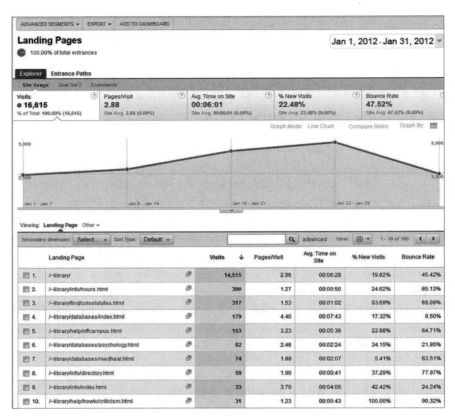

FIGURE 4.1
Landing Page Report, Google Analytics,
University of Colorado Colorado Springs

bounce rate, then it now knows it should target new visitors. Further analysis of referring sources can help target how the new visitors found the home page and identify whether there are trends in how new visitors find the home page.

Useful Segmenting Ideas

Segmenting is one of the most useful features a web analytics tool can provide. If your web analytics tool has a segmenting function, it will typically allow you to segment using standard metrics and possibly custom metrics so that you can combine several metrics as you desire. Here are a few suggested segmenting ideas to help libraries consider the different possibilities.

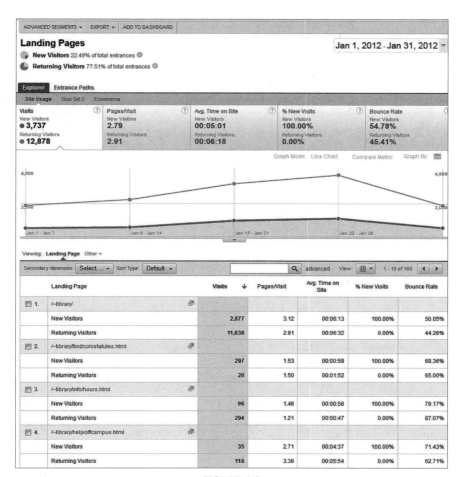

FIGURE 4.2
Landing Page Report with New Visitor and Returning Visitor Segment,
Google Analytics, University of Colorado Colorado Springs

Segmenting User Groups

Referring sources—Visitors can come directly to your site, find your site in a search engine, or link to your site from another website. By segmenting your reports using these metrics, you can learn how the different user groups access, use, and leave your site. Have a Facebook page for your library? You can segment the reports to look at visitors who are referred to your website from Facebook to see whether your posts are driving actual library use or just contributing to your bounce rate.

Does Your Tool Have a Segmenting Ability?

Most web analytics tools offer some segmentation capability. If you do not see an option to segment in your tool, check the documentation to see whether it is an option. In cases of open-source web analytics tools, you may be able to implement additional customizations to the software to enable this feature. For example, Piwik provides documentation on how to segment data using its application programming interface (API; http://piwik.org/docs/analytics-api/segmentation/). If you know that your web analytics tool does not offer a segmenting option, you can do most of the segmenting functionality by hand. Just export the data into a spreadsheet or data analysis tool and manually remove the sessions that contain the unwanted data. This requires additional work, but the results are often worth taking that extra step.

Geographic location—Segmenting by geographic location is particularly interesting if your library's website serves local users (e.g., residents of specific cities in a county library system) and/or distant users (e.g., distance education students in schools and universities). Although it is not possible to determine whether the visitor is affiliated with your library from geographic data alone, these data can reveal how local and nonlocal visitors browse and search for the content they need on your site.

IP address or service provider—Segmenting by IP address or service provider helps you narrow your data to a targeted user group. Segmenting by IP addresses is popular because you can remove unwanted traffic from certain IP addresses, such as library staff computers, to focus the on use data from actual library users. This segment may not always be useful in some libraries. At the University of Colorado Colorado Springs, any computer on campus, including library staff computers, department computers, and student computers, has a fluctuating IP range. Instead of segmenting by an IP range, the library segments by service provider because the university is the Internet service provider for all on-campus Internet access. This allows the university to compare the usage of the library's website from on-campus users and off-campus users but does not remove staff computers.

Mobile and nonmobile—Whether your library has a mobile-ready website or not, you should be checking to see the difference between how mobile and nonmobile visitors use your site. As chapter 7 highlights, this may give you ideas about what to include on your mobile site if you do not already have one or about how to improve it if you do.

Segmenting User Behavior

New visitor or returning visitor—Segmenting by types of visitor allows you to see whether users who are familiar with your website (returning visitors) have different use patterns than those who are new to your website (new visitors).

Nonbounced visits—Many standard reports include bounced visits in your total recorded visits. This is not particularly useful in some reports that are not focused on the bounce rate. For example, the page depth report shows how many pages per visit a user goes through. All bounced visitors would be recorded as having seen only one page per visit in the report, which adds little value to the data.

Visit duration or pages per visit—These engagement metrics help you segment the visitors that actually use your website. Although this sounds similar to the nonbounced visit segment, the added benefit is that you segment users who spent a specific time on the website or visited a set number of pages. The library website at the University of Colorado Colorado Springs was designed to facilitate access to a majority of the library's resources with two to three clicks. By applying a custom segment, it is easy to focus on the users who are on the site for only two to three pages and see whether the library is meeting that goal.

Segmenting Content

Individual page or selection of pages—Some web analytics reports combine the entire website's data when what you want to know is how one page or group of pages is being used. You can segment the report by content to get to the data of the web pages you need to analyze.

Difference between Using Filters and Segments

In the web analytics world, people refer to filters and segments, but those tend to mean two very different things, as highlighted in figure 4.3. A filter is typically a

57

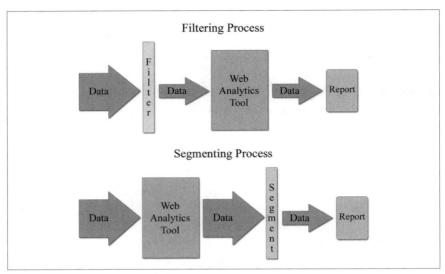

FIGURE 4.3
Comparison of Filters and Segments

method that identifies certain visitor traffic that you do not wish tracked in your web analytics tool. You apply the filter to the entire web analytics profile, so the data that you decide to filter are not collected in a report. A common filter applied to library websites is a filter that removes library staff computers by domain or IP addresses so the web analytics data collected reflects only library users. Since this filter removes all website traffic from staff computers (sometimes referred to as internal traffic), you would not be able to view that data within that web analytics profile. When you apply filters, remember to establish one master profile that has no filters applied so that it collects all data, and then create separate profiles for each of the filters you want to apply. This will ensure that you will not lose any important data.

Segments are different from filters because segments are applied after the web analytics tool collects the use data. All website traffic data are still collected and reported within one profile; however, you can apply a segment to the report to hide unwanted data from view. So, all data are present in the tool, but you decide which data you want to view and when. Segments can be applied to historical data, or to data that your web analytics tool has already collected, but filters cannot. If your library director comes to you and asks for data only from nonstaff computers, then you can provide this data by applying a segment that hides the identified domain or IP addresses to the web analytics report.

SEMICUSTOM REPORTS:
A STEP BEYOND STANDARD REPORTS

Even standard web analytics reports can be useful with some segmenting; however, you can learn even more about your website by using more customizable reports. Semicustom reports provide a unique view of your web analytics data by visualizing the data to enhance interpretation or by allowing you to create subsets of data by applying segments or additional metrics to standard reports. In both cases, the report is already prebuilt into the tool; you simply tell it which data to process. This section introduces click-density analysis reports, path analysis, event tracking, and conversion reports. All of these reports should be incorporated into a library's web analytics strategy.

Click-Density Analysis Reports

A click-density analysis report is a page-level report that shows where visitors click on a page. The report visualizes the website traffic by using a snapshot of the web page or the live version of the web page, and then it overlays that screen with the click data. These reports are extremely useful for studying how a web page is being used, which makes them ideal for optimizing individual pages. Since these are visual reports, they are easy to interpret, so even your director or coworkers who have little experience with web analytics can understand and interpret what visitors use on a page.

Many web analytics tools have some type of click-density reporting capability. Google Analytics has an in-page report, which is a site overlay style of report that displays the number of clicks a link received (figure 4.4). However, it does not show exactly where every click occurred on the page, and if a visitor clicked on a nonlinked object, such as white space or an image, those data are not displayed in the report.

Heat maps are another popular click density report. Heat maps generalize usage on a web page but use color to show areas of high and low traffic; the warmer the color (reds, yellows, and oranges), the more clicks there were in that area of the page (figure 4.5). Many tools now come with some type of heat map feature. Open Web Analytics contains a heat-map feature; Piwik users can apply a heat map plug-in that incorporates ClickHeat, a stand-alone, open-source heat map tool. If you are not satisfied with your tool's click density report, there are even separate web analytics tools, such as Crazy Egg, that focus on just providing heat-map and other click-density reports (Farney 2011).

59

FIGURE 4.4

In-Page Report, Google Analytics, University of Colorado Colorado Springs

Segmenting Click-Density Reports

Many click density reports have some form of segmenting capability that helps you advance beyond the bland aggregated data of all visits to focus in on how certain user groups are using that page. Have you ever wondered whether those visitors with smaller screen resolutions are fully using your website? If you can segment click density reports by screen resolution, you can see exactly where those users with small screens are clicking.

Usability Testing and Click Density Reports

There are usability testing tools that combine the functionality of click-density analysis reports with other user-testing features. For example, Mouseflow (http://mouseflow.com) is a commercial usability tool that can be implemented on a website during testing. It uses screen-capture software to record user movements on the site, and it generates heat maps based on visitor clicks and movements. Web analytics data should always be reviewed during usability testing. Heat maps or other click density reports are powerful for their simplicity—anyone on the

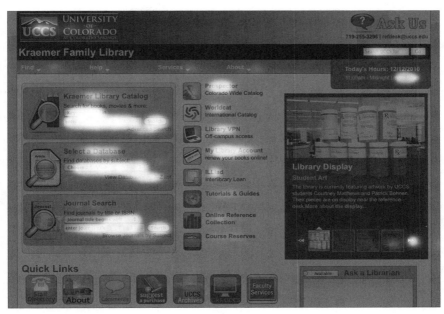

FIGURE 4.5
Heat Map, Crazy Egg, University of Colorado Colorado Springs

website redesign committee can interpret how visitors are interacting with that page. Library staff can create this type of report by implementing a click density tool on the website during testing to capture that click information.

Click-Density Analysis and Outbound Links

Always check your web analytics tool's documentation to understand which data are tracked in its click density report. Does it track all clicks, or does it report existing click data already collected in the tool? A majority of tools track individual clicks on the page, regardless of whether the click is on a link, an image, or white space. However, not all click density reports work the same way. Google Analytics' in-page report does not track outbound links or clicks on items that Google Analytics cannot track without additional customizations. Even if your website is configured to track outbound links as specified in Google Analytics' documentation, the in-page report still will not display those data. You will have to resort to path analysis reports to get to that data.

Path Analysis Reports

Path analysis, or navigation summaries, helps visualize how visitors navigate through a website (figure 4.6). At the web page level, path analysis reports show the page the visitors came from and the page they moved to next. Like the click density report, this report is useful for optimizing web pages because you can see whether visitors are navigating through the site as intended or are unexpectedly leaving the site. Most path analysis focuses on visits as the main metric; you can apply segments to these reports to further analyze specific users or behaviors.

There are website-level path analysis reports that show how visitors are navigating through the entire website beginning from their point of entry (landing page) to where they leave (exit page). Google Analytics' report on visitors flow is an example of a website-level path analysis report. As figure 4.7 demonstrates, this report makes it easy to segment the data so you can see exactly how new visitors are

FIGURE 4.6
Navigation Summary, Google Analytics,
University of Colorado Colorado Springs

navigating the site. Many entered the site directly from the website's home page, but more than half of those visitors left the site automatically (bounced), and the rest continued navigating to database pages, the library catalog, the library's hours page, and more. Also, note that second-largest group of new visitors landed on a wide arrange of pages humbly reported here as (more than eighty-three other pages). Clicking this link reveals exactly which pages were landed on and which pages had more click-throughs to other pages or contributed to more drop-offs (bounces).

Caution Regarding Path Analysis Reports

A problem with path analysis reports is that even though websites are designed with designated paths in mind, users may have completely different ideas on how to move through the site. Consider a person coming to the reference desk and asking for a journal article on a topic. There are many routes one could take to answer that question: use one of any number of the article databases, go directly to an electronic journal and start searching, use Google Scholar, and so on. Some answers may be better than others, but the point is that there is not just one way to answer the question. The same holds true for a website; there are many routes a visitor can take to get to the desired end point. Although path analysis reports

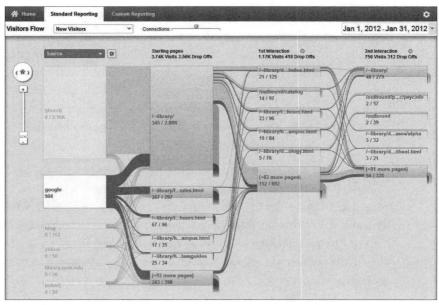

FIGURE 4.7
Visitors Flow, Google Analytics, University of Colorado Colorado Springs

63

can be useful in identifying some user behaviors and can provide ideas on how to improve the navigation or structure of your site, they are not the only reports you should use to review visitors' use of a website.

Event Tracking

Web analytics tools track website use by page views. When a page view is triggered, the tool starts collecting the data. Yet there are probably many items on your library's website that are used but do not trigger a page view because those items are not necessarily a web page. Kaushik (2010) refers to this as a pageless experience; when visitors interact with pageless objects, it is called an event. In web analytics, events include the following:

> **Outbound links**—Outbound links send visitors to another website. While the link takes the user to a web page, the page itself is not within your website, and your web analytics tool may not be able to track it. Some web analytics tools contain a standard report that can track outbound links automatically. If your web analytics tool has this feature, then there is no need for you to track outbound links as an event.

> **File downloads**—PDFs, text files, podcasts, and other types of documents are files, are not web pages, so they do not trigger a page view when clicked. If your library has a job application form as a PDF on your website, each time a visitor downloads the file, your web analytics may not be able to track it. Again, some web analytics tools do automatically track file downloads in a standard report; however, if your tool does not, you will need to implement event tracking on the downloadable files to record usage if this information is important to you.

> **Dynamic scripts and embedded objects**—Flash, JavaScript, Ajax, and embedded multimedia widgets and objects are elements within a web page and thus do not trigger a page view on their own. Sites with dynamic scripts or embedded players must use event tracking to track the use data on these objects. You can track how many times a video is played, the number of clicks an object receives, or even how often a visitor hovers over an object.

Some web analytics tools automatically track some events, but this is not consistent across tools. If your web analytics tool tracks events, you will need to first add the event-tracking code to the events you wish to track. After that is implemented, the data will be collected when users interact with that object, and the data will then be displayed in an event report. The next section is an overview of event tracking in Google Analytics and Open Web Analytics.

Tracking Events in Google Analytics

In Google Analytics, there are two options for tracking pageless objects: as virtual page views or as events. You can track virtual page views by implementing the track-page-views script (http://support.google.com/analytics/bin/answer .py?hl=en&answer=1136920) for each item you want to track. When a visitor clicks on the link with that script, it generates a fake page view that can then be tracked. The problem with this method is that it inflates the page views for the website because of all the fake page views generated. The inflated page views are then incorporated into other Google Analytics reports, so you will need to either segment the individual reports or create a separate filtered profile if you want to analyze the more realistic count of page views.

The preferred method is to track pageless objects as an event by adding the event-tracking script (http://code.google.com/apis/analytics/docs/tracking/ eventTrackerGuide.html) to each object that you want to track. Objects that are tracked as an event do not generate fake page views but report the action by the visitor. These data are viewable in a separate event report. So how does event tracking work? First, decide which objects to track and add the tracking event script to them. Google Analytics' event-tracking script allows you to customize the information tracked by four variables: category, action, label, and value:

Category—A name for the set of objects you will track. To track a series of outbound links, you could use "outbound links" as the category name. Likewise, to track a group of embedded videos using "videos" for the category.

Action—What visitors will be doing with the event. This can be as simple as "click" if tracking outbound links, the name of the buttons on the video player ("play" or "pause"), or a button in an online form ("submit" or "clear").

Label—The unique name of the object being tracked, for example, the name of the video, link, or file you are tracking. This is optional, but the event report will clarify which individual objects are used.

Value—Another optional variable; this one assigns an integer or numerical value to the event being tracked. One potential use is to assign monetary

65

value to each interaction with the object. This is particularly useful for libraries that like to monitor and report data on return on investment for online resources or services.

You need to implement the tracking script on *every* element you wish to track as an event. Here is an example of the tracking script that tracks the clicks an image in a jQuery slide-show viewer receives. The actual tracking script is called the "onclick" function. In this case, "spotlight" is the category, "click" is the action, and "Faculty Pubs" is the label. No value variable was assigned:

```
<img src="MasterPages/images/spotlight/faculty_image.jpg" alt="Faculty Name"
    onclick="_gaq.push(['_trackEvent', 'spotlight', 'click', 'Faculty Pubs']);"/>
```

Figure 4.8 demonstrates an events report that tracks the same jQuery slide-show viewer, which is prominently displayed on the library's home page. This jQuery object is set to automatically transition between a set of images, but visitors can click on a thumbnail image to make the slide-show viewer display that image. The Google Analytics event report is showing only data tagged with the category "spotlight," which is the name of the entire slide-show viewer being tracked. In

FIGURE 4.8
Event-Tracking Report, Google Analytics,
University of Colorado Colorado Springs

this category, two actions are tracked: click and hover. The events report shows total interactions, such as the total number of clicks the thumbnail images received. By adding event tracking, library staff can view the number of times each of the images in the slide-show viewer is clicked on or hovered over; this lets web staff check whether visitors are noticing the feature (hovering) and interacting (clicking) with it.

The event report also includes unique events, also referred to as visits with an event, which counts only the visit that triggered an event on a specific object. Adding the label variable is important because it allows Google Analytics to determine the difference between separate objects and unique events. In the slide-show viewer example, all of the thumbnails have the same action, but they have different labels, such as "Faculty Pubs" for faculty images, whereas library event images are labeled "Library Events." Since the images often change, it was more important to track which type of spotlight feature triggered more events. In this example, a visitor can click on the thumbnails labeled "Faculty Pubs" multiple times in one session, and that would record only one unique event because it stems from one visit. Yet if that same visitor clicked on a "Faculty Pubs" thumbnail and then a "Library Events" thumbnail, that would count as two separate unique events because the images have different labels. Remember, only one unique event can be triggered per label in one visit.

Tracking Events in Open Web Analytics

Action tracking (http://wiki.openwebanalytics.com/index.php?title=Tracker) is Open Web Analytics' version of event tracking, and it functions the same as Google Analytics' event tracking; you add an additional tracking script to what you want to track and the data gathered are reported in the action-tracking report. The action-tracking script has four variables: action_group, action_name, action_label, and numeric_value. These variables function exactly as Google Analytics' event-tracking script variables. So, action_group is similar to category, action_name is action, action_label equals label, and numeric_value is value. Again, this report is fairly similar to the Google Analytics event-tracking report, so you can drill down into specific action groups and labels to see the total events that are recorded.

Does Your Web Analytics Tool Automatically Track Events?

A handful of web analytics tools come with an ability to track some events automatically. Piwik has a nice functionality for tracking outbound links and file downloads out of the box, which means no extra setup is required to track this information. However, other events are not automatically tracked, so if you want to monitor usage of embedded videos, online form submissions, and other pageless events, you need to check Piwik's documentation. Regardless of the web analytics tool you choose, check the documentation to see which event-tracking options the tool provides.

Conversion Reports

When it comes to goal reporting in web analytics, goals are more commonly referred to as conversions. We use the term *conversions* when talking about web analytics goals so as not to confuse strategic planning goals and a tool's goal-tracking capability. Conversions are extremely useful because they help libraries focus on the outcomes and results that are important for libraries. It is easy to become overwhelmed with data in web analytics, but conversions are essential components in a web analytics strategy because they help measure the success of the website. Recall that a conversion is simply a visitor completing a desired task or behavior on your website. Conversions will be unique to each library, and they should directly tie into the website's purpose and objectives. The next chapter talks more about measuring website goals using web analytics; this section is designed to cover the basics of conversions and how they are incorporated in a web analytics tool's reporting. Since library sites are not typically e-commerce sites, this section does not cover conversions specific to e-commerce, such as transactions or per-visit value. E-commerce conversion information may be found in almost any other web analytics book.

Since conversions are unique to the organization, all conversions are based on that organization's desired outcomes. For example, if your library would like to increase the number of visitors that connect to the library's catalog from its main website, the desired outcome would be to increase clicks on the library catalog link; the conversion would be the clicks on the library catalog link. If your library's catalog is hosted on a different web server or domain from your library's website, you may need to track that catalog link as an outbound link either using virtual page views or as an event.

The total number of conversions in itself does not reveal whether your website is successful until those conversion are put into context. Enter the conversion rate, which is the total number of conversions divided by the total visits or unique visitors to the website. If the library's website tracked 800 page views to the library's catalog and 8,000 unique visitors during the same period, the conversion rate

Deciding between Visits or Unique Visitors for Your Conversions

When it comes to calculating conversions, you must decide to either use visits or unique visits as your measurement of overall site use. If you use visits as your denominator, your conversion rates will reflect all visits (sessions) on the site and will help you gauge the overall website use. The other option is to use unique visitors, which more closely align with an individual person using the website; this means that you are taking into account that a visitor does not always visit your website for the same purpose (Kaushik 2006). If the visitor converted once, then you have succeeded even if that visitor returns to the site for other purposes.

To demonstrate both possible methods, we use an example of a library wanting to measure the use of a specific article database on its website. In one month, 700 conversions took place involving that database, and the website received 24,000 visits and 8,000 unique visitors. Using visits, the conversation rate would be 700 divided by 24,000, or 2.9 percent. For unique visitors, the conversion rate is 700 divided by 8,000, or 8.75 percent. Naturally, there is a difference between the results; however, both are correct conversion rates. Regardless of which method you choose for your library, you must clearly report what this metric represents. If you used visits, you need to report that 2.9 percent of the entire website's traffic for that month visited the database. If you used unique visitors, you would report that 8.75 percent of your website's visitors accessed the database. Select a method and use it consistently for all conversion rates so that it is always clear what the number actually means (Kaushik 2006).

would be 10 percent (or 800 divided by 8,000). This means that 10 percent of the visitors that month came to the library's website to get to the library's catalog.

So, what is a good conversion rate to aim for? There is not a standard rate that can apply to all libraries. In general, the conversion rate is low; it is commonly 10 percent or lower. Since conversion rates are unique for each library, one way to evaluate them is to compare them with a previous month's rate. By benchmarking, or comparing, the conversion rate over time, you can determine whether the site is improving. We further discuss the concept of benchmarking in chapter 5.

Macro and Micro Conversions

Conversions are tied to a website's desired outcomes. Before approaching conversions, you should understand what your library's main goal or purpose is and how you intend to measure it using web analytics. However, a website serves multiple purposes that also need to be measured. Macro conversions focus on the website's overall purpose, and micro conversions help analyze the additional purposes it serves. For example, a library website's main purpose may be to provide access to research resources (macro conversion), yet the site might also attract visitors because of job postings, community information, or research assistance (all potential micro conversions). Depending on the website's goals, one macro conversion accompanied by several micro conversions can help you put into context how the site is being used.

Conversion Reporting in a Web Analytics Tool

Most web analytics tools include some type of conversion reporting integrated in a goals report. Again, the goals report should not be confused with a website's goals or goal planning, because conversions tracked in the goals report tend to be much more limited in scope. Web analytics tools often simplify conversions into visitors viewing a specific web page, measuring engagement metrics, or tracking an event; however, conversions can be whatever library staff desire to measure, and a website's goal may not always be measurable by web analytics alone. For example, a library wants to measure the impact of the website's marketing of a workshop on the workshop's attendance. You can track the visits or unique visitors to the advertisement for the library workshop on the website, but the important outcome is the number of attendees at the workshop, which is not recorded by the web analytics tool. The conversion rate would be workshop attendance divided by the number of unique visitors who viewed the website's advertisement. Sounds like good data to have, but these are not exactly the type of data that a tool's goals report automatically captures. At this point, it may even more beneficial to just poll the workshop attendees to find out whether they viewed the online advertisement before deciding to attend the workshop.

Yet conversions reveal a great deal of interesting data. The following section describes the typical conversion types included in a goal report.

Goal Type: Time on Site

The goal of time on site is fairly straightforward, as it is designed to trigger a conversion whenever a visit meets the condition requirement for the length of time spent on the site. This goal could track visits over a few minutes or track visits that do not last as long as desired on the site. Why monitor this conversion when you can just see the average time on site? Averages generalize use data and can be misleading. An average time on site of two minutes could potentially be a range from a lot of visits that last fewer than ten seconds averaged with the few visits that lasted more than an hour on your website. The average does not show how many visits actually lasted at least two minutes on your site. With the time on site goal, you can create a simple conversion to report the total visits that last longer or shorter than the length of time you specify for your website.

Goal Type: Pages per Visit

Similar to the time on site goal, the pages per visit goal creates a conversion whenever a visit meets the condition you created for the number of pages viewed in one visit. With this goal type, you can track the number of visits that view or do not view the number of pages you desire them to view in one session. Like the time on site goal, this goal is designed to help measure visitor engagement into a conversion and is much more robust than the metric of average pages per visit that is displayed in standard reports.

Goal Type: URL Destination

A URL destination goal identifies a specific web page or group of pages, sometimes referred to as a goal page, that triggers a conversion when viewed. A goal page can be a real web page on your site or a virtual page created to track outbound links.

A goal funnel is a unique feature of the URL destination goal report, and it tracks the anticipated series of pages that visitors will navigate through to reach the goal page. Funnels are particularly useful, as they illustrate where visitors enter and exit while navigating toward the goal page. By monitoring the early exits, you can identify potential problems in your website if you notice a large amount of unexpected exits where visitors abandon the outlined path to the goal page. This works well for goal pages that have clearly identified pages that must be navigated through to get to the goal page. For example, when you order something online, you typically start the process by putting an item in your shopping cart (step 1), and you then go to the checkout page, where you must first put in your shipping information (step 2) and then your payment information on the payment page (step 3). After you submit your payment information, you typically see a confirmation page (step 4) that confirms your order. In this example, the confirmation page would be a clear goal page because it marks the end of a successful transaction. The funnel includes the shopping-cart page, the shipping page, and the payment page because each is a required step and cannot be skipped in the purchase process. The funnel tracks the entrances and exits at each step, outlining where visitors are exiting before hitting the goal page. A company would be very interested in seeing where in that funnel they are losing visitors so that it can target those pages for improvement and increase their overall conversion rate, and in turn, increase purchases.

Setting up a goal page and funnel for a library is bit more abstract, as a library's goal page may not have a clearly defined path to it. If your goal page is a page that can be navigated to through various different routes, then you may not be interested in defining a funnel for that specific goal. However, you can still implement a funnel if you have a desired path to the goal page for your visitors to follow. This allows you to test the usefulness of that path. Keep in mind that, just like the path analysis reports, there is not one correct route to the goal page.

Figure 4.9 demonstrates a URL destination goal report to a library's psychology-related subject databases. The goal page is any of the database links, and since all are outbound links, each is configured for tracking. The funnel is tracking the perceived best route to the goal page, which starts at the library's home page, which leads visitors to the psychology subject database page and finally to the goal pages. Notice that many visitors started the conversion process at the library's home page but exited before the second step, which involves going to the database by subject page. This is not too surprising, as the home page receives a major flow of traffic, and not every visitor is interested in using psychology databases. However, the third step highlights that the visitors who proceed to the psychology database page are highly likely to click on one of the psychology databases to trigger the conversion. The psychology database page is successfully navigating users directly to the databases. Although the funnel is useful for identifying potential problems with the flow of a website (in this case the library could target the home page to better promote the psychology databases), it also can verify that website users are also finding what they need.

Goal Type: Event

The event goal triggers a conversion when a visitor performs an event (which you have already defined with an event-tracking script). Unlike the URL destination goal, the event goal does not include a funnel option because events are not necessarily tied to a specific end page. Note that a conversion occurs only once per visit for that unique goal, so if you set a conversion that involves an event that could potentially happen multiple times per visit, such as watching a video several times on your website, it will be counted as only one conversion per visit. You will need to check your event report to see the total number of times the event was triggered.

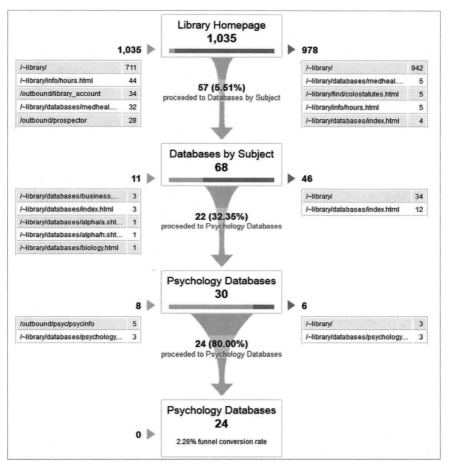

FIGURE 4.9
Funnel Visualization, Google Analytics,
University of Colorado Colorado Springs

Adding Value to Conversions

A benefit to using conversions is that most web analytics tools allow the association of a value to each time the conversion is triggered. In the business world, this makes perfect sense: even if the conversion does not result in the company directly making money, such as a visitor subscribing to an RSS feed, the company wants to track the return on investment it receives from that action. The value the company would associate with that conversion is rarely arbitrary; for the RSS example, the value could be calculated from past experience in how many of those RSS subscribers ultimately purchased an item and then dividing that figure by the amount of money those purchases brought into the company. Suddenly, value is associated with an RSS subscription! By goal tracking the RSS feed subscriptions, the web analytics tool can track the number of conversions taking place in addition to totaling the value that conversion brings to the company.

In the library world, adding value to conversions is not as easily defined. After all, how can we put a price on the use of information? Publishers and database vendors have done this for years, and libraries have also jumped on this bandwagon (Mezick 2007; Tenopir 2010, 2012). The question remains: should you use a goal value to help monetize your library's conversions? That is a question each library should answer for itself. Some like using the goal value to help convey to directors or administrators the perceived value from measuring the transaction, whereas others feel that putting a price amount on a library service or resource for conversions is a waste. If your library selects to implement the goal value, then make it a realistic goal value and not some meaningless number. It does not have to be an exact value, but a decent estimate will help make the goal value a useful asset in your conversion reports.

A simple example of calculating a realistic goal value is the cost per access for a vendor database; take the subscription cost for one year of access to the database and divide it by the total visits to that database received for that year. Your database vendor should be able to provide these data. Now you have the cost per access for that database, and you can associate it as a value in a conversion. Again, this is an estimated value, but in a year's time, you can determine whether the conversion value exceeds the database's price tag to see if the library earned more value from higher use to that database than anticipated.

CUSTOM REPORTS

Segmenting is a useful ability to apply to premade reports to gain additional discoveries in the data, yet there will come a time when you realize that no matter how you apply your segments, you are still not getting to the data you need using those standard and semicustom reports. The next step is to use custom reports, which empower you to select the exact metrics you want to analyze. Libraries can save time by building their own custom reports to help them focus on the data that matter. Custom reports are so useful that you may decide to abandon all other web analytics reports in favor of custom building your own.

Many web analytics tools allow for the creation of custom reports within the tool itself, but not all do. If your web analytics tool does not have a type of internal custom report feature, check to see whether it has data-export capability so that you can import your web analytics data into spreadsheet software or data analysis software, such as SPSS or R, to create custom reports. This requires more work but is worth the effort if you have a functional custom-reporting ability. Piwik's Analytics Data API (http://piwik.org/docs/analytics-api/) gives you the option of exporting data collected in Piwik. You can customize the export by selecting the metrics and adding segments to the data output.

Creating a Custom Report in a Web Analytics Tool

When you create a custom report in your web analytics tool, it is typically stored within that tool so that it instantly updates with new data as they are collected. This also means that it includes historical data, so whatever website use data your tool already collected can also be displayed in these reports. You create the custom report once and access it each time you need it. Although different web analytics tools may use different terminology and slightly different options, the process of creating a custom report across tools is basically the same. We use Google Analytics to demonstrate how to create a custom report.

To create a custom report, go to the "Custom Report" feature in Google Analytics. From here, you can view previously created custom reports or opt to create a new one. Click the "New Custom Report" button to begin the process. Name your report and report tab—in Google Analytics, each tab can hold a single report, and each custom report can contain up to five tabs, or five different reports. Select how you want the report to be displayed; your options are the explorer table, which lets you drill down further into the data, and a flat table, which reports the data into a single table. Next, select the dimensions, the main variable being reported (represented as rows of data), and the metrics that quantify the dimension (represented as columns of data)—an in-depth explanation is available on the *Webucator* blog (http://seo .blogs.webucator.com/2010/08/27/metrics-and-dimensions-in-google-analytics/). Some dimensions and metrics cannot be combined, and Google has documentation showing how you can test the possible options (https://developers.google.com/ analytics/devguides/reporting/core/dimsmets). After you select your metrics and dimensions, you have the option of applying a filter and selecting the profile you want to apply to the custom report. Be sure to save the custom report once you are done implementing your preferences.

Custom Report Filters and Regex

Regex stands for "regular expressions," which is a pattern-matching tool used to match a string of text. The filters for custom reports allow you to filter the report using a majority of the metrics Google Analytics provides. By using regex, you can tell Google Analytics which data to include or not include in the filter. This provides more control over the filtering abilities for the custom reports. Regex can be complicated for those who have not dealt with regular expressions before. If you have questions about using regex, Google Analytics provides a basic guide (http://support.google.com/analytics/bin/answer.py?hl=en&answer=1034324).

Custom Reports and Conversion Reporting

Custom reports provide a great deal of potential for library staff to develop useful web analytics reports, but like conversions, custom reports are unique to each library. This makes it difficult to prescribe the best custom reports, because each library needs to develop reports that are useful locally. To start this process, develop a list of the information you want or need to know about your website, and develop a plan for how you can measure it using website use data. Although the list will vary by library, it is highly recommended that each library consider building custom reports that incorporate its conversions or goals. The goals report is limited to showing how many times a conversion takes place. With segmenting, you can get a little more information about who is making the conversion. But what if you wanted to know if there is a trend in which landing pages tend to lead to a higher conversion rate? This requires a custom report to answer that question. Figure 4.10 shows the landing page (dimension) with some basic metrics—visits, bounce rate, and page per visit—as well as a goal of conversion rate. Now it is clear which landing pages helped trigger the conversion for that goal. The bounce rate helps interpret how many of the visits ended the conversion process at the first page. The pages per visit metric identifies the average number of pages the visitors click through on the website from the landing page, which reveals a bit of information of the visitors' paths. While all of this information is interesting, the main objective of this report is to identify the landing pages that contribute to the successful conversions.

In Google Analytics' custom reports, if you use the explorer table, you can add a secondary dimension to the report that lets you drill down even further into the

Landing Pages and Conversions Jan 1, 2012 - Apr 30, 2012 ▾

Advanced Segments | Edit Email BETA Export ▾ Add to Dashboard

● 100.00% of total visits

| Psychology Database Conversion | Pages Per Vist Conversion |

Basic Stats

Visits ▾ vs. Select a metric   Day Week Month

● Visits
8,000

4,000

Feb 2012   Mar 2012   Apr 2012

Visits	Bounce Rate	Pages/Visit	% New Visits	Psychology Databases (Goal6 Conversion Rate)
88,550	**30.67%**	**3.29**	**21.89%**	**2.33%**
% of Total: 100.00% (88,550)	Site Avg: 30.67% (0.00%)	Site Avg: 3.29 (0.00%)	Site Avg: 21.89% (0.00%)	Site Avg: 2.33% (0.00%)

Primary Dimension: Landing Page

Secondary dimension ▾ Sort Type: Default ▾   🔍 advanced

Landing Page		Visits ↓	Bounce Rate	Pages/Visit	% New Visits	Psychology Databases (Goal6 Conversion Rate)
1. /~library/		77,937	27.51%	3.41	19.92%	2.29%
2. /~library/info/hours.html		1,435	84.95%	1.36	24.11%	0.00%
3. /~library/find/colostatutes.html		1,218	71.51%	1.51	93.10%	0.00%
4. /~library/databases/index.html		1,155	9.26%	3.95	12.73%	4.94%
5. /~library/databases/medheal.html		534	30.15%	2.00	7.49%	0.56%
6. /~library/help/offcampus.html		523	60.42%	3.07	22.56%	1.34%
7. /~library/databases/psychology.html		480	37.71%	2.26	33.12%	37.71%

FIGURE 4.10
Custom Report, Google Analytics,
University of Colorado Colorado Springs

data. Using the custom report in figure 4.10 we added another subdimension called source, which is a referring-source metric that shows what referred the visitor to the website. When you add a subdimension, you can click on the original dimension in the custom report—in this example, any of the landing pages—and it will take you to another level in the report that reveals the referring sources along with all the metrics included in the custom report for that specific landing page. It is clear which individual sources helped contribute to the conversion rate for that specific web page.

Segment Your Custom Reports

The major theme of this chapter is that segmentation is essential. Even in custom reports you can still gain additional value by segmenting the data. Using the same example of a custom report, we can add a custom segment to see whether visitors are able to trigger a conversion (in this case, clicking on a psychology database) in fewer than thirty seconds. Now you can get an idea not only of which landing pages contribute to higher conversions but also whether website users can make the conversion fairly quickly on the site.

CONCLUSION

Customizable reports are the strongest assets in a library's web analytics strategy, but only if the library takes the time and effort to develop them correctly. Remember, the closer you connect your web analytics strategy to your library's and website's goals, the less likely you will be distracted by the nonessential data. This involves planning what you want to get out of your website use data and configuring your web analytics tool to properly collect it. This chapter covered the basics of customizing your web analytics reports and data using segmentation, semicustom reporting features like conversions, and finally custom reports. The next chapter takes you beyond the mechanics to practical applications of these custom features for your library.

REFERENCES

Farney, Tabatha A. 2011. "Click Analytics: Visualizing Web Site Use Data." *Information Technology and Libraries* 30, no. 3: 141–148.

Kaushik, Avinash. 2006. "Excellent Analytics Tip #5: Conversion Rate Basic & Best Practices." July 13. *Occam's Razor.* www.kaushik.net/avinash/excellent-analytics-tip5 -conversion-rate-basics-best-practices/.

———. 2010. *Web Analytics 2.0: The Art of Online Accountability and Science of Customer Centricity.* Indianapolis, IN: Wiley.

Mezick, Elizabeth M. 2007. "Return on Investment: Libraries and Student Retention." *Journal of Academic Librarianship* 33, no. 5 (September): 561–566.

Tenopir, Carol. 2010. "Measuring the Value of the Academic Library: Return on Investment and Other Value Measures." *Serials Librarian* 58, nos. 1–4: 39–48.

———. 2012. "Beyond Usage: Measuring Library Outcomes and Value." *Library Management* 33, nos. 1–2: 5–13.

Chapter Five

Action-Oriented Analytics
Turning Data into Decisions

Customizing your web analytics reports is a foundational strategy to refine your data into useful insights on how users access and utilize a website. Those data are meaningless unless you take the steps to turn insights into actions. Marshall Breeding (2008) defines the concept of action-oriented analytics as the process of using web analytics data in the decision-making process. He points out that web analytics data "allow you to make changes, measure their impact, and make a decision about whether to keep or roll back the change based on the user response" (Breeding 2008, 22). Action-oriented analytics is sometimes referred to as actionable web analytics or data-driven decision making. Each implies the same thing: the use of web analytics reports to help implement and evaluate changes to a website. This concept highlights the main purpose of web analytics: to go beyond collecting data to putting that data to use.

This chapter covers how to convert data into actions. We discuss using benchmarks and a formal web analytics strategy to measure the effectiveness of a library's website and success of the actions taken to improve them. We conclude the chapter with additional actionable uses for web analytics data.

BENCHMARKING TO DETERMINE SUCCESS

Have you ever made a change on a web page and wanted to know whether it had the impact you intended? To answer this question, you must first understand the typical pattern of use of whatever you are measuring, and then compare that with the new use data. A benchmark is simply a standard for comparing or measuring change. Benchmarks are your best ally in determining success, or lack thereof, in website use.

Benchmarking is all about putting data into perspective or context. If your website received twenty thousand visits in a month, how can you tell if that number is good or bad? With no other context, you cannot. However, if your analytics tool revealed that website received twenty thousand visits in a month, up from the seventeen thousand visits it received during the same month last year, now you have a good sign of success.

Benchmarks are also necessary to test how effective a change or revision is to a website. For example, a library wants to improve access to its online catalog, so it builds a catalog search widget and embeds it on the library's home page. Rather than assuming that the widget is improving access to the catalog as intended, the library can compare the number of click-throughs to the catalog before and after the widget was added to determine whether there was an increase in use—a positive indication of success in this example.

How to Benchmark

In web analytics, benchmarking usually implies competitive benchmarking, where site use data are compared to those of similar organizations' websites; however, it is important to self-benchmark, also known as internal benchmarking, which is the process of comparing a website's use data against itself. Both processes can help you understand your site's ideal use patterns and contribute to making your web analytics reports actionable.

Self-Benchmarking Basics

Before you can start benchmarking your own website, you must first understand the site's normal usage patterns. This may take a few months' worth of data—or even a year's worth of data—to see the use trends. By understanding the norm, you can measure how changes to the website have an impact on normal use. If usage increases after the revision, it is usually an indication that the revision had a positive impact; however, a decrease in use, an increased bounce rate, or more unexpected exits could be telltale signs of negative impact. Further analysis is required to figure out the source of the issue; additional revisions can then be made, and retesting of those revisions is necessary to determine success.

It is important to select comparable and useful time spans of data when you benchmark. Comparing apples to oranges will only skew the results. If your benchmark is based on one week's worth of data, then the data you will compare to that benchmark should also be one week's worth of data. Similarly, consider the time spans you are comparing. Track time spans that typically have close to the same use. An academic library's website tends to receive more use during the academic semester than during the summer or break periods when classes are not in session. It would not make sense to benchmark data from a week during the semester to compare with a week during the break, because the two weeks of data are not comparable in terms of usage.

The best time spans to use for benchmarking data vary depending on the situation. A benchmark can be based on a day, week, month, or even year of data. If you are comparing a revision to a web page, a week or month of use data should suffice. Sometimes it takes longer for a revision to fully take effect, so it may be necessary to look at more longitudinal data.

However you decide to self-benchmark, most web analytics tools make it easy to compare different ranges of data. Figure 5.1 compares the same months of data from 2011 and 2012 for an individual web page in Google Analytics. This web-page-level report compares several page-specific metrics: page views, unique page

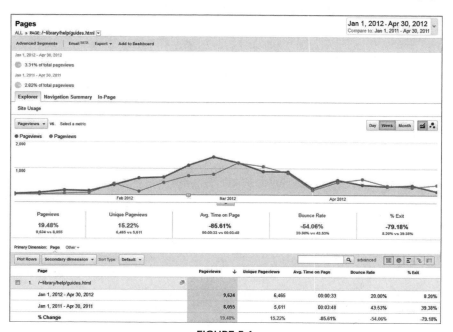

FIGURE 5.1
Comparing Data by Date Range, Google Analytics,
University of Colorado Colorado Springs

views, average time on page, bounce rate, and percentage of exits. All of these metrics are compared between the two different years, which makes it easy to discern the differences on this page. For additional comparisons, apply additional segments to this report to compare usage by different user groups or behaviors.

Notice that figure 5.1 shows a major difference in the page's bounce rate and average time on page. What caused that shift? It is not clear by looking at the data; however, looking at the full data set, an annotation explained that this web page was redesigned in late 2011. This revision has had a clear impact on how the web page is used, but that would not be obvious if the annotation were not present. We recommend using annotations in your web analytics tool when you want to track the impact a revision has on the site's use. Annotations can be any type of information that you would like to include, such as noting when a major website revision was implemented, when a new web feature or service was introduced, or when a marketing campaign began. If your library maintains a blog or online newsletter or journal, you can make note each time the site publishes

Data Decay and Self-Benchmarking

Website use data is not a like a fine wine; it does not age very well. When you are benchmarking data, you are comparing older data with new data, which may not be a perfect comparison because the usefulness of data decays over time. By understanding how data go bad, you prevent misinterpreting comparisons. Here are some issues to be aware of when comparing old, longitudinal (usually more than one year old or older) data to current data (Kaushik 2010):

- Web analytics tools or their methods of tracking data may change.

- Visitors and the way they navigate through a website changes.

- Design and content on a website are occasionally drastically modified, which changes users actions and behavior on the site.

Each of these reasons may affect internal benchmarking, but before you throw out your old web analytics data, there are some web analytics reports worth keeping. Avinash Kaushik (2010) recommends keeping at least reports that reveal the weekly trend of visits and unique visitors, the top ten referrers by month, the monthly bounce rate, and your critical metrics—your important conversions and other key data. All of these reports are useful for internal benchmarking and should be archived locally.

a new post or issue. You can compare the impact new content has on the usage of the entire website—are you increasing or decreasing your readership over time? Benchmarking data will show this. Additionally, if your library undergoes a marketing campaign, make a note of it in your web analytics tool so you can measure the potential impact of the marketing. Google Analytics has an integrated annotation feature, but if your web analytics tool does not have one, we suggest that you keep a separate, internal document of the dates and annotations so that you have that information readily available.

Benchmarking against Other Libraries

Competitive benchmarking, also referred to as external benchmarking, is the process of comparing your web analytics data with the data of other similar organizations. This is particularly handy in the commercial realm because companies want to compare their use data with those of their competitors. Libraries are not typically in competition with one another, but competitive benchmarking can still be useful, as it puts in perspective a library's website usage. Competitive benchmarking can reveal areas for improvement on the website that may have gone unnoticed, and it helps establish new usage goals for the site.

To start the competitive benchmarking process, select a library that serves a similar purpose, size, and audience. Next, check to see which web analytics data from that other library are available to you and start benchmarking away! It sounds easy, but it can be more complicated than that—sharing web analytics data is not a common practice. If you happen to get your hands on that data, the data tend to be a basic report containing few standard metrics, such as visits, and little else. Additionally, libraries may have different web analytics tools, which makes it difficult to compare data since each tool has its own method for collecting and analyzing the statistics.

Getting Other Libraries' Website Use Data

Despite all these complications, there are benchmarking tools available that can help. Note that most of them are commercial, fee-based tools, such as Hitwise (www.hitwise.com/us), which focus mainly on e-commerce or high-traffic websites. Benchmarking tools for libraries and other nonprofit organizations are not readily available, but many of the commercial tools offer free demonstrations that are worth checking out. Note that these tools work only if the library websites reside in their own domains, and even then, the tools are not always perfect. Useful commercial tools you can try for free include the following:

83

Alexa (www.alexa.com)—This tool reports website use data as a percentage of all global traffic, so even though it may not show you the exact number of visits or page views, it provides data on pages per visit, bounce rate, average time on site, top search keywords, and basic user information. Most data are limited to the previous three months, but historical data are available for the high-traffic, ranking websites.

Compete (www.compete.com/us)—Compete shares unique visitors by month and other sites that visitors accessed. Other options may be available in the future, such as heat maps, depending on the site.

Both tools help provide perspective on how other library websites are being used. This gives libraries an idea of what to expect for usage from their own sites.

Since benchmarking tools are limited, another solution is to simply ask another library to share data. This is an excellent alternative solution because you can ask that library for the specific metrics that your library wants to benchmark. If you are interested in this approach, make sure your library and the benchmark library candidate both use the same web analytics tool in order to increase the precision of comparing the data. Remember to be a good benchmarking library partner and return the favor by sharing your data.

Besides benchmarking with individual libraries, there are also industry benchmarking reports that combine and average the website use data of many similar organizations into one report. Some hosted web analytics tools come integrated with a benchmarking option. Google Analytics used to have a benchmarking report option, but it was retired in favor of sending quarterly, industry-specific reports for organizations that opt in. These reports do not discern the different types or sizes of the organizations, but they provide a broad overview on user behavior on similar organization's websites.

Benchmarking is not a silver bullet that will cure all of your website woes; it is merely a guideline to measure use and to put your data in perspective. It is far from a perfect practice. There will always be discrepancies between the data comparisons because library website users and their behaviors differ by the library—and that, of course, affects the website use data.

DEFINING YOUR LIBRARY'S WEB ANALYTICS STRATEGY

One of the best ways to ensure that web analytics data is instantly actionable is to develop a web analytics strategy. This book is designed to help library staff develop a web analytics strategy, but what exactly is a web analytics strategy? A web analytics strategy is the structured process of identifying and evaluating your key performance indicators on the basis of an organization's objectives and website goals—the desired outcomes, or what you want people to do on the website. Key performance indicators, or KPIs, are the ways you measure the success of meeting the designated goals. Your edits or revisions to the website are all based on meeting or surpassing your goals.

If are you planning on creating or revising a web analytics strategy, which we strongly recommend that you do, it should be embraced by the entire library—or at least by your administrators and anyone who has the ability to edit the website's content or design. This means that everyone is on the same page on how to contribute their support to meet those goals. Administrators can focus on implementing or expanding services that complement the web analytics strategy. Content creators and web developers understand where to focus their efforts on improving the site's design and content to help achieve the goals. Your strategy is not set in stone but instead should be flexible to adapt to the library's changing needs. Plan on reviewing it periodically to ensure that it still fits the library's needs.

Web Analytics Strategy Example

Web analytics strategies will be unique to each library. Some libraries may have common goals but completely different KPIs. To give you an idea on how to write a web analytics strategy, here is an excerpt from the strategy of the library at the University of Colorado Colorado Springs:

> *Library's Mission:* The Library enhances our users' ability to access information and develop critical research skills by creating physical and virtual pathways for them to interact with Library resources and staff at the most opportune times in their learning processes.
>
> *Website Goal 1:* Connect users to a majority of the library's online databases quickly and efficiently.
>
> *KPI 1:* 80% or more of the users that accessed library databases did so in three or fewer click-throughs on the site.
>
> *KPI 2:* Over half the visitors are able to find a library database in less than a minute from entering the site.

The use of *quickly* and *efficiently* in the goal implies time and ease of navigation through the site data, which makes it natural to use visitor engagement metrics like

Visitor Type	Visits ↓	Pages/Visit	Avg. Visit Duration	Database Usage (Goal11 Conversion Rate)	Database Usage (Goal11 Completions)
1. Returning Visitor					
Less than 60 seconds	43,083	1.70	00:00:08	6.19%	2,667
All Visits	69,161	3.27	00:07:56	7.06%	4,886
2. New Visitor					
Less than 60 seconds	13,265	1.61	00:00:07	3.72%	493
All Visits	19,389	3.36	00:05:27	5.39%	1,045

FIGURE 5.2

KPI 2 Represented in a Segmented Goal Report, Google Analytics, University of Colorado Colorado Springs

pages per visit and time on site in the KPIs. Notice that none of the KPIs is a simple, standard metric—all are conversions and may require additional segmentation. To implement KPI 1, you could create a URL destination goal report (remember those goal types!) and then segment that report with the pages per visit metric. For KPI 2, you could use that same URL destination goal report and apply a different segment for extracting time on site, as shown in figure 5.2. You could also consider building a custom report to organize these data. Since your web analytics strategy will contain multiple goals, each having its own KPIs, creating a custom report for your strategy helps you organize your KPI data in one report and location.

Your web analytics strategy can have as many goals for a website as necessary. Each web presence in the library (e.g., website, blog, online catalog, other web-based services) should have its own set of goals, because different web presences serve different intended purposes. All goals will have their own unique KPIs to measure the desired outcome. Do not let your web analytics strategy grow out of control. Remember to focus on the goals that really matter: your macro conversions and micro conversions. Develop no more than three KPIs for each goal, to keep them manageable. Additionally, ensure that the KPIs you develop are actionable— if you see your website is not meeting your KPI's standard, that should trigger a reaction in the library to make revisions to the website to solve the issue or to reevaluate the appropriateness of the KPI.

Putting Your Web Analytics Strategy in Action

After creating a web analytics strategy and implementing it in a web analytics tool, libraries should regularly monitor the data. Devise a schedule for reviewing the KPI reports to ensure that the library is still on track with its goals. We suggest monitoring your KPI results every two to three months to best keep track of the site. Be prepared to monitor overall visits, conversions, and bounce rates for signs of problems—and remember that decreased usage or increased bounce rates are typically not a positive sign. Also, some KPIs will have their own indicators of success. Using KPI 1 in the earlier example, if that library noticed a significant increase in the number of clicks it takes users to get to a database goal page, then that could be a sign that users are getting lost or distracted from their original intent. The library could review KPI 2 to see whether there is a correlating increase there to confirm that there is a problem. Using both KPI data, the library can track to determine the approximate date that the increases started to incur to see whether they are related to a specific revision to the website. The data may reveal the problem, but you need to identify and fix the problem. After edits have been made, you can review the KPI data to ensure that the revisions made the desired, positive impact.

While setting a regular schedule for reviewing the KPI reports is useful, libraries should also plan on reviewing these essential data after major revisions are made to a site that could alter how the website is used. Does the revision help or hinder the site's ability to meets its goals? By benchmarking a portion of the data before the revisions were implemented with data gathered after the revisions, you can effectively compare the two on the basis of the goals and KPIs for your library's website. Measuring the effectiveness of an edit is as simple as seeing whether the site performs better with the selected KPI.

This type of web analytics strategy is the main driving force behind the site's development. Any edits to the site should be designed to improve the site's KPI performance. Major edits or redesign initiatives should be clearly linked to a specific KPI. If you are completely redesigning a website, it is the perfect time to also reevaluate its goals and KPIs. Are the goals still appropriate? Do the KPIs continue to measure the goals effectively? Addressing these questions during the redesign process keeps a web analytics strategy relevant and up to date.

SOLVING PROBLEMS WITH DATA

The web analyst John Lovett (2009) remarked, "Strategic Web Analytics goes beyond merely pointing out problems to actually solving them." A web analytics strategy helps you monitor the overall effectiveness of a website and identifies potential problems. If your site is not meeting the targeted KPI, web analytics data can play a central role in providing context for an identified problem and then assisting you in deciding how to fix it and testing the fix to see if it worked as intended.

Using Web Analytics to Find Solutions

Web analytics can be incredibly useful for identifying potential solutions to a problem, but it requires you to ask the right questions and to select and analyze the useful metrics. Using the earlier web analytics strategy example, let's say the library's website failed to meet KPI 1 and is hovering around only 60 percent of visitors who entered a research database in three or fewer clicks. To better understand why 40 percent of visitors do not make it to a database in a few clicks, the library needs to find out how those users navigated to the database destination. Where do they enter the site, and what path do they take to get to the database? To answer these questions, you need to review several reports. In Google Analytics, we recommend using the landing pages report to apply a customized segment for the KPI you want to track (labeled "DB Event" in figure 5.3). Now, you can see that a majority of users who use the library's databases enter through the site's home page, but on average, they view five pages before leaving the site. Using the "Entrances Paths" tab, you can track to see where those users go from the library's home page, thus creating a type of navigation summary. Although some users are going directly to

	Landing Page		Visits ↓	Pages/Visit	Avg. Visit Duration	% New Visits	Bounce Rate
☐	1. /~library/	⊕					
	DB Event		4,940	5.01	00:08:39	18.60%	0.00%
	All Visits		42,736	3.44	00:08:16	19.08%	21.64%
☐	2. /~library/databases/medheal.html	⊕					
	DB Event		188	1.89	00:03:55	5.32%	0.00%
	All Visits		265	1.78	00:03:00	7.92%	21.51%
☐	3. /~library/databases/index.html	⊕					
	DB Event		141	3.79	00:04:22	10.64%	0.00%
	All Visits		660	3.87	00:04:40	12.58%	9.24%
☐	4. /~library/databases/business.html	⊕					
	DB Event		38	3.24	00:09:37	5.26%	0.00%
	All Visits		64	3.08	00:07:58	10.94%	15.62%
☐	5. /~library/databases/education.html	⊕					
	DB Event		28	3.36	00:09:22	10.71%	0.00%
	All Visits		78	3.17	00:05:45	6.41%	29.49%
☐	6. /~library/databases/sociology.html	⊕					
	DB Event		28	6.07	00:09:03	35.71%	0.00%
	All Visits		73	3.52	00:04:08	53.42%	38.36%

FIGURE 5.3
Landing Pages Report with Custom Segment, Google Analytics,
University of Colorado Colorado Springs

the database, even more are exploring other portions of the website, including help guides, before clicking on one of the database links.

There is more than one way to solve this problem, but you use web analytics to gain more insight into the problem and formulate a solution. For this example, the library can target the top landing and secondary pages to prominently add a direct link to the databases on those pages, and then see whether that helps those users find the database in fewer clicks. Once the fix is in place, the library can test its effectiveness to see whether the website's performance improves for KPI 1.

Error-Reporting Example

Nothing is worse than navigating through a website and suddenly hitting a web page with a message "HTTP 404: Page Not Found"—for users, it is like slamming into a brick wall. An easy way to improve a user's experience is to prevent this from happening. You can track these error pages using web analytics. Start by adding the tracking script to the error-page template; each time a visitor ends up on an error page, it triggers a page view, which will be tracked in the tool. By viewing the error-reporting pages, you can identify dead links and where users stumbled on them, and then get them fixed fast. Such a quick and easy solution to an annoying problem!

Web Analytics in the Testing Process

Testing a site or page determines whether it is functional; this can be as simple as making a revision on a page and then monitoring that page's use data to determine whether it was improvement. To test a site using web analytics, you must clearly define what you are measuring and then measure it. Consider it like setting up a goal and KPIs for a specific task; once the task is completed, you no longer need to keep track of that goal or KPIs. For example, a library wants to increase the number of chat references it receives through its chat widget, so web staff add the chat widget to each of the top landing pages on the website in addition to its current locations. After a few weeks or a month, you can compare the number of chat references before and after the chat widget was added to the selected pages. The goal is to increase chat interactions, so the measurement (KPI) would involve the total number of chat references received, but another KPI should focus on the total chats generated from the new pages versus the original pages—does it show a significant difference in use? Which pages generate the most chats? The testing process needs to be designed to fit what is being used.

Testing a Marketing Campaign

Libraries can market their services or events in many ways and can just as easily track the success of their marketing campaign using web analytics. It requires some planning at the beginning, but once implemented, this sheds more light on which marketing strategies work best for the library. We offer a method for testing online marketing and print marketing; however, neither is the only way to measure a campaign's effectiveness. These are suggestions to give you an idea of how to approach this issue.

Tracking online marketing efforts is fairly straightforward. As an example, your library is hosting a donation drive in which visitors can donate money online. Your library has a web page dedicated to the information about the drive that contains a place for visitors to donate money. If you advertise the donation drive on your library's Facebook page, blog, or other websites, you can track the referrals those sites send to the donations page. You can take it a step further by setting up a conversion to trigger each time a visitor finishes the donation process. Then, you can compare not only which referring sites sent your donations page traffic but also which of those sites led to a higher conversion rate. From these data, you can target your poor-performing referring websites to enhance the marketing message or decide to improve your marketing effort in other locations.

You can also track a print-based marketing campaign that uses mainly flyers or newspaper advertisements. Doing so requires more planning, but it's worth it since print-based marketing tends to cost more than online marketing. Using the same example of accepting online donations, we suggest using an intermediary redirect page embedded in a shortened URL or Quick Response (QR) code, to refer visitors to the donations page on the print-based advertisement rather than a direct link to the page. The potential donor would see the ad, go to advertised page, and then be quickly redirected to the correct donations page. The redirect can happen so fast that visitors will not even notice the transition, but the major benefit is that a web analytics tool would report these visitors as being referred from that redirect web page. You can track the visits that occurred from the print marketing campaign by tracking visits from those redirect web pages. Now your web analytics tool can help track print-based generating referrals!

WEB ANALYTICS IN THE REDESIGN PROCESS

Another fabulous actionable use of web analytics data is to put it to work during the redesign process. A study found that combining website statistics and user testing greatly improved the redesign committee's ability to make design decisions (Arendt and Wagner 2010). While the case studies in chapters 8 and 9 highlight in-depth how two libraries used analytics data in redesign projects, the next section provides an overview of incorporating web analytics in a redesign process and suggests some specific analytics reports to consider.

The obvious use of web analytics for a redesign process is to provide valuable background information on the website's users and their behaviors. Here are a few questions to answer with web analytics data:

- What content do your users use?
- How do your users access the site?
- What type of technology would their browsers support?
- How long and/or deeply do users navigate through the site?
- Are there noticeable trends in how users navigate through the website?

These questions demonstrate how visitors are already interacting with the site. They are designed not to incite actions but to support some basic decisions. For example, if a website receives a sizable portion of visitors who are using an older version of a browser, you may decide that it is still necessary to support that browser and plan the redesign to accommodate it. Similarly, if you notice that a significant amount of the visitors have their Internet browsers set to a language that is not English, your library may want to consider translating the library's website into the top languages to accommodate those users.

A more actionable use of web analytics in a redesign process is to identify major problems with a website that can be fixed during the redesign. Before starting a redesign, it is useful to determine the purpose and goals of the redesign. Why is the redesign necessary? What is it trying to accomplish? If your library has a web analytics strategy, then the obvious reason for the redesign is to improve the site's KPI performance. Here are common reports that can reveal problems that may hinder a website's KPI performance:

Pages with high bounce rates—As you now know, high bounce rates are rarely a good sign because they indicate that visitors are refusing to even interact with a page and are instead leaving your site. Find out what is contributing to those bounces, and then segment the report by referring sources to see whether a specific user group is responsible for the bounces.

Unexpected exit pages—Inevitably, visitors have to leave your site, but it is better when they make a "good" exit, or one that is designed into the website, rather than a "bad" exit, by leaving the site in an unplanned page. Examine your top exit pages in a standard report, and review any funnels set up in URL destination goal reports.

Poorly performing goal or conversion reports—Since conversions are unique to each library, it is not easy to advise on how to identify problems or solutions. If you find that your conversions do not meet the desired expectations, be prepared to think long and hard about why this is so. Formulate questions, and look for potential answers in web analytics data.

Low-use web pages—Just because a page does not receive much traffic does not make it a potential problem. The real issue is when a page does not receive the traffic you think it should. There could be a disconnect between what you and the users think is valuable content, or perhaps the page is buried and needs better promotion.

Once you have identified problems, you can develop and implement solutions and then measure their effectiveness using data.

There are several ways to measure the success of a redesign process, and each involves measuring goals. If you created a redesign strategy in which you defined the purpose and goals for the redesign, then you should also create a subset of KPIs to measure the success of the redesign. This process borrows the general philosophy of the web analytics strategy, but it focuses specifically on the redesign process. Even if you did not create a redesign strategy, you can still measure the success of the redesign by comparing the use of the old site to the redesigned site on the basis of the goals and KPIs outlined in your library's web analytics strategy. The purpose of a website redesign should never be just to prettify the site, but rather to improve its overall functionality—it should perform better against its KPIs than the old version of the site. If it does not, then your redesign was not an improvement, or your site's purpose has changed so much that it is time to update the website's goals.

CONCLUSION

Turning data into actions is the ideal practice in web analytics. If you do not do anything with the data, then what is the purpose of even collecting data? By making the effort to put your data into context by benchmarking them, you can track changes in use and visitor behavior on your website. These changes could identify whether the edits implemented were a success. However, that is just the beginning. A true action-oriented analytics practice requires understanding the intent of the website, selecting what goals or outcomes are desired on the site, and knowing how to measure those goals using KPIs. This helps libraries focus on the actions necessary to improve the effectiveness of their websites. Using data in the processes of testing and redesign is an additional way to put data to use.

Although this chapter has focused solely on what actions you can take with web analytics data, you will find that data alone are not always enough to make decisions. Consider adding usability testing to gather additional useful data. You must go beyond your web analytics tool to understand the intent behind users' actions.

REFERENCES

Arendt, Julie, and Cassie Wagner. 2010. "Beyond Description: Converting Web Site Usage Statistics into Concrete Site Improvement Ideas." *Journal of Web Librarianship* 4, no. 1: 37–54.

Breeding, Marshall. 2008. "An Analytical Approach to Assessing the Effectiveness of Web-Based Resources." *Computers in Libraries* 28, no. 1: 20–22.

Kaushik, Avinash. 2010. *Web Analytics 2.0: The Art of Online Accountability and Science of Customer Centricity*. Indianapolis, IN: Wiley.

Lovett, John. 2009. "Defining a Web Analytics Strategy: A Manifesto." *Web Analytics Demystified*. http://john.webanalyticsdemystified.com/2009/12/22/defining-a-web-analytics-strategy-a-manifesto/.

Chapter Six

Communicating Website Usage within Your Library

By now, you are already comfortable with analyzing website use data. However, the true web analytics process involves converting data into actions. In chapter 5, we highlighted several cases on how to put that data to use, but we realize that not every action—not every decision about your library web site—is within your control. Some actions require the input and movement of others within your library, and perhaps even a parent organization, to make the changes happen. For example, many libraries use content management systems, such as Drupal, to manage their websites. A content management system, or CMS, is often implemented to make it easier for more users to contribute content to the website. To implement changes to websites with multiple "content contributors," you may need to share your web analytics data and knowledge to help those contributors make effective content decisions. Even if you are one of the content contributors in your library, helping your fellow contributors make better content or design decisions will reduce the time spent fixing potential problems on the website. Content contributors are only one example of a user group that could benefit from web analytics data; no doubt, there are other groups that could use the data to improve library services, particularly if those services have online components.

Before sharing all the great data collected in your web analytics tool, you should decide who needs the information and how to share it with them. We discuss the best practices of sharing web analytics data in addition to covering how specific web analytics tools export data. This chapter will help you identify some basic user groups in the library that could benefit from access to customized web analytics reports, identify the data they could use, and provide the data to them in an easy-to-read format.

WHO NEEDS ACCESS TO WEB ANALYTICS DATA?

The people who need the data will vary by library. We developed a generic list of groups you may have in your library that may need this data. These groups include people who create code or manage a website (the coders and managers); people who contribute content to a website (the contributors); people who have decision-making power over a website (the decision makers); and, of course, library administrators (the administrators). Some libraries have individuals fulfilling multiple roles, so you may have people in your library who fall into two or more of these categories. It is important to identify people who are in each of these categories, as their web analytics needs differ depending on their roles.

Coders and Web Managers

This group includes your web services department, or more specifically the web programmers, website administrators or managers, systems administrators, and any person who has the power to edit and create the code for a website or directly oversees a website. These people most likely implemented the web analytics tool your library uses; however, it is not safe to assume that everyone in this role has access to the web analytics tool or its data. For libraries with large web services departments, perhaps only a select few have actual access to the tool(s) and data.

Since these are the people who build and maintain the websites, it is essential that they are informed about how users are actually interacting with the website. Data can reveal website errors or areas in which code needs to be fixed on a website, in addition to highlighting trends in user behavior on a website. This information can help your coders and managers develop more user-centric websites.

Contributors

As defined already, contributors are the people who create and post content on a website. Your library may have multiple content contributors working on different websites. Besides content management tools like Drupal, blogging tools make it easy for multiple people to contribute content to a library blog. There are also systems like LibGuides (www.springshare.com/libguides/), a CMS that allows librarians to develop and share web-based library guides. These tools require no experience in web design or programming to create online content, so anyone familiar with word-processing software can add and edit content on a website. Content contributors' skills differ; some may have web design or programming skills, and others may be completely new to these concepts. It is important to show your content contributors how users interact with web content because they can use the feedback to improve their contributions to the site's content and layout.

Sharing web analytics data with content contributors can be murky if it is not clear who is responsible for maintaining the content. In LibGuides, it usually is obvious who owns one of the online guides, since that person's name and contact information is attached to that guide. When it comes to other systems, content ownership and responsibility is not always transparent, as many contributors may have permission to edit an entire website, and the system may not track which author edits which page. If this is the case, then work with the website's manager to convey the web analytics data with the intent that person passes along the information to the necessary contributor.

Decision Makers

Decision makers are the people who have the power to make decisions about a website's design (or redesign) and purpose. This may sound vague, but consider the people who serve on a website oversight committee or redesign committee, or those who serve as a website owner. This user group may or may not have access to edit the specific website, but it does have the influence to approve or veto the website's appearance and purpose, which affects the content that goes on the site. Committees are easy to identify since they are an established group, but they can be temporary—for example, a group convened to serve for the length of project—or permanent. "Website owners" may be a little ambiguous; essentially, they are people who had a website created for them for a specific purpose. For example, at the University of Colorado Colorado Springs, there is one web services librarian who maintains several websites for the library; however, there are multiple website owners. The library has two online information literacy tutorials that two other librarians manage. While the web services librarian assists in the technical maintenance and troubleshooting, the other librarians determine the tutorials' purpose or goals and maintain the content. Whomever you identify as your decision makers, sharing web analytics data will help them make informed decisions on the design or layout of a website and could potentially help them create website goals to measure the effectiveness of the site.

Administrators

The "administrator" group includes library administrators, ranging from department heads to deans or directors of a library to whoever has administrative authority in your library. Academic libraries have a dean or director; public libraries have directors and a library board; school libraries have principals or school district administrators; and for special libraries, it varies by organization. Most administrators probably are too busy administrating to be concerned with a library's website, so why is it important that we share web analytics data with them? Administrators may require these data as part of library's annual usage reports. We report other use data, such as gate counts for physical visits, so it makes sense to track those virtual visits on the library's website. However, web analytics data can be used for so much more at the administrative level. Laura B. Cohen (2003) recommends that library administrators analyze website use data to understand library website users' needs; to justify, add, or eliminate library services or online resources; and to modify library operational hours or library staffing. An informed administrator can make educated, data-driven decisions to improve library services and resources, which can have an impact on the entire library.

IDENTIFYING WEB ANALYTICS NEEDS

Now that you have an idea of who needs access to the web analytics data, the next step is to consider the specific data that those individuals actually need. It is very likely that most of the people you will work with have little to no experience with web analytics. They will probably not know their own web analytics needs, and they are even less likely to know how to identify and meaningfully use that data. It is your job as the local web analytics expert to understand these needs and connect them to the useful reports that can help. Dazzle them with relevant data, and they will be more likely to develop a sense of ownership of the data that are pertinent to their job responsibilities or aspirations. They can use the data to recommend or make improvements to a website they work on.

So, what is relevant web analytics data? That can be tricky, since it depends on the individual or group you work with. Your best bet is to actually talk with these people—do not ask them directly what their web analytics needs are, as you will get blank stares, but do ask how they are involved with a website's maintenance and what they see as the purpose or goals of that website. From there, you can apply your web analytics knowledge to identify the data that are useful for their needs. If you need help to get the conversations started, we recommend asking some basic questions, including the following:

- What is your role in maintaining this website?
- What do you want to know about your website's users?
- Why do users come to your web page or website?
- What do you think is most important about this website?
- What are your goals for the website?

Even if they do not have specific answers to these questions, think about questions the individuals or committees may have about the website and then use website statistics to answer them. Since your colleagues may not be familiar with analytics tools or which kinds of data and reports are available, a demonstration of the tool in use is a good way to spark some ideas and get the discussion under way.

We provide several examples of identifying web analytics needs with the user groups we identified earlier: coders and managers, contributors, decision makers, and administrators. For each user group we selected three web analytics reports to use as jumping-off points, and we discuss how each meets a potential need for that group. The examples are not all-encompassing, but they are designed to help you identify user needs and the process of connecting those to specific web analytics reports. We also recommend using these examples as you meet with these people; it may help illustrate what you are trying to do for them, and it gives you an opportunity to prove how web analytics data can be useful.

Data for Coders and Managers

Since coders and managers are the people who build and maintain websites or other online library services, their primary responsibility is to keep the website(s) functional. Their web analytics needs will most likely involve identifying potential problems with a website. Website use data offer a few ways to track possible glitches on a website. You could provide your coders and managers with reports that track error messages, such as the "HTTP 404: Page Not Found" error messages your users stumbled on, as discussed in chapter 5. Depending on your web analytics tool, you could show how your users navigate to the error page. With this knowledge, coders and managers could identify missing or dead web pages that are causing the error. Additionally, these data can be used to recommend where to set up redirects to help connect users to the right web page.

By now, you understand that a high bounce rate is not a good sign for most web pages because it indicates that users go to a web page only to automatically leave. Although web analytics cannot tell you why your users instantly navigate away from a page, the bounce rate should send up a red flag, and your coders and managers may want to review those pages (and possibly do some actual usability studies!) to see whether it is a technical issue with the page or whether there is an issue with the page's layout or content. As you work with the coders and managers, you should clearly explain what could trigger a bounce to put these data into context. Chapter 2 covers the bounce metric and how it could be misleading if your web analytics tool is not configured to track it correctly.

Coders and managers should also review the visitor technology reports that outline the type of web browsers, operating systems, and screen resolutions that your website's visitors use. It also reports whether their web browsers support Flash and Java. All these data are useful for designing a cross-browser test in which someone (again, likely your coders and managers) views a website in different browsers and technology settings to ensure that it is usable. Why guess which web browsers to test a website in when you can easily use the data in the visitors technology report that shows you which web browsers frequent the website? Beyond usability testing, your coders and managers can use this report to identify their mobile-device users and justify either development or expansion of a mobile-compatible website or mobile applications—more on this in chapter 7.

Data for Content Contributors

Content contributors are mostly interested in data from the web pages they edit, so most of the web analytics data they need are found at the web page level. You may need to provide some website-level data to put the data into context (think self-benchmarking again), such as comparing the total number of visits to the site to the number of visits that a particular web page receives helps put into perspective how popular that page is on the site; however, the main emphasis is on the specific web page(s) that the contributor maintains. Since most contributors want to know how a web page is being used and who is using it, we recommend three page-level reports that provide these data.

Click-density reports, which are further discussed back in chapter 4, are effective web analytics reports that show the links or areas clicked (and not clicked) on a web page in one report. The report is typically a screen shot of the web page, with the click data overlaying that image, which makes it easy even for web analytics novices to see what content is being used on a web page. There are a wide range of click-density-type reports, ranging from heat maps to site overlay features; figure 6.1 illustrates the confetti view report in Crazy Egg that displays each click as a tiny colored dot on the web page. Your contributors can look at click-density reports and see which content is actually being used and which is not. This may help contributors decide how to rearrange content on that page to make it easier for users to find the links or information they need and delete unnecessary (i.e., low-use) content.

Contributors should also know the total volume of traffic that a web page receives, along with some additional basic user information. Understanding the number of visits a web page receives (total visits) may indicate the importance of the page; the higher-traffic pages should be regularly monitored to ensure that the content is current. However, contributors need to know more about their users than just total traffic. One popular request is to know whether the users are

FIGURE 6.1
Confetti View, Crazy Egg, University of Colorado Colorado Springs

in the library or on campus or whether are they accessing a web page remotely. This is especially important if the web page contains links to the library's online, subscription-based resources. At the University of Colorado Colorado Springs, the campus uses a virtual private network (VPN) to authenticate users when they are not on campus to access the library's restrictive, online resources. If the person accessing the web page is not in a specific IP address range, the links to online databases, e-books, and other online sources will not work for that person. Content contributors at this university's library can use these data to see how many users are not connected to the VPN before clicking on those links. Although it is not possible to discern whether the users are affiliated with the university, the contributors can take extra steps to include information about the VPN with instructions on how to use it, or they can make the information more prominent if it is already present, to alleviate potential user frustration for students and faculty.

The bounce rate is also useful for contributors because it shows the lack of interaction on a web page. Identify the web pages with a high bounce rate, and contact the necessary content contributors that there may be a problem with that web page. Perhaps the web page's content needs to be updated or its design could be improved. It may not be clear what is causing the bounces, but content contributors should be aware that there is a problem. Individuals with web design experience could evaluate the page and offer suggestions for improvement, which the contributor could implement. You can further monitor the page to see whether the bounces remain high or decrease over the following month. If there is not a significant decrease, then usability testing should be implemented to identify the underlying issue.

Data for Decision Makers

The web analytics needs for decision makers will depend on what decision they are in the process of making. They will be interested in a mixture of website-level reports and web-page-level reports. Decision makers working on a website redesign project will want a blend of data that report content usage and user behavior.

One useful content report is to list the most and least used web pages on a website. Since websites vary in size, we suggest reporting between 10 percent and 15 percent of your highest-use and lowest-use web pages in a single report and listing their total visits and visitors over an extended period—six months' to a year's worth of data will give an idea of trends in use. Decision makers need to understand what content is used by website users in order to make informed decisions on which content to keep, remove, update, or reorganize on a website.

The high-use web pages are important to know because decision makers can take steps to ensure that content remains findable on a website during the redesign process. Reporting the low-use content is just as important because it may notify the decision makers that the content is not as important and can be (gasp!) weeded from the website during the redesign; or, perhaps those low-performing pages are deemed valuable by library staff and then efforts should be directed toward making these pages easier to find on the site or improve their content. If the information is important to staff, consider moving it to an intranet or similar internal space.

Another useful web analytics report is to identify trends when visits occur—is there a specific time of day, day of week, or time of year that the website is in high demand? This type of data identifies optimal times to release major edits or a redesign without large disruption to the website's users. An academic library website may have fewer visits during June and July since fewer students are taking summer classes, but rather than relying on anecdotal information, you can pull website use data by the hour, day, week, or month to prove it. Figure 6.2 demonstrates Google Analytics' ability to track visits by the day of the week; if your

103

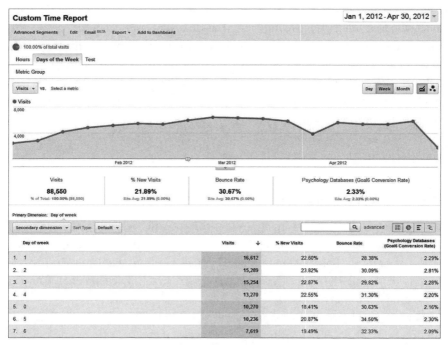

FIGURE 6.2
Visitors by Hour, Google Analytics, University of Colorado Colorado Springs

web analytics tool does not have the ability to segment by time, with more effort you can still pull this information by coding web server logs.

Decision makers should also have access to user behavior data so that they can understand how users actually interact with the website. Web analytics is chalked with user behavior data, but we recommend starting with how users navigate the website. Where do they enter the site? How many pages do they click through before leaving the site? Where do they leave the site? These are all questions that should be answered, since understanding how users navigate your website can affect decisions about the design and information architecture of a site. If you see that a majority of a website's users directly link to the site's home page, then decision makers will be more inclined to focus resources on redesigning the home page. Libraries may notice that a large percentage of users search for the site via a web search engine and enter the site through a secondary page, such as a database listing page. Then decision makers may want to focus energy on redesigning the top entry pages to make sure that they contain the information the users need. Once users are on the site, how deep do they go into the site—one page, two pages, or more? By analyzing a site's page-depth metric, you can determine how many pages users navigate through before leaving the site. If you find that users typically look at a few pages and then move on, then decision makers may want to redesign the information architecture of the website to assist users in locating what they need in just a few clicks. Last, are users leaving the site on pages designed to be natural exits to a website, or are they unexpectedly abandoning the site on pages you had not anticipated? Examine the top exit pages to determine where users are leaving. By pulling together these separate web analytics metrics and reports, you can create your own custom navigation summary report on how users find, interact, and leave your site.

Data for Administrators

Administrators are the least likely to be involved with a website's development; however, they are deeply invested in websites because they are a major service access point for the library. Administrators' needs range from standard web analytics reports that can be used for those annual reports to highly customized data for evaluating library services.

For standard reports, administrators will be interested in overall traffic data—so the total number of visits, visitors, or page views that a website receives over a year. These data are hardly exciting and not particularly useful in making decisions regarding a website; however, they are typically collected and recorded for annual reports within an organization or association. Library administrators collect this information because it shows use of library resources. Although administrators will need data for a one-year period, you can also impress them by showing several years' worth of data to show trends (and possible increases) in website use.

Web analytics is more than just a reporting tool; it can keep administrators informed on what users need from a website. The report on top content is a great report to share with them because it lists the most used web pages on a site. Administrators can see the content the library users want, or at least use, on the website. Although this report is informative, it may also help administrators decide where to focus library resources, such as assigning individuals (those content contributors) to monitor high-use web pages for accuracy. Administrators could also justify increasing funding for specific areas on the basis of the top content reports. For example, if web pages designed to link to online resources, such as

What Does the Board Want to Know?

Public libraries are beholden, for better or worse, to their boards of directors. Determining what to report at this high level can be tricky. Too much information can be overwhelming, especially if board members are not given proper context, but too little, and the web may not get the support and buy-in required for healthy growth. At the bare minimum, we recommend reporting visits, unique visitors, and page views at the same interval that other use statistics, such as gate counts and circulation totals, are reported (i.e., monthly or quarterly). This is analogous to reporting physical visits, physical visitors, and physical material use—nonweb metrics with which the board members ought to be quite familiar with already.

For a more progressive or tech-savvy board, consider also reporting the following:

- top content

- mobile use (top devices and top content accessed by mobile users)

- percentage of new visits

- bounce rates (with the understanding that you will need to define and contextualize it)

- a brief summary of any trends that have emerged during the month or quarter vendor databases, are consistently among the library's most used pages, then they could allocate more money toward those areas on the basis of their use.

Conversions, or goals, reports are useful for administrators to focus on outcomes a website produces. Before there can be conversions to report, the library must identify clear website goals that can be measured with website use data. In the previous chapter, we discussed how website goals and their KPIs can measure a website's effectiveness. With these goal-oriented reports, administrators can easily determine whether the website is performing as it was designed. If the website is performing poorly on its conversions, they can task others (coders and managers, contributors, or decision makers) with addressing this issue.

SHARING WEB ANALYTICS DATA: BEST PRACTICES

Before you start throwing web analytics reports at your unsuspecting coworkers, design an approach for sharing all the data. In his blog, Kaushik (2011) suggests, "When you are doing that data regurgitation it is important to try to make life for the person at the other end (typically your boss, or worse your boss's boss) as easy as possible." You want that person to use web analytics data, but if it is too complex, he or she will mostly likely ignore it because it is too time consuming to interpret or is not clear what actions need to be made. How you deliver the web analytics data can help or hinder this process, so the following are a few suggestions.

Keep It Simple

Since most individuals and committees with whom you will share web analytics data are most likely not web analytics experts, remember to keep the data simple to read and interpret. By "simple," we mean accessible, not watered down. Give them metrics and reports that will be helpful and useful to them, but remember to clearly define the web analytics jargon, because even seemingly intuitive terms, such as *visitors*, can have a wide range of meanings to different people. For example, you may need to clarify the basic differences between visitors and unique visitors, and why your colleagues might prefer to use one over the other for their purposes.

Second, present the web analytics concisely. Avoid trying to impress with extravagant but unreadable charts; charts are designed to help express information simply, not complicate it. Pie charts are rarely a good option for expressing data, especially when it comes to comparing data, because they contain so much

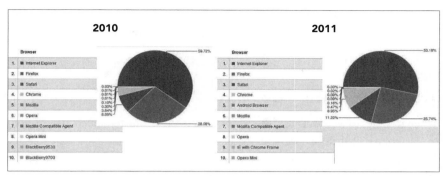

FIGURE 6.3
Pie Charts Comparing Web Browser Type in 2009 and 2010,
University of Colorado Colorado Springs

information that it makes it difficult to interpret it all (Kaushik 2011). Figure 6.3 compares the visits by web browser over a two-year period using pie charts. To compare the data, you constantly need to look back and forth between the two charts to see the actual comparison. You could display this information more effectively using a different method, such as a line or bar chart, or even just display the data in a simple table (as shown in table 6.1). Although the table is not as colorful as the pie chart, it ends up conveying the same information without the strain of having to compare graphs.

Visualizing web analytics data is an important aspect of sharing web analytics data. Just because your web analytics tool formats the data in specific charts does not make that the correct way. Many tools are full of pie charts or other types of

TABLE 6.1
Comparison of web browser types in 2010 and 2011

Browser name	Visits		Change in visits (%)
	2010	*2011*	
Internet Explorer	143,350	128,816	–10.1
Firefox	67,405	62,346	–7.5
Safari	19,316	27,677	**+43.3**
Chrome	8,744	21,677	**+147.9**
Mozilla	713	395	–44.6
Opera	252	207	–17.8

NOTE: The data cells with boldface text indicate which browsers received an uptick in usage in 2011.

poorly designed graphs that are not practical for comparing data. If you want to explore ways of graphing data, we suggest a few resources to learn more about effectively representing data at the end of this chapter.

Avoid the Information Overload

When it comes to web analytics, there is a problem of sharing too much information. In the library profession, we love to share information, but we are also wary of information overload: providing so much information to the point that it is difficult to determine the important data from the worthless stuff. As a super web analytics user, you know not to waste your time sifting through all the data; rather, you can identify and target the metrics and reports that are meaningful for you. Apply this same principle as you share web analytics data with others. Only connect them to the data that matter by using custom reports. Keep it simple and to the point; do not detract from this information by adding unnecessary metrics. This helps avoid overwhelming them with useless data and assists them in focusing on interpreting the information so they can implement improvements to the website.

Suggest Actions Based on Results

The reason for sharing web analytics data is for someone to actually do something with the data. As you share data, help others understand what actions need to be made by clearly listing them. Also, remember to connect the data to specific recommendations. You are making the decisions on the basis of the data you provided, not a guess. If you feel uncomfortable making suggestions, work with a person who is comfortable with web design and development. Explain what the web analytics data reveal, and your web design expert can help you formulate recommendations on what needs to be the next step.

Be Prepared to Talk

Most web analytics tools make it fairly easy to create reports to export and share with others—more on that in the next section—but just sharing reports is not the best way to communicate the data, especially for those not familiar with web analytics. Even if you took the time to simplify the reports, Kaushik (2010, 409) cautions, "You can't expect that they'll figure it out." Rather than sending web analytics reports and hoping that the receivers understand it, take the time to explain the data results and recommendations by talking with them. Although this requires more commitment from you, it also provides you with an excellent opportunity to ensure that they understand the data and what the next steps are that they need to take. Additionally, you can ensure that the data met their needs and answer any other questions they may have regarding web analytics. Given some time, you will have the ability to convert your coworkers into true web analytics believers.

SHARING WEB ANALYTICS DATA: THE TECHNOLOGY

Talking with each individual and group about web analytics and providing those people with recommendations is not a practical option each and every time data needs to be shared. We recommend talking with the individuals at least for the first few times to clarify what the results imply; after that, if your coworkers feel comfortable working with the data and creating their own data-driven decisions, then you have several options to distribute web analytics reports to them via your web analytics tool or with slight intervention by you. Sharing data on website use is as easy as providing direct access to the web analytics tool, but it can also be more complicated requiring you to manually export the data or configure some type of automatic export for it. Each of these options has pros and cons you must consider before implementing them. Most of these options depend on your web analytics tool, so check your tool's documentation to see what it offers.

Providing Access to the Web Analytics Tool

The easiest solution for you is to give your coworkers direct access to the web analytics tool so that they can pull the data they need when they need it. Set-up procedures for providing access to a web analytics tool will differ depending on the tool. Basically, you either can create an account for each individual who needs access to the tool, or you can create a generic account for multiple people to access using the tool's interface. Check your tool's help section for information about adding user accounts. Once the account is created, your coworkers can directly log in to the web analytics tool when they need it. If your web analytics tool distinguishes between administrator and general user roles, consider making others general users to avoid the accidental deletion of customized settings or data.

Evaluation

Providing direct access to the web analytics tool is an obvious solution, but it may not be a practical solution for all libraries. After the initial creation of the account(s), your job is done; it is now up to the others to access the tool and get the data they need. This reduces your workload for sharing web analytics data and empowers your fellow library workers to customize the data as they see fit—in a perfect web analytics world. However, unless those people take the time and effort to actually learn the tool, they may not be comfortable with using it. Web analytics tools are designed for use by people who understand web analytics, which makes it easy for web analytics beginners to get lost. Although the data are technically available to them, they may well be beyond their comprehension.

Additionally, if your web analytics tool collects IP addresses, you have an extra responsibility to protect that information. If applicable, consider providing training on how to handle IP addresses in the tool. Another option is to secure the data so that they cannot be viewed, exported, or both by general users.

A few web analytics tools allow you to provide others with access only to reports that you select for them to view. This helps cut down the confusion, but it still requires the individual to log in to the tool's interface and figure out how to use the reports within the tool. Overall, although providing direct access to a web analytics tool is a simple solution, it is not feasible unless the people you are giving access to the tool are familiar with web analytics or are motivated to learn it.

Manually Exporting Web Analytics Reports

Most web analytics tools have some type of data-export feature. This is usually the case with commercially hosted tools because they require a means of getting the data out of the tool. Data are typically exported as a CSV (comma-separated values) file that can be imported into spreadsheet-reading software like Microsoft Excel, iWork Numbers, or Open Office Calc. Your tool may have other export options, such as PDF, which takes a screen shot of the reports and converts them to PDF format. Again, check your tool's documentation to understand the complete offering of export options.

Implementing a manual export process depends on the tool; however, if possible, we recommend creating customized reports within the tool and then manually exporting the customized data—doing so will save you time. If your tool does not create custom reports, then you may find it necessary to export web analytics data into a spreadsheet and further customize the report by rearranging the data. This process could involve removing unnecessary data, reorganizing metrics, or performing some basic mathematics to create percentage rates or averages. You may also want to convert the spreadsheet data into charts or other graphs as necessary to make the data as accessible as possible to the end receiver. It is necessary to repeat this process as often as needed, so you may want to develop templates in your spreadsheet software.

Evaluation

If the process of exporting reports manually sounds too time consuming for you, then it most likely is, and you should skip to the next section that discusses options for automating the export process. Yet, this option is easier for those receiving the web analytics reports because they do not have to learn to use the web analytics tool's interface. To make this process more time manageable, create a schedule of how often you will send the reports. Discuss the options with the recipients of the data and develop a time schedule that works for you and them. Overall, this option does require more work on the part of the person sharing the web analytics data, but it is ideal for the data recipients because it connects them to the data they need with very little effort on their part. The ease of access to the data will increase the likelihood that the data will be used.

Automatically Exporting Web Analytics Reports

There are several ways to automatically export web analytics data. This includes scheduled emails or alerts that send reports to the assigned person as well as application programming interfaces (APIs), which include specific code designed to pull and report data from a web analytics tool, allowing you to create customized dashboards outside your tool. Unfortunately, not every tool offers automatic export features, so before you get excited at the possibilities, be prepared to research your options. Begin by exploring your tool's documentation and then searching additional web analytics resources (e.g., books, blogs) for ideas. Google Analytics is an advanced web analytics tool in the export arena. We will use Google Analytics to illustrate ways to export web analytics data because of its export features.

Automatic Email Reports

An automatic email report is a feature that allows you to email reports created in a web analytics tool on a regularly scheduled basis. The reports are typically sent as an attached file (either CSV, TSV, or PDF), so that the recipient can view the report without having to log in to the tool. Google Analytics contains a scheduling option for emailing reports on daily, weekly, monthly, or quarterly intervals, and it specifies what day of the week the email is sent. This feature makes it a breeze to create custom reports and share them automatically, so the reporting process is convenient for both the sender and the recipient(s).

Google Analytics also has an alert feature that automatically sends an email to you when an event is triggered. For example, you can monitor a web page's bounce rate, so if a page receives a high bounce rate (you determine the rate that is deemed too high), you will be sent an email to notify you about the issue. The alert feature is available for most of Google Analytics' reports, and you can set up multiple alerts to monitor different reports in your profile.

Google Analytics APIs

Google Analytics has two powerful APIs (management API and core reporting API) that allow you to directly export data from a Google Analytics account and customize how the data are displayed. These features make it possible to create personalized web analytics dashboards or reports and integrate them into a library's web-based intranet, an internal website, or other web tools. Google provides excellent documentation and examples (https://developers.google.com/analytics/devguides/) on how to program using the Google Analytics APIs, but there are also several third-party tools that can provide libraries the API functionality with no programming skills required. For example, Excellent Analytics (http://excellentanalytics.com) is a free, Google Analytics plug-in for Microsoft Excel. Once installed on a computer, the plug-in integrates into MS Excel 2007 or 2010. Users can log in to their Google Analytics account, search, and retrieve data found in their Google Analytics profile all from the comfort of Excel. This plug-in uses the APIs to remotely log in to the profile and retrieve the data; however, to actually use the plug-in, you only need to be able to log in to a Google Analytics profile. While you would need to install the Excellent Analytics plug-in on the computers of every staff member who wanted access to it, you can build and save custom web analytics queries and reports using your Google Analytics data on a local computer. When a person wants to view the report, he or she can click the update query button to automatically refresh the report with the latest data collected in tool.

Excellent Analytics is just one example of using the Google Analytics APIs. Interested in building a custom dashboard or other creative mash-up using data gather in your Google Analytics profiles? You can do so using the APIs. The management API exports a data feed about a Google Analytics profile, so it includes profile settings and goal configurations, whereas the core reporting API exports the actual web analytics data collected. Most likely, you will be interested in the core reporting API for automatically exporting your web analytics data from Google. To use the API, you must be comfortable in web programming in one of the recommended client libraries: JavaScript, Java, .Net, or Python. If your eyes are starting to glaze over, but you are still interested in what the API has to offer, you may want to bring a web programmer into this conversation.

An in-depth explanation of the API implementation process is beyond the scope of this book, but briefly, it is a two-step process that requires an authorization script and another script to pull the data. Currently, Google recommends the OAuth 2.0 authorization method, but the OpenID authentication process is also accepted (https://developers.google.com/analytics/devguides/reporting/core/v3/ gdataAuthorization). Each option offers a different authentication procedure that is further explored in Google's documentation. The authorization method must be included in whatever script is developed to access the API. Once the authorization script is in place, you add the script that communicates with your Google Analytics profile(s) to query and display the data. You control the data that are searched and how the data are displayed. Essentially, you could create a dynamic, personalized web page to share web usage statistics.

Evaluation

Automatically exporting web analytics data, whether it is a simple procedure like setting up instant email reports or using an API to completely build your own reporting tool, saves you time in developing and delivering custom reports on a regular schedule. For libraries that have the knowledgeable programming staff and necessary technology, utilizing Google Analytics' APIs is an opportunity to have more control over the web analytics data, including how they are displayed and who in the library can access them. It does require time and effort to build your own internal reporting tool, but once it is in place, the API should automatically update the data for you and your colleagues.

CONCLUSION

Communicating web analytics within your library is more than just waving around some charts and reports; it requires planning to ensure that you connect the most useful data to the right people. Take the time to assess who in your library could use web analytics data to make more informed decisions; once you have identified them, consult with them to find out exactly what data they need. Decide how you will share that web analytics data and let the data sharing begin. Last, follow up with these individuals or groups to ensure that their needs are met, answer any follow-up questions, and make certain they follow through in using the data. Do not be afraid of starting small—identify the people who you feel could make the most impact with the data—and develop your own web analytics communication strategy that fits you and your library.

FURTHER READING

Few, Stephen. 2006. *Information Dashboard Design: The Effective Visual Communication of Data*. Cambridge, MA: O'Reilly.

Tufte, Edward R. 2001. *The Visual Display of Quantitative Information*. 2nd ed. Cheshire, CT: Graphics Press.

REFERENCES

Cohen, Laura B. 2003. "A Two-Tiered Model for Analyzing Library Website Usage Statistics, Part 1: Web Server Logs." *portal: Libraries and the Academy* 3, no. 2: 315–326.

Kaushik, Avinash. 2010. *Web Analytics 2.0: The Art of Online Accountability and Science of Customer Centricity*. Indianapolis, IN: Wiley.

———. 2011. "Data Analysis 101: Seven Simple Mistakes That Limit Your Salary." October 31. *Occam's Razor*. www.kaushik.net/avinash/data-analysis-101-seven-simple -mistakes/.

Chapter Seven

Mobile Analytics in Libraries

More and more libraries are developing mobile websites and applications. As with any new tool, it is essential to assess use, in this case, by tracking the usage of these mobile tools like any other traditional or desktop tool. This chapter discusses some of the challenges of mobile analytics, new metrics added for mobile analytics practice, and how library staff can track mobile usage of their sites and leverage mobile analytics in mobile site development. In other words, even if your library does not currently have a mobile site, analytics can help identify how mobile users are interacting with your current website to gather actionable data in order to develop a demand-driven mobile site. Analytics can provide important information about mobile use that helps determine whether a mobile site or application should be developed; which platform(s) should be used for mobile development; which website content should be selected and adapted for use by a mobile audience; and whether additional vendor tools optimized for mobile should be purchased. Finally, once a mobile website is launched, it requires a separate tracking process and analytics strategy of its own.

First, however, we need to define what we mean by "mobile users." Simply put, they are library users who arrive on our websites using a browser-enabled phone, smart phone, or tablet. The same person may visit the full website in addition to the mobile, but—as you may have guessed by this point—we have no way of tracking the same person's use on both full and mobile sites. For example, a student who is browsing an academic library's subject guides on a laptop, but then decides to check what time the library closes on her iPhone will count as a visitor once on the "regular" desktop website and once on a mobile website.

CHALLENGES IN TRACKING MOBILE USE DATA

As Avinash Kaushik acknowledges, mobile analytics is still an emerging field. Kaushik (2010, 250) notes, "We have not seen a massive adoption of mobile analytics yet because the industry has not settled on how to collect data from mobile platforms." Although some of the challenge of mobile analytics practice stems from the relative newness of mobile computing and assessment of it, other challenges are technical in nature.

What are limitations of standard desktop tools for tracking mobile data? For starters, older mobile devices do not support JavaScript and HTTP cookies in the way that traditional desktop browsers do, which makes collection of even the simplest visitor data complicated and, worse, potentially inaccurate. For this reason, mobile analytics products tend to prefer the web-beacon method of tracking. Recall from chapter 3 that a web beacon is a small, invisible image added to a site as a marker to track website use data. If a browser is able to load images, then that browser can be tracked using a web beacon. Some experts contend that users of older devices that have limited Internet-access capabilities do not matter as much in terms of mobile analytics, since their owners understand that they are not likely to have a full, browser-based experience on these devices. We recommend monitoring the usage from all devices, but remember to focus mainly on your website's more popular devices, since they will most likely represent the majority of the site's users.

An additional problem for tracking mobile use data is that the IP address sent from devices using wireless networks is often the gateway access for the service provider; as a result, your geographic reports could mysteriously show that 100 percent of your BlackBerry use comes from New York City. This is because BlackBerry users may rely on their subscription data plan rather than a local wireless network. BlackBerry's main ISP (Internet service provider) is based in New York City, so even if a person was physically in the library in Iowa but connected to the Internet via this data plan, the mobile device would geographically register as New York City. Recall, however, that IP tracking for desktop analytics is problematic for similar reasons: an ISP for a large metropolitan area may provide access to users in surrounding cities or towns, but the IP that registers for those users will show the city in which the ISP resides. In spite of these shortcomings, there are techniques and tools that can be used to create accurate pictures of mobile use for all of the good reasons that we have discussed in previous chapters: observing and learning about user behavior, sharing that information with colleagues, and making important content and development decisions. As we have shown with traditional analytics in previous chapters, understanding how the technology works (and does not work) can help account for technological shortcomings yet still provide us with access to a great wealth of data.

MOBILE METRICS, REPORTS, AND TOOLS

The first step in tracking either mobile users or mobile websites is to select a web analytics tool that is capable of tracking those data. With Google Analytics' popularity, it is natural to see its mobile-tracking functionality, but we also examine Percent Mobile, which is a tool that specializes in tracking mobile visitors.

Google Analytics

In October 2009, the industry leader Google Analytics added two mobile-specific reports, overview and devices, for all customers. The overview report contains two results, simply no and yes, in answer to the question, "Is this website user coming to the site on a mobile device?" (figure 7.1). The device report lists all of the different devices that accessed the site during the reported period (figure 7.2).

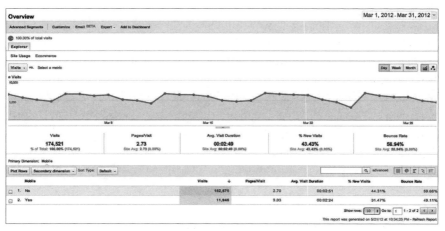

FIGURE 7.1
Mobile Overview Report, Google Analytics, Arapahoe Library District, Englewood, Colorado

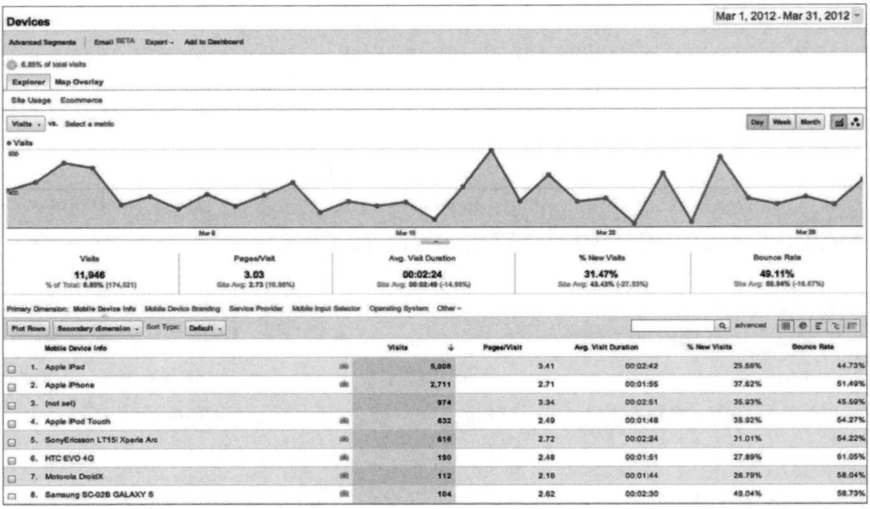

FIGURE 7.2
Mobile Devices Report, Google Analytics,
Arapahoe Library District, Englewood, Colorado

Although these two reports might seem scanty for something as significant as mobile, Google Analytics' powerful advanced segmentations and custom reporting features allow them to be combined with other data for more complex queries, as is demonstrated here.

Mobile analytics practice takes advantage of the same traditional metrics that you learned about back in chapter 2. This means that we can still gather data about visitors, visits, demographics, traffic sources, referrals, and content, and take advantage of tools like conversions and KPIs; here, though, we are merely focusing our analysis of those things to the mobile realm. The practice of mobile analytics, however, adds a handful of new data points to Google Analytics, which we define briefly here. These include device, branding, service provider, input selector, operating system, and screen resolution—all information specific to the type of handset or device being used, and thus they are included as dimensions in the device report:

> **Device**—The name of the mobile device (e.g., Apple iPhone, Motorola DroidX, T-Mobile myTouch4G, LG LS670). You may be surprised to learn just how many types of devices are out there in your users' hands.

Depending on the size of your audience, there will be many, possibly hundreds, of devices listed.

Branding—The name of the company that created each device (e.g., Samsung, HTC, Apple, Motorola).

Service provider—The name of the service provider that gives access to the device. Some of these are device specific (e.g., Sprint Nextel Corporation), and others are local ISPs or networks (e.g., Comcast Cable Communications, Cherry Creek School District), for devices that accessed the Web via a Wi-Fi network.

Input selector—The type of input a mobile device uses (e.g., touch screen, click wheel). Do not be disappointed if most of the data in this metric show as "not set"; this just means that there is currently not enough information provided for the analytics tool to differentiate the types of interfaces other than the two mentioned.

Operating system—The name of the mobile operating system the device uses (e.g., iOS for iPhones and iPads, Android for Droid phones and some tablet devices, BlackBerry, Windows Phone).

Screen resolution—Like its nonmobile cousin, the dimensions of mobile-device screens, such as 768 × 1024, 320 × 480, and so on. Larger devices such as iPads and tablets will obviously account for the larger resolutions.

Although these reports are available in Google Analytics traditional implementation, it should be noted that there is a preferred method of tracking mobile users with Google Analytics (see https://developers.google.com/analytics/devguides/collection/other/mobileWebsites). This method requires server-level access to install a script and minor changes to the information in your tracking code. However, it makes it possible to track mobile devices that Google Analytics cannot track because of JavaScript loading problems.

Percent Mobile

Percent Mobile was another web analytics tool dedicated to tracking and reporting web analytics data specifically on mobile use of a website. Percent Mobile ended its service in July 2012; however, it was used in this original case study and provides

119

FIGURE 7.3
Percent Mobile Report for Auraria Library, Denver, Colorado

a great example of a mobile-specific analytics tool. This study used the free version of this product that provided data for the previous thirty days only. Since Percent Mobile was a product developed specifically for gathering mobile web-use data, it overcame some of Google Analytics' limitations with regard to mobile tracking, most obviously in its use of the web beacon (versus Google Analytics' JavaScript tracking) tracking method.

Percent Mobile presented mobile-specific reports up front, and no knowledge of custom report creation (as is the case with Google Analytics) was required (see figure 7.3). Finally, Percent Mobile also included pictures of the devices, which made identifying and assessing their capabilities easier. For example, the pictures could help identify which devices use touch screens, which have full keyboards, and which may still rely on Text on 9 Keys (T9) for text entry. This type of information is also available through the mobile dimensions in Google Analytics. However, as a relative newcomer, Percent Mobile had not yet integrated as seamlessly into popular CMS products like Drupal, WordPress, and LibGuides; you had to insert the web-beacon tracking code into website templates.

Looking for Other Mobile Analytics Tools?

Most comprehensive web analytics tools, such as Google Analytics and Piwik, are capable of using web beacons. If a library is willing to put in some development time, it has the opportunity to enhance mobile tracking with the tool it is already using! Check the documentation for the necessary customizations during the server installation process. Yet there are still mobile-specific tools that libraries can easily add to their site. Bango (http://bango .com/mobileanalytics), KissMetrics (www.kissmetrics.com), and ClickTale Mobile (http://research.clicktale.com/ClickTale-Mobile-Beta.html) are out-of-box mobile solutions but fee-based products that require a monthly subscription, which may not be practical for many libraries. Other advertised mobile analytics tools are designed to track mobile applications rather than a mobile version of a website—tracking mobile apps is a hot trend in web analytics, but it's not useful for monitoring usage from a mobile website. So, what is the best solution for tracking mobile websites and visitors? Since most modern mobile devices (iOS, Android, and recent BlackBerry systems) all can handle JavaScript and cookies, the need to have a separate tool to track mobile website usage will slowly disappear. Until that time, for libraries determined to capture all of their mobile traffic, whether or not the mobile device has JavaScript or cookies enabled, we suggest that they use either a web beacon tracking tool or a traditional web log parser.

Using Both Tools

There is no rule that you cannot use both of these tools as part of your mobile analytics assessment strategy; as discussed at length in chapter 3, there is no one-size-fits-all tool, and different tools should be implemented as the library's needs and the tools' strengths dictate. For example, if a library has been using Google Analytics for several years, the mobile metrics and reports can be used for historical mobile data (from October 2009 forward), whereas a tool like Bango could be implemented in tandem to give a fuller, more immediate picture of recent mobile site use and the types of mobile devices that visitors are using.

WEB ANALYTICS IN MOBILE DEVELOPMENT

In the planning stages of a mobile project, as with any web project, it is important to ask questions. Corresponding web analytics queries can then be developed to provide data to answer them. Questions to ask regarding a mobile development project include the following:

- Should we develop a mobile site? How many of our website users are already using mobile devices while visiting our desktop site?
- Assuming that we decide to develop a mobile site, should we consider catering to a specific platform? Should we develop platform-specific apps, or should we develop a platform-free mobile version of the site that detects which device is accessing it and adjusts accordingly? What can we realistically take on, given our current level of resources, human and fiscal?
- What are users doing or attempting to do on our existing site via their mobile devices?
- What content should we select and optimize for mobile access?
- Should we purchase and/or implement mobile versions of our other tools, such as our catalog and other electronic resources, to complement the mobile site that we build?

As a mini case study, we consider Google Analytics reports for the Arapahoe Library District (ALD), a medium-size public library district in southern suburban Denver, Colorado. The district outsourced development of a web app for specific popular devices in late 2011, but the library does not yet have a mobile website. We look at data to determine the mobile use of the site and whether the development of a mobile site would be a sound investment of resources.

Mobile Traffic Considerations

To answer the first development question, "Should we build a mobile site?" we can look to the amount of mobile traffic on the existing desktop site as a convenient indicator of mobile use, or if statistics are available over longer periods, we can look to whether or not the traffic has been increasing. For many libraries, the decision to develop a mobile site is a chicken-and-egg conundrum: do we have low mobile use because we do not have a mobile site or, at the very least, a mobile-friendly site? Will a mobile site increase mobile usage? To gather data in support of this "Do we or don't we?" decision, simply compare Google Analytics' mobile overview report from two analogous time periods. Figure 7.4 shows a comparison of mobile use of the ALD website (http://arapahoelibraries.org) in March 2011 and March 2012.

This basic report reveals some interesting information. First and foremost, while overall visits to the library's site are down 7.39 percent, mobile use has increased

Visits	Pages/Visit	Avg. Visit Duration	% New Visits	Bounce Rate
-7.39% 174,621 vs 188,483	6.16% 2.73 vs 2.57	19.69% 00:02:40 vs 00:02:21	80.14% 43.43% vs 24.11%	-7.06% 58.94% vs 63.41%

Primary Dimension: Mobile

Plot Rows Secondary dimension ▾ Sort Type: Default ▾   🔍 advanced

Mobile	Visits ↓	Pages/Visit	Avg. Visit Duration	% New Visits	Bounce Rate
1. No					
Mar 1, 2012 - Mar 31, 2012	162,575	2.70	00:02:51	44.31%	59.66%
Mar 1, 2011 - Mar 31, 2011	183,670	2.57	00:02:21	23.81%	63.63%
% Change	-11.49%	5.38%	20.86%	86.15%	-6.24%
2. Yes					
Mar 1, 2012 - Mar 31, 2012	11,946	3.03	00:02:24	31.47%	49.11%
Mar 1, 2011 - Mar 31, 2011	4,783	2.63	00:02:15	35.58%	54.97%
% Change	149.76%	14.97%	6.63%	-11.55%	-10.65%

Show rows: 10 ▾ Go to: 1   1 - 2 of 2 ◂ ▸

This report was generated on 5/21/12 at 3:34:40 PM - Refresh Report

FIGURE 7.4
Mobile Overview Report, Comparison of March 2011–March 2012,
Arapahoe Library District, Englewood, Colorado

by 149.76 percent. More good news in terms of mobile user: visitors are viewing more pages (pages per visit has increased by 14.97 percent) and staying on the site slightly longer (average visit duration is up slightly by 6.63 percent). New visits have decreased by 11.55 percent, and the bounce rate is down 10.65 percent, both of which could mean that fewer people are turning away on their initial encounter with the site. All of these data points seem encouraging for mobile development!

If you are in a more technologically conservative library environment, there may be anecdotal claims that "no one uses our site on mobile," or mobile development may not be a priority for other reasons, web staffing and limited resources being top among them. Providing mobile-use statistics could confirm or deny any assumptions and give you the boost necessary to receive the blessing from administration and get the development of a mobile site into your strategic plan.

Mobile Platform Considerations

In an ideal world with unlimited resources, libraries would be able to afford (in terms of staff time or contractor budgets) both a mobile version of the website and platform-specific apps for the most common devices owned by its users. In the real world of limited library resources, however, the choice often comes down to how to best serve the most users given the status quo of resources. Analytics tools can determine the dominant devices—if there indeed are any—for a website, which eases this otherwise-tricky decision. In Google Analytics, the devices report, as shown earlier in figure 7.2, is a simple and easy way to get this information. This report shows that the Apple iPad is the clear leader among devices used to access the library's website, at 5,008 visits in one month. The iPhone and iPod Touch are the next most popular, with 2,711 and 632 visits, thus demonstrating a clear preference for iOS devices among library users. Given these data, paying for a contractor to develop device specific apps, including an iOS app, was money well spent. In terms of development of a mobile site, the ALD web staff would do well to consider how to display a mobile site on a 768 × 1024 display—the resolution of the iPads that visited the site.

One final note regarding the mobile platform decision: in an environment in which a single device does dominate—for example, an academic campus on which all students are expected to own and use a common device for their studies, or in a work environment in which employees are officially issued a specific device—it may make sense to develop an app specifically for that device. Mobile analytics can help support the decision to invest (or not) in platform-specific development.

Mobile Content Considerations

Not all of the existing content on a library or any other type of website needs to be, or should be, on a mobile version of the site. Often, visitors using a smart phone are looking for quick bits of information, like a library's open hours, or want to perform a time-sensitive task quickly, like renewing library books. In an academic environment, top content pages are likely to be library hours, directions to the library and maps, and the A–Z list (or other variations of listings) of your databases and other electronic resources. Public library staff can expect to see branch location and hours information, as well as programming and events information, in their top content reports.

Tracking the top content that mobile users access on a desktop site takes the guesswork out of the content selection process, which saves time that can be used adapting or modifying the content to fit the smaller screen of a mobile experience.

Setting Up a Top Content Report in Google Analytics

There are multiple ways to set up a "top content" report for mobile devices in Google Analytics. The easiest method is to use the site content standard report that shows the top web pages view by all visitors to the site. Apply the mobile traffic default segment, and you instantly have your data! Another option is to use a filtered profile that reports only mobile user visits; this would focus all the standard reports on mobile users. Finally, the option we selected was to build a custom report, which we highly recommend, because it allowed us to create several mobile-specific reports in one location. Figure 7.5 demonstrates a simple custom

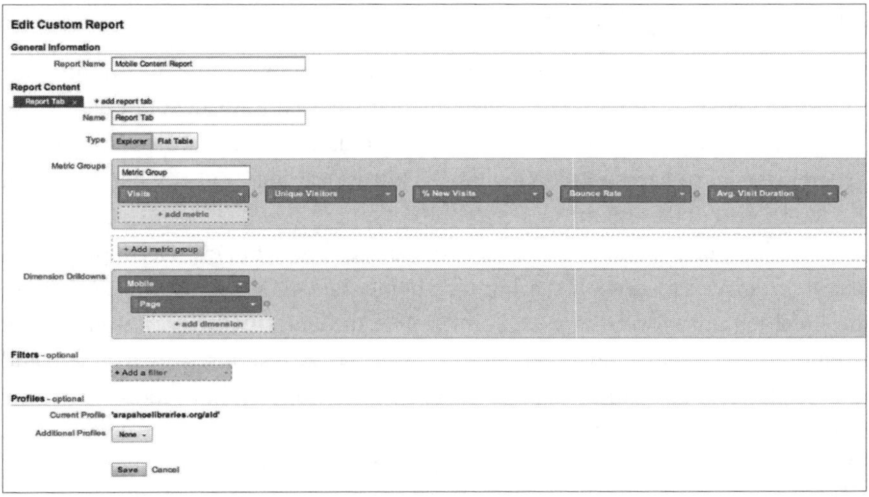

FIGURE 7.5
Configuration of a Top Mobile Content Custom Report

	Page	Visits ↓	Unique Visitors	% New Visits	Bounce Rate	Avg. Visit Duration
1.	/ald/	6,728	4,908	29.35%	42.15%	00:02:35
2.	/ald/locations-and-hours	494	1,182	32.19%	71.66%	00:01:41
3.	/ald/location-details?location=sm	406	356	51.97%	61.08%	00:01:21
4.	/ald/aldsearch	328	1,717	7.32%	59.76%	00:03:29
5.	/ald/location-details?location=ko	243	231	51.85%	50.21%	00:02:00
6.	/ald/content/borrow-renew-pay-fines	225	219	26.22%	50.67%	00:02:01
7.	/ald/books	175	872	22.29%	34.29%	00:03:16
8.	/ald/programs-and-classes	97	292	24.74%	62.89%	00:01:40
9.	/ald/jobs-at-the-library	89	59	30.34%	65.17%	00:00:48
10.	/ald/location-details?location=sg	62	70	46.77%	58.45%	00:01:05

Show rows: 10 Go to: 1 1 - 10 of 6223

FIGURE 7.6
Top Mobile Content Custom Report, Arapahoe Library District, March 2012

report that uses standard metrics of visits, bounce rate, and visit duration, but uses mobile as its dimension and page as its subdimension. Basically, this custom report reveals the total mobile and nonmobile users and the specific web pages they view.

Figure 7.6 shows the pages subdimension view for mobile users. Although the ALD's home page receives the most mobile traffic, four of the top ten results are requests for information about branch locations and hours. Also noticeable is that mobile users are looking up specific types of information, such as information on renewing books or paying fines and library programs. So, most mobile visits involve finding information about the library.

Mobile Usability Considerations

Regarding user intent and desire, the same is true for mobile and nonmobile analytics analysis: web analytics can provide us with a great deal of quantitative data but not so much in the way of qualitative data. In other words, we can tell where users have been on mobile devices, but we cannot predict what they want to do. Enter mobile usability.

Usability practices are beyond the scope of this book, but even a simple single-question survey placed on the library's home page—"What would you like to do on the library's website with your mobile device?"—will reveal a great deal about possible mobile development directions. Leave responses open ended, and they will help determine where to focus web development and tool-purchasing decisions. More complex user-testing sessions, in which you observe your users accessing your library's site, will no doubt prove eye opening as well. Regardless of your testing methods, you will likely find that users want the ability to perform some tasks related to their library accounts, such as renewing library materials, which are generally not supported by the library's website. This may require purchase of additional mobile products or enhancements for your integrated library system (ILS).

TRACKING MOBILE USE OF A MOBILE SITE

Although all of the reports and example from above show how to track use of mobile visitors on a desktop site, if you are given the green light to develop a mobile site, or if you already have one, you will need to track it separately when it becomes its own entity. Remember to define a separate set of goals, related to the purpose and/or scope of the mobile site. Establish goals and convert them into conversions and measurable KPIs that are geared toward your mobile site and how your users are interacting with it. For example, an easy goal is to monitor visitors' engagement with the mobile website. Is there a high percentage of returning visitors? How many web pages are visitors viewing, or how long are visitors on the site? These are all questions that can help measure engagement on a website and make easy conversions. Just remember not to benchmark your mobile website against the desktop website—a mobile website should not replicate the full website, so the content and structure will be different, thus making it difficult to effectively compare the two.

Another way to "test" the effectiveness of a mobile website is monitor the bounce rate. Is there a high bounce rate tied to a particular device or web page? If so, consider digging deeper to find out what is going wrong. Also, if your mobile website uses interactive features, such as forms, be sure that your users can actually use them. Do users without touch screens have trouble filling out forms? Use the form confirmation screen as a goal page, and build a funnel to visualize where users are getting lost in the form submission process.

Tracking Mobile Apps

We have focused mostly on mobile websites, but libraries are also busy developing mobile apps for specific devices. Tracking mobile apps using web analytics tools is far from seamless, since most mobile apps do not generate web pages, which tools require to track users. Currently, there are not even standards in place on how to track mobile apps. The common practice is to develop separate tracking mechanisms or tags for different platforms: Android, iOS, Blackberry, and others. Most traditional web analytics tools are just not built for this type of functionality. There are a few specialized web analytics tools, such as Flurry (www.flurry.com), which is a free tool that generates its software development kit (SDK) for the popular mobile platforms. The SDK serves as the platform-specific tagging code that must be added to the mobile app's code in order to track and report data. For libraries that already use Google Analytics, it also offers an SDK for iOS (https://developers.google.com/analytics/devguides/collection/ios/) and Android (https://developers.google.com/analytics/devguides/collection/android/). This SDK code requires additional programming to a mobile app but keeps all the data collected in a Google Analytics profile.

127

No matter how you decide to track your mobile apps, just know that the analytics data and features from a mobile app are typically not as robust as tracking a full website, since an app has less content and usually serves only one purpose, such as searching the library catalog. Flurry and Google Analytics provide different data, so take the time to evaluate them (or whatever mobile app analytics tool you select) to determine the best one for your library.

CONCLUSION

While industry-standard best practices continue to evolve, we recommend the following three practices for mobile web analytics practice in library environments. First, use multiple analytics products to complement one another for mobile tracking and data capture; second, complement quantitative analytics data with qualitative user input; and third, integrate your mobile analytics strategy into your overall web analytics strategy.

Regarding use of multiple products, tools such as Google Analytics and Bango each bring advantages and disadvantages to the table. These two products use different methods of data capture, and as previously mentioned, they report data differently, so the use of both is not redundant. Many library web developers have been using Google Analytics for a while now, which can offer more retrospective data, but a mobile-specific tool can provide easier mobile-specific reports without the extra step of creating custom reports. Once you have a mobile site, use mobile-specific tracking tools for it. Regarding complementing quantitative analytics data with qualitative user data acquired through usability testing, we still cannot divine user satisfaction and intent from statistical data. In other words, analytics can tell us a lot about where users have been and where they go on an existing site, but it offers little insight into user motives. And finally, regarding integration of mobile assessment into web and general assessment practices, make sure that you are treating mobile sites as separate entities with different goals. The development of mobile analytics best practices and standards will be an especially interesting and exciting facet of web analytics practice to watch in the coming months and years.

REFERENCE

Kaushik, Avinash. 2010. *Web Analytics 2.0: The Art of Online Accountability and Science of Customer Centricity*. Indianapolis, IN: Wiley.

PART 2

Using Web Analytics in Libraries Case Studies

The Right Tools for the Job
Using Analytics to Drive Design

Joelle Pitts and Tara L. Coleman

When building or moving to a new house, you would never sign the paperwork without a thorough investigation of the property. Questions about the home's ability to cater to your unique lifestyle invariably arise: Does it have enough closet space? Is the garage big enough for my Hummer? Is there enough fenced yard for my dog? Can this kitchen accommodate my collection of ceramic chicken plates? Surveys, appraisals, water tests, inspections, and other data are also collected and analyzed as part of the home-buying process. In many ways, websites serve as our digital homes and environments, but unfortunately, many libraries fail to investigate the features, spaces, and usage of digital environments before they begin to make design decisions.

Web analytics should be the foundation for any web redesign project, but it is important to begin the project with an understanding of the type of data that will be collected. Different analytical tools provide you with different types of data, with different levels of granularity. Even the best analytical tools will not be able to provide data on certain aspects of your website, especially those elements that are hosted in other domains. Tools like AWStats and Google Analytics are wonderful for providing snapshots of web traffic on various pages and how your users navigate them. However, these tools will not show how useful the information on a given page is, or how easy it is for your patrons to find the information they are seeking. In cases when no data are available or when the data gathered are not robust enough to use in the decision-making process, it is important to combine web analytics with usability testing, surveys, and other types of qualitative data to ensure that you have an accurate picture of how your users interact with your site before you even consider the first redesign decision. This ensures that you do not design a beautiful, spectacular web interface that your patrons cannot or will not use.

Data-driven decision making relies on the collection and analysis of various types of data and sources of information pertaining to your collections, patrons, and organization's ability to connect the two. Data on usability, link navigation, and page views are crucial to understanding why your site must be redesigned in ways that meet your users' needs while upholding your organizational goals. For example, you need to know that when your patrons click on your "digital collections" link, they are really looking for e-books. Using existing data to plan, to make critical decisions, and to legitimize decisions during a website redesign is an efficient and user-centered approach to a project of this magnitude. Although the data-gathering process can be daunting and frustrating, the use of data to make and reinforce decisions informs your entire project and facilitates each phase in the process. This case study examines Kansas State University Libraries' approach to gathering and utilizing data from various sources in preparation for a website redesign.

OUR REDESIGN TOOLBOX

It is important to create a web redesign toolbox before you begin a large-scale project. Our redesign toolbox consisted of some traditional and some unconventional tools to create a comprehensive picture of how patrons interacted with our site before the redesign. These tools also allowed us to make decisions based on data, both qualitative and quantitative, collected from a variety of sources.

AWStats

The first set of data gathered on the existing website at Kansas State University Libraries was completed using AWStats (http://awstats.sourceforge.net/), an open-source web analytics tool (figure 8.1). AWStats allowed the redesign team to gather information on every web page publicly accessible online. AWStats is a great analytical tool to quickly get the number of page views into a single document and to sort the information to see what was used and what was not. AWStats was established as the primary K-State Libraries web analytics tool in the early 2000s to gear up for the previous redesign. The tool worked with our local Apache servers and met the needs of the web team during that period. The web redesign team

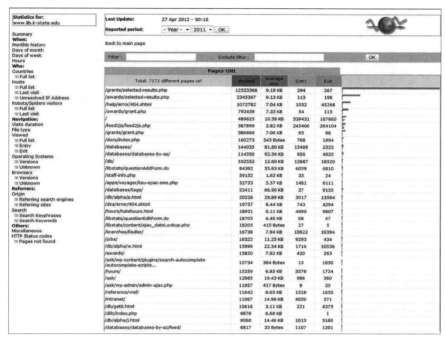

FIGURE 8.1
AWStats, Kansas State University Libraries

determined that the data provided by AWStats were sufficient to go forward with the current redesign and did not necessitate a search for a different primary tool.

The major drawback to AWStats is the lack of context associated with the data you can pull from the system. Without knowing how and why patrons got to the page and where they went when they left, results can be skewed during analysis and lead to ill-informed decisions. For example, Hale Library is Kansas State University Libraries' main and largest library. The public computers located in Hale are actually owned and maintained by the university's central IT department, and therefore every Internet browser defaults to the university home page, not the libraries' home page. Three of the smaller Kansas State University branch libraries own public computers that default to the individual branch home pages. AWStats identified that all of the branch home pages were among the top ten most visited library pages in the domain. Out of context this would seem to show that the branch libraries' home pages are highly used, thus skewing the statistical results of the program.

Comparing AWStats and Google Analytics

AWStats (http://awstats.sourceforge.net)—Collects page view data from your existing website for easy sorting/auditing

- BENEFITS: Price (free), ease of use, and ability to quickly collect data from a specified period of time

- DRAWBACKS: Lack of context associated with extracted data

Google Analytics (www.google.com/analytics/)—Gathers detailed site navigation and time-on-page data

- BENEFITS: Price (free), ease of use, ability to provide some context to raw click data, and visually friendly reports

- DRAWBACKS: Requires customization to gather analytics on out-of-domain (outbound) links

Google Analytics

Google Analytics was the second major toolbox addition at Kansas State. We installed Google Analytics into library web pages in 2008 for two reasons, the first being the cost: it is free. Library staff are encouraged to investigate and employ freeware or open-source programs to manage operations. The second reason is, at the time, Google Analytics was being touted as the premier web analytics software. The features and reports included in the out-of-the-box implementation seemed to augment the data gathered in AWStats by providing the context behind the raw data. In addition, some features, like outbound link tracking using the virtual page views method, inflated page views (http://support.google.com/analytics/bin/answer. py?hl=en&answer=1136920), which made it undesirable to customize at that time. Since AWStats met basic analytics needs at the time of the redesign, no effort was made to explore the features added to or improved on in Google Analytics since it was originally installed. The redesign team used Google Analytics to determine how often page links were clicked on, how long patrons stayed on a page, how they navigated to a page, and where they went next.

LibQual Lite

Although not a web analytics tool per se, the LibQual Lite survey administered to the Kansas State University community in the spring of 2011 served as a baseline for an analysis of the Libraries' website. LibQual responses and comments are based on user opinion and desired level of service. LibQual is designed to provide a holistic view of the perceptions and needs of patrons regarding all library services, resources, and spaces, both physical and digital. Web-specific questions can be added to an implementation of the LibQual survey, but they are not the focus. However, LibQual is a nationally recognized and high-quality system, so any web-related results derived from it are especially valuable. After a quantitative and qualitative analysis of the data, the redesign team found that the libraries' website was the most unsatisfactory aspect of library service for every patron group (undergraduate, graduate, faculty, staff, and community member) (figure 8.2). LibQual measures perceived service and desired service. Respondents rated the item "a library website enabling me to find information on my own" to be the

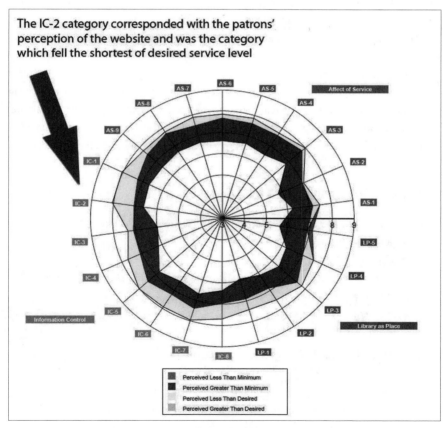

FIGURE 8.2
LibQual Affected Service Graph, Kansas State University Libraries

most desired service enhancement, yet this was also the one patrons perceived as in most need of improvement.

There were several negative comments associated with the library website, varying in degree from mild annoyance to outright contempt. In many cases, patrons confused the online public access catalog (OPAC) system Voyager with the library website as a whole, which negatively skewed the results. However, comments from the website-specific LibQual questions were used to augment the data gathered from our web analytics tools and to justify the time and resources required to completely redesign the website.

LibStats

LibStats (http://code.google.com/p/libstats/), a Google application used to track reference questions, was also used as an analytical tool during the redesign decision-making process. LibStats is an open-source application that is relatively easy to download and install on your server, if you have some basic programming knowledge. If you do not, it is helpful to ask a programmer to step in and complete the installation for your library. LibStats runs on Linux or Windows operating systems. Once installed, you can customize your interface to include various categorization or tagging functions. For example, the Kansas State University Libraries installation includes a location, patron type, and question type, as well as a

Comparing LibQual and LibStats

LibQual (www.libqual.org/home)—Gathers qualitative data regarding user perceptions and needs for your digital spaces

- BENEFITS: Visual representation of use satisfaction with various points of service, qualitative data derived directly from library users, and users often provide comments

- DRAWBACKS: Price (thousands of dollars), length of time to implement, and not web focused

LibStats (http://code.google.com/p/libstats/)—Gathers detailed information regarding reference questions and patron needs

- BENEFITS: Price (free), ability to customize interface, robust reporting feature, and ability to analyze data from select time periods

- DRAWBACKS: Need programming experience to install or customize

way to indicate the amount of time spent answering a question, the format in which the question was asked, and a write-in space for librarian initials and dates. LibStats also allows you to run detailed reports, which are also customizable. Again, it is helpful to have a programmer on hand to make these types of customized changes.

LibStats is not a traditional web-based analytical tool, but it is one that informed time-sensitive content decisions after overall content and style decisions were made. The application allowed the team to determine which reference questions are asked most frequently during different periods in the academic year. LibStats records patron questions at their time of need, revealing more specific aspects of patron use than the LibQual survey can uncover. For example, we record instant-messaging transactions and email questions in LibStats verbatim (minus any personal identifying information) and can return to those transactions at a later time. Although many questions are common throughout the year, such as printing and interlibrary loan questions, many occur most frequently during specific time frames, which allowed the group to decide which content should utilize valuable home page real estate during different times in the semester and which content would always be featured. In this way, LibStats can provide qualitative information in a more time-frame-specific way than other tools like LibQual. LibStats also allows us to gather qualitative data from patrons who may not have received the LibQual survey or those who chose not to participate or share in-depth experiences (figure 8.3).

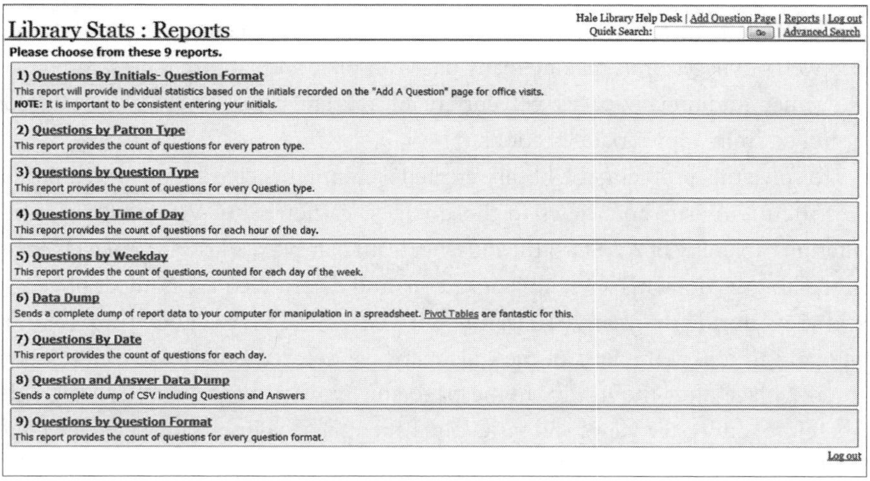

137

Library Stats : Reports
Hale Library Help Desk | Add Question Page | Reports | Log out
Quick Search: [Go] | Advanced Search

Please choose from these 9 reports.

1) Questions By Initials- Question Format
This report will provide individual statistics based on the initials recorded on the "Add A Question" page for office visits.
NOTE: It is important to be consistent entering your initials.

2) Questions by Patron Type
This report provides the count of questions for every patron type.

3) Questions by Question Type
This report provides the count of questions for every Question type.

4) Questions by Time of Day
This report provides the count of questions for each hour of the day.

5) Questions by Weekday
This report provides the count of questions, counted for each day of the week.

6) Data Dump
Sends a complete dump of report data to your computer for manipulation in a spreadsheet. Pivot Tables are fantastic for this.

7) Questions By Date
This report provides the count of questions for each day.

8) Question and Answer Data Dump
Sends a complete dump of CSV including Questions and Answers

9) Questions by Question Format
This report provides the count of questions for every question format.

Log out

FIGURE 8.3
LibStats Reports, Kansas State University Libraries

REDESIGN DECISIONS

The LibQual survey results showed that users were literally *demanding* a more user-friendly website, which provided the stimulus for a complete redesign. A designated redesign team led the library's redesign process. The composition of the team focused on the skills needed to get the job done: programming, web design, graphic design, data interpretation, and experience working directly with users. This team had access to the necessary data to assist in the redesign process. The qualitative data collected in LibQual and LibStats identified potential problems on the website and provided suggestions on how to fix it. The quantitative data gathered via the web analytics tools were used to investigate and analyze known issues with the website. With these data, the team was able to review important content on the website, revise the home page, and improve the site's navigation.

Content Audit

At the time the redesign began in spring 2011, Kansas State University Libraries hosted a staggering 3,500 published web pages on the main website. Many pages were unlinked, buried deep in the website, or simply did not provide helpful information to patrons. In addition, many of the pages contained internal information that was not necessarily intended for public view, or had content that had been written for print documents and had not been converted to web-friendly language. It was apparent that a large portion of the pages were created and uploaded during the previous ten years by staff with changing responsibilities and web privileges, thus making many pages obsolete and, in some cases, forgotten altogether. Additionally, pages with current authors and content were not promoted or linked from appropriate locations.

To solve this problem, the library created a comprehensive list of its web pages and the total visits and views to those pages, gathered in AWStats. Using the filtering capability of AWStats, the redesign team compiled a list of every web page in the library's domain (www.lib.k-state.edu) and determined the number of views and visits during the year 2010 (figure 8.4). Given the overwhelming size of our site, and to follow the lead of the university, we decided on a rolling migration, to take place after the library home page and internal pages were redesigned. Therefore, only page views and visits, time spent, and bounce rate were collected for top-level pages before the redesign, to facilitate the wide-scale deletion of redundant or out-of-date content. This tactic served as a time-saving device, in that large-scale analysis of web data was not conducted on content destined to be deleted. More in-depth web analytics would be collected and analyzed during the rolling migration into the new content management system in order to ensure that each migrated page had been thoroughly analyzed.

The team used these data to help sort web pages for use in an upcoming comprehensive content audit. Our library's content audit is based on advice from Nick DeNardis (2010), who recommends inventorying every page on a site and compiling a document with components such as page title, owner, last updated, visits, and currency. Once the data were compiled, the team should inspect the data, remove outdated content, and revise content for consistency. The original goal of our audit was to identify which pages were online, to remove out-of-date and irrelevant information, and to update pages determined to be of value to the organization.

The team quickly discovered that the content audit was going to be a challenge because of the size of the organization, the specialization of the information online,

139

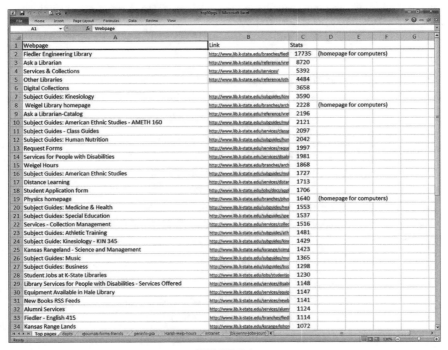

FIGURE 8.4
AWStats Top 50 Pages Report, Kansas State University Libraries

and the large number of published pages. The content audit was distributed among library staff, and pages were grouped together by department or content owner or expert. The web services librarian reviewed pages that had no obvious content owner. Each content owner was sent a list of his or her pages and asked to review and identify pages to be deleted. Content owners were asked to decide whether pages should be kept online, with the understanding that they would be either updated if necessary or archived and deleted. In other words, the pages would be taken offline, but a copy of the local file would be kept for archiving purposes. From the content audit, we discovered that sometimes low-use pages were not used because they were hard to find. Other times, they were not used because the content was out of date, poorly written, and so on. Regardless, it was difficult for staff to delete pages. These factors contributed to a very lengthy, frustrating process, which prevented the website redesign team from moving forward on schedule.

Overall, the audit highlighted the amount of content on the public site. It highlighted the need for a consistent voice and the need to remove redundancy. Much redundant content was removed or consolidated before the migration, and an internal architecture team was formed to address content formation in the future.

Home Page Revisions

The data from Google Analytics helped guide the team's decision making, especially when the redesign team decided to remove links from the home page. At the beginning of the redesign, the library home page had twenty-three links to other library web pages, one link to another campus department housed in the main library, and four links to social media. Of the twenty-three links on the home page, several were repeated links. There were two links to the catalog and two links to the database page. The links in the global navigation were used more than the links further down on the page. There were three links to the "Ask a Librarian" page—two of them were hit more than the other (one in the top navigation and one an image link). We discovered later that these two were linked slightly differently from our Apache server—pagename/index.html instead of pagename/—which allowed Google Analytics to track the links separately. This happy accident helped verify that it is not necessary to repeat links as often in order to drive patrons to the desired page and that graphics can help guide patrons to the appropriate links.

Qualitative data gathered from LibStats were also useful in identifying information that needed to be on the home page during different times of the semester. LibStats was also handy in determining the best avenue for promotion. For example, each semester, our Anthropology 200 course consists of more than two hundred students who have trouble finding their class guide. To address this, we created a slide show addition for the course that includes the link to the class guide and is displayed during the week the assignments are due. Printing was another frequently asked question in LibStats; thus, we created a permanent link to the printing help page from the left-hand home page navigation.

Improving the Site's Navigation

Information from LibQual and LibStats showed us that navigation was a challenge for many of our patrons. While librarians and library staff understand the difference between the catalog, the website, interlibrary loan, and our chat service, our patrons do not. That means that it is important for us to use the same voice and language across platforms to improve overall navigation between them

We addressed these concerns in several ways. One way was making a concerted effort to use less jargon or to connect necessary jargon with common language, for example by adding the language "aka the 'checkout' desk" whenever we mention our circulation desk. We also made sure to key match pages in the libraries' Google Search Appliance so that terms like *printing* matched the official printing pages maintained by the university's IT department and *late* and *hours* matched the main libraries' hours page.

COMMUNICATING THE DESIGN DECISIONS TO LIBRARY STAFF

Communication was a crucial aspect of the project charge, and the redesign team agreed on incorporating it into each phase of the project. Each team member was responsible for updating assigned departments and units when appropriate. In addition, there were weekly updates to library administration, and monthly in-person updates at librarywide staff meetings. The redesign team also hosted several open forums for library staff to voice their opinions on different aspects of the redesign as the project unfolded. This allowed the organization as a whole to share feedback on the public face of the libraries while simultaneously providing a platform to educate the staff regarding the data-driven decision-making process.

However, despite the team's broad communication plan, many individuals expressed concern regarding links and content that would be affected by the redesign process. It was important to communicate that decisions were prompted by data gathered from analytical tools, not the relative importance of the content or link—a process made much easier with the data in hand.

When communicating data-driven web decisions to library staff and stakeholders, it is important to have some very visual representations of your data. If you are conducting a content audit and want to encourage departments and units to update and clean out their areas more efficiently, provide them with not only the Excel spreadsheet listing all of their pages but also a pie chart representing the percentage of pages they are responsible for. Pie charts are helpful for purposes of visualizing some data, but they are not always perfect. We communicated to library staff about how data-driven decisions were made by showing them screen shots of the Google Analytics in-page statistics reports for various pages, the LibQual affected service chart, and statistics from AWStats.

Although the communication process will be different at every institution and every library, a good rule of thumb is to communicate often and to the right people. The best place to start is with your library administration. Talk with the deans or directors who will be able to back you up and support design decisions based on web analytics. It is important also to keep your administrators in the loop at all times. Part of what made the data-driven redesign so successful at Kansas State University Libraries was the depth of support from upper administration.

If your project team comprises members from each division or department, task each member with communicating design decisions after each meeting. Present milestones to all library staff at organization-wide meetings. At Kansas State University Libraries, the full library staff was informed that the redesign was taking place and that the team was relying on data to drive decisions. At the beginning of the project, staff were shown a mock-up of the initial design and overview of which content would go where toward the middle of the project, and they were introduced to the final design just before the release. We also held smaller open forums regarding specific content areas of the site so that staff could ask questions and provide input. All communications made reference to data-driven decision making and provided visuals of data collected, and data were kept on hand to answer questions regarding content and design decisions. Having the data on hand will also help solidify a case when recommendations or decisions are made that displease others, such as removing pages or highlighting one page over another.

CHALLENGES AND SOLUTIONS WHEN USING DATA TO DRIVE DESIGN

The Need for Usability Testing

Although the redesign team had data backing most of its decisions, that did not guarantee a high degree of usability in the proposed redesign site—it is still necessary to test the usability of the site. We conducted a usability study on the redesigned site. The study included members of the faculty, staff, and student populations. Questions were formed in collaboration with the libraries' Office for Planning and Assessment.

Usability testing is an essential qualitative component of any web project and must be counted in your web analytics toolbox. You can also utilize screen-capture software like Screencast-O-Matic or Jing to augment the data you collect from your participants verbally. This information, combined with the classic web analytics from Google and AWStats and data gathered from LibStats and LibQual, provides a holistic, complete, and positive analysis of the essential content and design elements included in a redesign.

143

Screen-Capture Tool

Screencast-O-Matic (www.screencast-o-matic.com)—Gathers qualitative data and records user navigation of your beta site

- BENEFITS: Visual and audio record of user navigation through your site, which can augment users' answers to usability questions, and price (free version)

- DRAWBACKS: Can record for only fifteen minutes, which may not be enough time to capture an entire usability session

Incomplete Data

During the Kansas State University Libraries' redesign, there were links and content for which web analytics data were unavailable and circumstances wherein the data gathered were not robust enough to use in decision making. One major challenge the redesign team faced was the absence of data on the usage of library social media and external applications. As mentioned already, the analytical tools utilized for this project included Google Analytics, AWStats, LibStats, and LibQual. Although these are all excellent data analysis tools, they do not track everything; thus, the decision-making process was stalled when such sites and applications were encountered during the redesign.

For example, a Twitter feed is synced directly onto the libraries' home page and was originally envisioned as the avenue used to alert patrons (both Twitter followers and home page visitors) and staff of current events and building issues, such as fire alarms. We placed the feed on the home page so that people would be kept informed without having to have a Twitter account. Although we are able to find out how many people are following us using their own Twitter accounts, unless a patron clicked on a link in the Twitter feed, the redesign team was unable to gather usage data on how often people checked the feed on the home page. The team decided that because social media has been identified as a major promotional avenue and the statistics could never account for the number of patrons who read the feed on the home page but never clicked on it, the Twitter feed would remain live on the home page and would be included in ongoing usability studies.

Managing Organizational Politics

Campus and library politics can also challenge the use of web analytics in a redesign. Prompted by a new university vision, the campus's Office for Communication and Marketing introduced new university web standards about three weeks before the proposed launch date for the redesigned library site. The redesign, of course, did not meet those standards—most notably, in the form of the newly required web template that included a very specific header and footer. The analytics we had gathered up to that point become null, and the implementation of the new library website was delayed by several months. This is a perfect example of how politics can undermine the careful collection and analysis of web data. Staying connected with library and university offices and committees responsible for online environments is one way to avoid lengthy delays, but politics can sometimes stand in the way of your perfect online space. And in cases like this one, sometimes you just have to follow the regulations. Our redesign team complied with the branding standards but persisted on using web analytics and usability testing to ensure that our site is as up to date and user-friendly as possible.

CONCLUSION

If you use the right tools and processes to move out of your old home and into your new one, it should be a smooth process. A functional, effective, and timely website project is possible with the right tools and great communication. Qualitative and quantitative tools can be used to gather the data necessary to redesign a website, and web analytics can be used to legitimize the decisions made at every step in the process. Conventional web analytics tools like AWStats and Google Analytics can be used to collect use data and provide context as to how users may be utilizing your site, and library-specific tools like LibQual and LibStats can gather direct feedback from users. Last, usability testing can provide additional qualitative data.

Although pleasing everyone is impossible, you will please no one if you do not communicate the decision-making process to your colleagues and staff. Web analytics can be used to legitimize the decisions made at every step in the process. Often, staff are surprised to learn what web data uncover about user activity. The first step in the communications process is to get support from your administrators. Be prepared to share your data and design mock-ups with your administration and periodically with your entire staff. Structured open forums are helpful in giving library staff the opportunity to voice opinions. Head off potential political issues by having your data in hand and being prepared to discuss data-driven decision making. Overall, these steps can help make the transition to a redesigned website a much smoother process.

145

REFERENCE

DeNardis, Nick. 2010. "Spring Cleaning: Finding Your Lost Stock." *eduGuru*. http://doteduguru.com/id4939-spring-cleaning-finding-your-lost-sock-the-guide-to-content-audits.html.

Chapter Nine

Using Web Analytics Tools to Revise a Humanities Library Website

Harriett E. Green, Jordan Ruud, and Andrew Walsh

T his case study examines the use of web analytics to assess and revise the website for the newly created Literatures and Languages Library at the University of Illinois at Urbana-Champaign. Through the use of Google Analytics and StatCounter, we collected data on the new Literatures and Languages Library website as well as the transitional usage of its predecessors, the websites for the former English Library and Modern Languages and Linguistics Library. With this collected data, we revised the Literatures and Languages Library website to develop an effective suite of online resources specifically targeted toward supporting the unique research methods of the humanities scholars in our campus community. This chapter discusses the creation of the Literatures and Languages Library's website, with a focus on how we installed and implemented web analytics tools on the new library's website and the former departmental libraries' websites in order to strategically assess and relaunch the site. We discuss the challenges and findings from the collected data and best practices for using web analytics tools.

BACKGROUND

The Literatures and Languages Library (www.library.illinois.edu/llx) opened in January 2011 as a new departmental library within the University of Illinois Libraries as a result of a merger of the former English and the Modern Languages and Linguistics departmental libraries. A critical facet of the library merger was a unified web portal—a website that, in the words of the Literatures and Languages Library Implementation Plan, "aims to be a robust library gateway and online portal to support research and disciplinary scholarship of the patrons served by the Literatures and Languages Library" (www.library.illinois.edu/nsm/lit/index.html). A useful and robust website was particularly important to the launch of our library for two primary reasons. First, recent library and information science research literature by William Brockman (2001), Carole Palmer and Laura Neumann (2002), and Claire Warwick and colleagues (2008), among others, strongly suggests that today's humanities scholars increasingly integrate digital resources into their research. Second, web statistics, reference statistics, and a planning survey of users from affiliated campus departments such as English, French, German, and Classics documented that our users across the University of Illinois Library most frequently interacted with library resources and services through the library's websites.

The Literatures and Languages Library website was planned and built in a compressed time frame of approximately three months at the end of the fall 2010 semester, after the construction schedule and opening of the new library was confirmed. The website was launched in conjunction with the physical Literatures and Languages Library's mid-January opening. Given the short rebuild time frame and the minimal amount of time we had to prepare users for the changes, the library's Web Technologies department recommended that we allow access to the English and Modern Languages and Linguistics libraries' websites in the form of live archived web pages. These two archived sites from the closed libraries remained live and available to the public as "archived resources" for a twelve-month transition period in 2011.

Given these circumstances, we installed two web analytics platforms, Google Analytics and StatCounter, on all three websites: the Literatures and Languages Library website, the former English Library's archived web pages, and the former Modern Languages and Linguistics Library's archived web pages. Because of limitations of staff resources and time, the web analytics platforms were installed in their basic out-of-the-box configurations. The goal of installing two web analytics platforms on the three websites was to gather a broad amount of web analytics data on the fullest spectrum of our users. For the months following the opening of the new library, users' online activity usage was distributed across the three websites, because users who had bookmarked pages on the departmental libraries' archived websites were still able to access and use the old web pages. Otherwise, the university library website directed users to the Literatures and Languages Library website for resources in literatures and linguistics. Google Analytics and StatCounter enabled us to gather enough data to begin revising the Literatures and Languages Library website from its basic initial design to a robust web portal for research.

WHY USE TWO WEB ANALYTICS TOOLS?

The purpose of installing both the Google Analytics and StatCounter web analytics platforms on the Literatures and Languages Library website was to gain a sizable amount of data in a relatively short time for comparing the usage of the new website to that of the former departmental libraries' archived websites. In particular, we needed to gather data on how users were accessing the various sites, which archived web pages still had high usage, and how users navigated through the new website compared to the old websites.

149

These two web analytics platforms were chosen because their out-of-the-box configurations provided the complementary data we needed. Most notably, StatCounter offers reports on exit link activity that effectively track detailed exit and referral link activity to help understand users' browsing behavior. By comparison, Google Analytics required configuring every outbound link on the website with a specific script to mark them as exit links. Because of limited staff resources, we could not immediately code the hundreds of outbound URLs on the three websites to track all user exits properly. Yet Google Analytics offers, by far, the most robust and long-term option for gathering web analytics data for free, whereas StatCounter's free version retains data for only the four previous days, which requires frequent downloads of data. The free versions of these web analytics software platforms were utilized in this study to explore the most cost-effective options for libraries; however, a minimal subscription for StatCounter provides longer sets of data and may be worth considering for long-term solutions. For libraries that have similar staff and time constraints, installing multiple web analytics platforms is a strategy to consider for gathering significant amounts of data without creating detailed customizations and configurations to the tool, such as tracking outbound links in Google Analytics.

IDENTIFYING AND ANALYZING USEFUL DATA

Google Analytics and StatCounter provide immense amounts of data in detailed granularity and breadth. However, not every data set is needed to evaluate your library website. The first step in using the data from your web analytics reports is to identify the goals for your library website and key performance indicators, as explained in chapter 5. Goals can be determined by asking questions such as the following: What is the primary purpose of our library website? Who are the audiences we are trying to reach with our library website? What are the target levels of traffic? What are the content and services that should be available to users for their research? What are the target levels of use for the content?

For an academic library website, the subject-specific focus can be critical to answering these questions and determining the valuable data from the web analytics reports. For the Literatures and Languages Library, we were aware that the humanities researchers we served needed to be able to seamlessly access bibliographies, catalogs, primary source documents, and research guides that enabled them to navigate between physical and digital resources for their research.

In this light, we immediately identified two major goals for the Literatures and Languages Library website: to provide users with efficient access to digital research resources for literature and to connect users to library services for advanced help with resources. In monitoring the three websites with the two web analytics platforms, we could identify which research resources were most frequently accessed and view the primary paths that users took to access research resources and library services on our website. This data were then incorporated into the strategies for revising the Literatures and Languages website. We determined three questions to be answered from our goals:

- Who are the library's users?
- How well do they navigate the website's architecture to find resources?
- What information needs do their searching and browsing behavior express?

These questions enabled us to identify the data sets that would allow us to assess our goals. The user traffic data, particularly for visits and referrals, was important because as a new departmental library, we needed to identify our user community and determine which research resources should be featured for the users in the demographics identified from the data. Data on how users navigated the website's

150

User Analysis Tips and Suggestions

Filter out IP ranges: For more accurate data, filter out IP ranges for staff computers and devices used to access or edit the website. You can exclude IP addresses or ranges through Google Analytics' account settings; StatCounter offers a similar option under "Config," providing options to "Create Blocking Cookie" and for "IP Address Labels" of particular users.

Adjust for seasonal patterns of library use: There will be fluctuations in usage of library resources based on the seasons and user communities. For example, most academic libraries will have fewer visits during the summer, whereas public libraries might expect more visits during the summer months. Libraries can supplement other methods of assessing library use, such as gate counts and circulation statistics, with analytics data as a way of noting consistent trends in website use.

Incorporate analytics into evaluation methods: Website usage data can supplement traditional methods of evaluation. Libraries can use these data sets to evaluate library user services. For example, a library could use IP address and location data to evaluate whether a community of users in a specific geographic location is finding and using the site. If your library does outreach in a community, location data can reveal whether the community uses your web resources.

structure enabled us to learn how users located resources. Additionally, keyword data provided information on users' content needs and assisted us in revising the site's content and research resources.

Because of the need to revise the website by the beginning of the fall semester, we used six months of data collected from February through August to analyze for the revision process. It should be noted that because the data were collected during a period that included the summer term, some trends may be influenced by an overall decrease in library use during summer months.

User Profiling and Demographics

Data on website users is crucial to assessing whether your website meets user needs. User data include the number of visitors to your site, how frequently they visit your site, where they are coming from, and which sections they most frequently use. We drew on several types of data to build a basic demographic profile of our website's users: the geographic locations of users, traffic volume, and how users found and accessed the site. These data would enable us to answer our first question on user demographics and to build a picture of the users of the Literatures and Languages Library website.

We found that Google and direct access were our greatest sources of visits. But we were particularly interested in the websites that directed users to our website. What specific and specialized websites referred users to the Literatures and Languages Library's website? What did this referral traffic reveal about the user communities served by the library? In Google Analytics, the sources for this type of information can be primarily found in four metrics: unique visitors, new versus returning, location, and referral traffic.

Unique Visitors

As defined in chapter 2, a unique visitor is a visitor counted only once regardless of how many times that visitor accesses a website within a specific period of time. In Google Analytics and StatCounter, the unique visitor metric can be viewed in a range of increments—from daily date ranges, to customized increments, to the entire breadth of recorded analytics—to gauge levels of unique visitors' interaction with your website during a particular period. These data are most effective for tracking trends in visitor type and visitor frequency. If you introduce a new resources page, the unique visitor metric can help determine whether visitors are frequently finding and using a particular page or resource. In Google Analytics, you can view the total number of unique visitors in the visitors overview report; however, we recommend that you view unique visitors data in relation to other data. This enables you to examine how your website retains and increases interest among the target population. Information on unique visitors combined with location data may not tell the full story, because many different users may enter a site from a single public terminal—in this case, each user would count as a separate visit to the site but would count as only one unique visitor because users share the same computer. In spite of this, the data still provide a general overview of how a website has increased in use and interest.

New and Returning Visitors

Google Analytics' report on new versus returning users augments the relatively simple unique visitors data by parsing the number of first-time visitors compared to returning users. The report includes additional metrics, such as average pages viewed per visit, time on site, and bounce rate. These data reveal how many users are new to your website versus the total returning visitors—ideally, both rates would maintain or increase over time. It should be noted that this report will be affected by repeated use of the website by different users at your library's public terminals, as well as by users who access the website from multiple computers or devices. It provides a basic overview of users' browsing patterns within the structure of the website. Do new visitors browse the same number of pages as returning visitors? Are new visitors more likely to bounce from your site rather than engage with it? These are all questions this report can answer.

The new and returning visitors report can be filtered to customized periods to track trends across months and years of your website's usage. This type of analysis was particularly useful for the Literatures and Languages Library website, as we created benchmarks to compare how our websites were used at the beginning of the term versus six months later.

Geographic Location

Google Analytics' location report helps to shape a profile of the user community that your library serves. This report contains the country and city data based on the geographic location where the users reside; the report shares the total visits, bounce rate, pages viewed per visit, and other related metrics for each country or city listed.

If the report reveals an unexpected geographic location using the library website, this information could provide the evidence needed to begin exploring outreach and partnerships in new communities. For the Literatures and Languages Library, the geographic location data were particularly useful in seeing whether other local and academic communities in Illinois and Indiana were using our website.

Referral Sources

Referral data allow you to gather information on the smaller user communities that are being directed to your website from other sites. Analysis of referral source data from Google Analytics and StatCounter reveals from which internal and external websites users are coming into your website. For this case study, it was particularly important to learn what campus departments and constituencies were directing users to the library website. This information was important because it enabled us to begin promoting our current library services to the specific departments that directly referred their students and faculty to our websites. Google Analytics' referral traffic report provides referring website URLs, visits, average pages viewed per visit, average time on site, and bounce rate. In contrast, StatCounter's "came from" report lists each referring URL and the entry page that referral directed the visitor. Together, these standard reports allow you to build a detailed portrait of how users find and access your site—with simple sorting of the data, you can find the top referral websites, track the most frequently accessed entry pages, and calculate the average number of pages viewed and time spent on your website. These data were useful because we were able to determine which pages users most frequently consulted and which referral sources were directing the greatest numbers of users to the site. Another strategy to consider with this report is to segment the data by visitor type (new or returning visitor), generate report for a multiple-month time span, and examine the time spent per visit. Over a longer time period, the time spent per visit could reveal a possible correlation in the usefulness of certain web pages on your website.

Synthesizing User Data

When analyzed as a whole, these data sets (unique visitors, new versus returning visitors, geographic location, and referral sources) enable you to assess the reach and retention of your target audiences and to identify users consuming your library website's content and services. The focus of the Literatures and Languages Library's web services, which includes general bibliographic resources and specific disciplinary research guides, is for humanities scholars in the University of Illinois community. Our analyses provided a fairly accurate reflection of what at the outset we presumed to be the website's audience—the geographic location and referral data confirmed that the majority of the Literatures and Languages Library website users were located on the University of Illinois campus and in the Champaign-Urbana area.

Analyzing the total website visitors reported distinct usage trends. For example, we graphed monthly page views for the six-month period and tracked the average number of pages viewed by the total number of returning visitors and new visitors. Initially, the returning visitors' average was higher than that of the new visitors. As time progressed, the two averages grew closer to the point that both types of visitors viewed nearly two pages per visit on average. This suggested to us that new and returning users were attaining the same level of use on the site, given that both groups were steadily accessing more than one page on the site. Information like this analysis of the cumulative numbers of visitors is valuable in assessing whether your website has achieved a base of steady users.

For our analysis of the location data, we utilized monthly reports of city data and coded each location in a spreadsheet. "Local" were locations in the state of

Illinois or within fifty miles of the state border—this was based on the University of Illinois's stated mission: "dedicated to comprehensive excellence in the service of Illinois" (http://strategicplan.illinois.edu/documents/Illinois_StrategicPlan.pdf). We also included known border communities in Indiana and Wisconsin where our users reside. All other locations were nonlocal sites. We then sorted the data to determine the locations with the greatest number of visitors, lowest bounce rates, and highest percentage of new visitors. These data revealed the communities where our regular users resided—the locations with high numbers of visitors and low bounce rates. Although the visitor data revealed that users were coming from a wide range of global locations—a trend likely to be observed on most library websites—the actual number of visitors was concentrated in three to five relatively local geographic sites in and around the library. This trend was verified by the bounce rate, where bounces—particularly during the peak months of April and May—were significantly lower with local users compared to nonlocal users (figure 9.1).

Referral source data also provided a useful snapshot of our website's role as our public face to the various demographics we serve, ranging from new visitors who

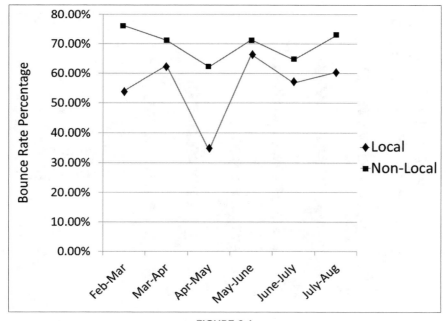

FIGURE 9.1
Bounce Rate, February 2011–August 2011, Literatures and Languages
Library Website, University of Illinois at Urbana–Champaign

visited the website once to regular and frequently returning visitors. For instance, in an analysis of the top twenty-five referring sites to the Literatures and Languages Library website recorded by Google Analytics data, the data revealed that websites with the domain of Illinois.edu in their URL clearly exceeded non-Illinois sites in the number of referral visits (figure 9.2).

We further coded the referring sites from the illinois.edu domain by category—department-specific websites, library websites, and general searches from illinois .edu—and tracked their frequency, as demonstrated in figure 9.3. But we realized that this analysis was more complicated than initially anticipated: the university's server structure includes numerous referring sites, including some library sites, and thus specific websites were subsumed under the "illinois.edu" in the recorded Google Analytics data. StatCounter provides a more accurate means of gathering this data by allowing you to label IP address ranges from known internal traffic sources. For libraries interested in analyzing referral data in detail, we recommend that you work with your web services manager to configure the web analytics software to label known IP ranges and implement other customizations that will allow you to analyze referral data in detail.

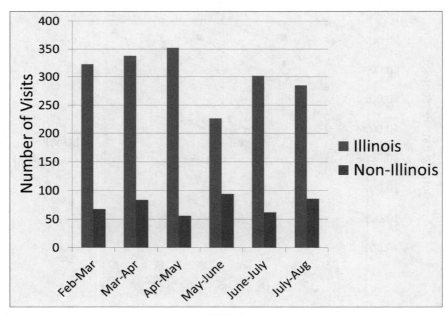

FIGURE 9.2
Referring Websites Coded by Domain. February 2011–August 2011, Literatures and Languages Library Website, University of Illinois at Urbana–Champaign

We analyzed the StatCounter "came from" report data by coding the referral websites by the following categories: "university library," "general University of Illinois," "Literatures and Languages," and "outside." In a four-day sample available through StatCounter's limited free account, the report indicated that 62 percent of the recorded referrals came from other pages on the Literatures and Language Library's website, and 35 percent originated from other web pages on the university library's website. With these data, we surmised that a large number of users found us through both library resources and affiliated departmental websites.

Website Architecture and Content Organization

After building a picture of our users, the next step was to explore how they navigated the website and accessed our content. To determine the effectiveness of a website's structure and content organization, entrance and exit reports pinpoint the sections of the website that are key to users' access and use of the site's resources. For this analysis, we combined the Google Analytics reports on landing pages and

157

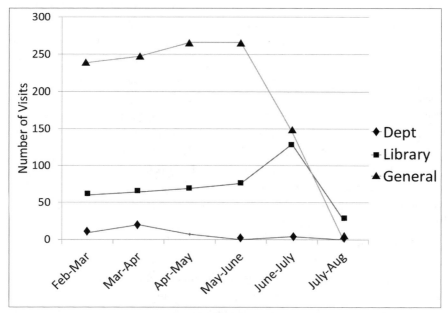

FIGURE 9.3
Illinois.edu Websites Coded by Type, February 2011–August 2011, Literatures and Languages Library Website, University of Illinois at Urbana–Champaign

exit pages with StatCounter's report on exit links and exit link activity to analyze use of the website's structure.

Entry Pages

Entry pages, also referred to as landing pages, can reveal which web pages visitors most frequently use as access points for the website. With these data, you can compare the effectiveness of entrance points for users. Do these entry pages lead users to actually using the site? In particular, you can use the data to evaluate the use patterns in landing on the library's home page compared to direct access of specific resource web pages.

This issue was particularly important for the Literatures and Languages Library because of an initial transition infrastructure that incorporated the former websites of the closed English and Modern Languages and Linguistics libraries. The archived websites were merged under the umbrella of the new website, to ease users' familiarity with former resource pages into use of the new site. The Google Analytics data allowed us to track entry pages from the archived web pages compared to the new home page and resource pages offered through the Literatures and Languages website. There were a few findings that indicated successful and unsuccessful transitions from the old websites to the new site. The research guides on the archived library websites and the Literatures and Languages Library website were identical at the beginning of the study. When the new library opened, we copied many of these resources from their original homes on the archived sites, maintaining both versions as live sites for users' convenience. In our examination of the analytics data, we found notable trends in the use of these guides. For example, the literary-theory research guide on the archived Modern Languages website saw a 52 percent decline in entrances, and an equally sharp increase in use of the new literary-theory guide on the Literatures and Languages Library website (figure 9.4). Similarly, the older Francophone research guide saw an 85 percent decline in entrances, and the new version of the Francophone guide received a cumulative 15 percent increase in entrances.

Another notable insight was the consistently high use of a comprehensive resource list, the "Online Resources and Databases" web page, from the former English Library's website. In response to the high entrance numbers, the library transferred this page to the new Literatures and Languages Library website and placed a prominent link to it on the home page. Subsequently in the fall of 2011, the relaunched library website featured a new comprehensive resource guide that reflected the structure and content of the former English Library resource page.

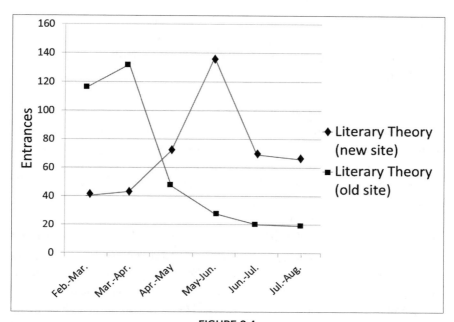

FIGURE 9.4

Usage of Literary Theory Guide on Archived Modern Languages Library Website versus Literatures and Languages Library Website, February 2011– August 2011, University of Illinois at Urbana.Champaign

Entrance data revealed the strong and consistent use of a web page and enabled us to respond to users' expressed needs for a comprehensive access point for research resources on the new website.

Entrance data can identify the strong pages in a website and assist you in focusing services and resources on high-traffic entry points. For our library website, the entrance data analysis in this form became a key method for evaluating other pages of the website and revising the website to more seamlessly integrate effective parts of the older websites' structures into the new.

Exit Pages and Bounce Rate

Analysis of bounce rate and exit data is a slightly more complex method of evaluating the site's structure. Clifton (2010) discusses in *Advanced Web Metrics in Google Analytics* how visitors' departures from the landing page are strong indicators of poor engagement and failure to meet the users' needs. Yet a key goal of the Literatures and Languages Library's website is actually to guide users to outside resources, but this can trigger a bounce in certain web analytics tools. Our installation of Google Analytics records some exits as bounces because we did not configure the tool to track outbound links during this case study. Since we knew the data were inaccurate, we had to be critical of the bounce rate Google Analytics reported.

We used the recorded statistics on StatCounter's exit links report to help us understand which web pages were contributing to the bounce rate and which were promoting proper exits from the website. StatCounter's exit links report does not include a bounce rate—in fact, this web analytics tool does not report bounces at all—but rather lists the outbound links and total exits (reported as hits) that link received. Outbound links can be grouped by domain, which makes it easier to analyze which websites your users are going to when they leave your site. Next to each link listed is a small icon that can be clicked to drill down to the date and time of the exit and the web page where the outbound link is found. StatCounter's report on exit link activity further augments the exit links report with data about the exit pages and the specific links that users clicked on to exit the library's web pages. Together, these reports can serve as useful tools in building an understanding of user interactions with exit links. Google Analytics revealed that the Literatures and Languages Library home page recorded a bounce rate of approximately 67 percent during a one-month period. This is high for a home page that is designed to navigate users to different areas within the site. But in StatCounter's exit links report for the same period, the data showed that of the 957 unique visitors to the library home page, 85 users (approximately 9 percent) exited the home page via its link to the MLA International Bibliography database. By combining the data from Google Analytics and StatCounter, we learned that our bounce rate for the home page was inflated, as some users were actually properly exiting the page to other library resources not on the library's domain.

Using data from the two web analytics tools improved our ability to analyze our site's use and helped make some design decisions for the website. We decided to place links to the MLA International Bibliography in multiple locations in the sidebar navigation included on a majority of the library's web pages and also the "Quick Links" section on the library's home page because of its high use. We wanted to ensure that users could find the database when they wanted it, regardless of where they were on the site.

Again, we did not have the resources at the time to configure all of our outgoing links with Google Analytics tracking code, and thus StatCounter was a useful complement to decoding our bounce rate and exits. Although we used StatCounter to compliment Google Analytics, we encourage libraries to follow Google Analytics' method to track those links to make it a more useful web analytics tool (http://support.google.com/analytics/bin/answer.py?hl=en&answer=1136920).

Users' Information Searching Behaviors and Needs

The core functionality of our library's website is how well it works as a conduit for connecting users to the e-resources and collection materials that they need. To determine the usability of a library website, you need information-seeking data. What are users looking for when they search for your website? The visitors flow and keyword usage reports from Google Analytics and the "came from" report in StatCounter all provide important data on content users seek.

Visitors Flow

The visitors flow report creates an effective visual guide to how users navigate and search the site. The report confirmed the initial findings we saw in the data on user traffic, exit links, and bounce rate, in which the number of users decreased as users moved deeper into the website's pages.

Keyword Data

Google Analytics' keyword data offers rich data sets of keyword queries from two different reports. The queries report, part of the search-engine optimization reports, provides actual search queries (keywords) visitors used to find your website; the queries are divided by impressions and click-through visits. The queries report requires the enabling of Google's webmaster tools, but you can also use the search overview report, which is available out of box, to see the keywords your visitors use to find your website. On the search overview report, change the primary dimension to "keywords" to see the top keywords and key phrases, including number of visits for each keyword phrase, the pages per visit, average time on site, percentage of new visits, and bounce rate.

In our analysis, we primarily used the keyword data found in the search overview report because they revealed the frequency and depths to which users explored the website by dominant search terms. However, we still referred to the queries report for data on impressions (the number of times the website appears in searches, regardless of whether a user clicked through), the average position of the website's pages in results for a given query, the successful clicks, and click-through rates. You can use the keyword and queries data to develop goals for creating new research guides, revising website content, and linking to online resources that meet these queries. For example, in response to a notable number of searches for "French film" and "German film," we expanded our cinema studies research guide to highlight studies of international film.

"Came From" Report

As discussed earlier, StatCounter's useful "came from" report records how visitors found your site. Knowing how users find a website and the pages in the website where they land can be valuable in identifying user needs—if a user lands on a research guide, we can make an assumption that the visitor needs research help.

Our library's came-from data sets were limited because of StatCounter's free account, which retains the data from only the previous four days of activity. The recorded URLs in the sample set for a four-day period in October were sorted by name and type, and then counted for frequency to assess how users accessed discipline-specific guides, databases, and other information on the website. In one example, the data revealed that eight visitors viewed the library's digital humanities research guide as a navigation progression from the home page, and more than fifty visitors viewed multiple pages of the French, German, and Scandinavian web research guides. Overall, approximately 65 of the 107 recorded visits (or approximately 61 percent) to the Literatures and Languages Library website involved content navigation to another page on the website. This type of analysis of users' browsing behavior through this report can provide valuable information on how users navigate through the website content and how frequently they access certain resources, and it ultimately provides defined areas of focus for the library to enhance web content.

CHALLENGES

The primary challenges we encountered in this case study were implementing an adequate installation of web analytics software on the Literatures and Languages Library website and interpreting the data. Each analytics platform had its benefits and drawbacks in the type of data it gathered.

Adding Web Analytics Tools to the Website

Successful implementation of analytics platforms required a high level of familiarity with not only the Literature and Languages Library website but also the university library's content management system and the library's related web services, such as LibGuides. Despite the limitations of the content management system, we found a solution to installing the tracking code on every page of its website by installing it within the "include" element on the website—the sidebar menu that appears across every page of the library website. Subsequently, the library solved the problem of tracking LibGuides traffic by inserting specific Literatures and Languages Library tracking code as an invisible element in the chat widget code of the user profile sidebar. Thus, our library's LibGuides had two Google Analytics codes: one for the university library and the other for our departmental library. Similar recurring elements, such as sidebars or chat widgets, can be effective carriers for analytics code; however, this is not the best practice for implementing a web analytics tool. Work with your web services department or manager to determine the best solution for tracking web analytics data or collecting it from the library's existing web analytics tools. Also, remember to read the tool's documentation to see how to best implement it.

Identifying the Targeted Audiences

Another challenge we encountered in the data analysis involved the breakdown of the visitor statistics between target users and outside users. It would be ideal to calculate the percentage of University of Illinois affiliates compared to the general public, but visitor statistics are difficult to parse in that manner. Students and faculty browse library resources from on- and off-campus IP addresses, and users arrive on the website from search-engine queries, outside websites, and many other diverse locales. Given those facts, an in-depth examination of visitor demographics requires a comparative analysis of multiple data sets, including location, IP addresses, entrance data, and referral reports. That process is likely the most effective way to paint a full picture of users.

Relatedly, the data analysis must also account for internal library traffic. The Literatures and Languages Library set up its Google Analytics account to filter the IP addresses of the library staff and unit public terminals that have the website as their default home pages, but the data still had to be sifted for visits from other staff computers in different library departments. We were able to identify other library staff computers by monitoring the frequency of hits from particular IP addresses and locations on campus at certain times of day. Although this method is not perfect, it did help us successfully narrow our analysis to actual users of the website.

Understanding the Bounce Rate

We also faced the challenge of analyzing the web analytics data in ways that reflected typical usage patterns of a humanities library website when most of the advisory literature, such as Brian Clifton's *Advanced Web Metrics with Google Analytics* (2010), advocates that ideal website statistics have a low bounce rate, drill-down goals for getting users as deep into the website as possible, and financially defined key performance indicators. But the users of library websites follow much more dynamic browsing and search practices, especially in the humanities. Brockman and colleagues (2001) note that humanities scholars engage in "chaining" and "footnote chasing" behaviors that facilitate the scholars' need to browse widely for research resources.

As such, a user may jump from the Literatures and Languages Library website to the MLA Bibliography and then to the library catalog within the same search, a series of activities that can be measured in a fully configured Google Analytics by exit activity and accessing the web analytics for the library catalog. This common type of use for our library website results in high exit activity and, depending on the web analytics tool, a potentially high bounce rate, but it does not imply that the library did not meet its website goals for the user. High exits may be a good sign if users are exiting where you anticipate they would leave the site.

Additionally, bounces can be caused by library staff or public terminals with their home pages set to the library website, or a web page may serve as a heavily used reference point for links to non-locally-hosted web guides, services, and research databases. Ultimately, an accurate interpretation of bounce rate requires deeper analysis with other exit page reports, navigation summaries, and other analytics reports. The basic visitor statistics and bounce rate reports from analytics data can provide insight only into broad user browsing patterns, traffic, and website structure.

FINDINGS AND BEST PRACTICES

By implementing two web analytics tools on the Literatures and Languages Library website, we created a multifaceted portrait of our web traffic and developed a more in-depth assessment than if we had only used one web analytics tool. The data sets from Google Analytics and those from StatCounter complemented one another and helped provide a broader picture of users' information needs and behaviors. By using data from both tools, we were able to set action items and goals for how to revise the website's design and content for optimal use by our patrons.

We also found that monitoring and analyzing keyword data is an extremely useful strategy developing more effective ways to guide users to needed resources. Users of a humanities library such as the Literatures and Languages Library conduct their research in a way that is notably different from users based in other disciplines. While scientists often will do known-item searches for a standard or handbook, humanities scholars conduct their research as a series of exploratory queries and browsing, as documented in studies by Massey-Burzio (1999) and Palmer and Neumann (2002). As such, their search needs may be best answered by a larger set of resources rather than being directed to a single resource. This included a reorganization of interdisciplinary research guides and resources on the relaunched website to match how users search for resources by language or subject, such as cinema studies. We also rebuilt the website architecture to be more navigable and responsive to the users. The structure changed from a home page linking to general subject-related pages to a portal with a sidebar menu that directly links to all of the website's major research guides and resources. This new sidebar connects the user to the resources at their immediate point of need.

Another strategic practice that we plan to implement in the future is to customize the website's implementation of Google Analytics. We will configure all of the website's outbound links with Google Analytics' tracking script to gather accurate data on exit activity for future website revisions and development of the library's mobile website. We are also exploring Google Analytics' event-tracking capabilities to track click behavior based on the specific links, not solely on the destination URLs. For example, if there are two links to the library's website—

Best-Practices Highlights

- Use multiple web analytics tools if your current web analytics tool is lacking the data or reports your library needs.

- Analyze keyword data to evaluate web content and user behaviors.

- Use Google Analytics' ability to track outbound links and events to better understand how users navigate through the website.

one in the sidebar and another in the main body of the home page—the events report can indicate which of the two links was clicked. Then the library can assess the best positioning of links and remove underperforming redundant links.

CONCLUSION

In this case study, using web analytics data enabled us to revise and relaunch the Literatures and Languages Library website with strategic targeting of user needs. Our analysis of visitor statistics, entry and exit pages, and keyword data enabled us to explore who was using the website, how they navigated its structure, and what content they were seeking. These data also provided us with one-year benchmarks for future revisions of the website in terms of the visitor traffic, navigation through the website, and use of exit links.

Concrete methods of evaluating library use are increasingly important, and web analytics tools offer a crucial way to capture data about the value of a humanities library's web presence and the resources it offers. In the case of the Literatures and Languages Library, data gathered by web analytics tools provided immediate guidance for revising the site's structure and evaluating the scope of the library's resources, and gave the library an enhanced understanding of its users' behaviors on its websites. Humanities libraries that implement web analytics tools may be able to make similar use of the resulting data, as they can use the data to quantify the effectiveness of the library's web services.

REFERENCES

Brockman, William S., Laura Neumann, Carole L. Palmer, and Tonyia J. Tidline. 2001. *Scholarly Work in the Humanities and the Evolving Information Environment.* Washington, DC: Digital Library Federation, Council on Library and Information Resources, 2001. www.clir.org/pubs/reports/pub104/pub104.pdf.

Clifton, Brian. 2010. *Advanced Web Metrics with Google Analytics.* 2nd ed. Indianapolis, IN: Wiley.

Massy-Burzio, Virginia. 1999. "The Rush to Technology: A View from the Humanists." *Library Trends* 47, no 4: 620–639.

Palmer, Carole, and Laura Neumann. 2002. "The Information Work of Interdisciplinary Humanities Scholars: Exploration and Translation." *Library Quarterly* 72, no. 1: 85–117.

Turner, Steven J. 2010. "Website Statistics 2.0: Using Google Analytics to Measure Library Website Effectiveness." *Technical Services Quarterly* 27, no. 3: 261–278.

Warwick, Claire, Melissa Terras, Paul Huntington, and Nikoleta Pappa. 2008. "If You Build It Will They Come? The LAIRAH Study: Quantifying the Use of Online Resources in the Arts and Humanities through Statistical Analysis of User Log Data." *Literary and Linguistic Computing* 23, no. 1: 85–102.

Chapter Ten

Web Analytics Applied to Online Catalog Usage at the University of Denver

Christopher C. Brown

L ibrary directors crave statistics. But uniform statistics are not easy to come by in the digital and Internet era. In an effort to bring uniformity to the "apples and oranges" vendor reports that have been supplied to libraries for many years, the COUNTER initiative (www.projectcounter.org) Counting Online Usage of Networked Electronic Resources and the Standardized Usage Statistics Harvesting Initiative (SUSHI) standard (also known as ANSI/NISO standard Z39.93) have brought a degree of uniformity to the electronic resource world (www.niso.org/workrooms/sushi/). What about uniformity in other statistical areas that concern library administrators? Outside of the electronic resource world, web analytical tools provide statistical uniformity across a wide variety of library projects, including the library website itself, reference guides, and library discovery tools such as online catalogs and so-called web-scale discovery services that provide access to a large swath of library-licensed content.

The task of relocating all library materials to an offsite storage facility while still providing access to all collections, combined with providing ease of access to materials via a web interface, presents a series of challenges. This is the story of Penrose Library at the University of Denver in 2011. The following sections discuss the challenges of providing access to library materials through two library catalog interfaces that use the web analytics tool Google Analytics to provide evaluative statistics to aid the decision-making process and determine a possible future direction.

BACKGROUND:
MOVING MATERIALS AND SHIFTING DEFAULTS

The University of Denver is a private nonprofit university with just under ten thousand students, roughly half graduate and half undergraduate. Penrose Library is the main campus library, with about 1.2 million books, 250,000 bound serial volumes, 850,000 federal publications, just over 1 million microfiche items, and online access to 2.5 million items (1.7 million online items with catalog records and 800,000 harvested records from the HathiTrust).

Two major changes occurred at Penrose Library during 2011: the entire physical collection was moved to an off-site storage facility to accommodate renovation of the library, and we gradually rolled out the Summon discovery tool and repositioned it as the primary search box on the library website.

Penrose Library began moving materials to an off-site storage facility in the early months of 2011. By early April, 29 percent of materials had been moved. The project was nearly complete in July, with 91 percent of materials off-site, and shortly after that, 100 percent of library materials were no longer available for browsing. The rapid removal of physical materials from the familiar open stacks of the library created a near-crisis situation among many faculty members and students who depend on shelf browsing as a research and discovery strategy. These realities motivated the library to focus on strategies to mitigate the lack of a browsing experience.

Since physical browsing was not possible during the renovation, virtual browsing was our only available option. To set up discussion of the statistical analysis from Google Analytics, an overview of the discovery tools used in this study is in order. Penrose Library migrated to Innovative Interfaces Inc. (III) for its integrated library system in 1997. At present, the library uses two separate III catalog interfaces: Millennium (also called the classic catalog in this study), and Encore, III's next-generation catalog interface. Encore lives on a separate server and pulls records in real time from Millennium. The Encore interface uses newer technologies, including Apache Lucene (http://lucene.apache.org/core/) for faster search capability and Apache SOLR (http://lucene.apache.org/solr/) for faceted result sets. Encore gives users the option of linking back to Millennium to view the classic catalog record. When users want to request materials, they click a button labeled "Request It" from within either Millennium or Encore. These requesting functions are actually being performed on the Millennium server, whether the request is initiated from Millennium or Encore.

Even though the Encore interface is more user-friendly and faster, we felt that we needed to provide as much virtual or visual browsing as possible in the catalog, so we subscribed to LibraryThing's Shelf Browse feature (www.librarything.com/blogs/thingology/category/shelf-browse/), which embeds cover images from books into the library catalog record, simulating a shelf-browse experience with books before and after the featured title. Users can click on a cover image and view the full catalog record. This feature is available only through the classic catalog. We added the service in October 2010, but it became more essential as materials were completely removed from patron access.

The Millennium catalog is searchable by author, title, subject, Library of Congress call number, Superintendent of Documents number, journal title, ISN (ISSN and ISBN), and genre headings. Each of these searches is "left anchored," which means that the string entered by the searcher is executed against the left-most part of the field being searched (as opposed to a keyword-type search, in which words are searched regardless of their location in the field being searched). Keyword searching is possible across author, title, subject, and notes fields. These searches are not anchored, which means that the terms can occur anywhere within a given field, not being restricted to the left-most location. Because of functionality and interface design, users determine the kind of search they want to do first, and then they initiate the search. The classic interface does allow for limiting after the initial search by clicking the "Limit this Search" button on the results page. Users can then limit by publication date, format, language, publisher, or location. They can also sort results by year. Figure 10.1 displays the Penrose Library discovery environment in a conceptual manner.

In contrast, the Encore interface allows only for keyword searching but provides "facets" to encourage postsearch manipulation of records. Facets are a dynamically generated clustering of results by categories (e.g., location of search term such as

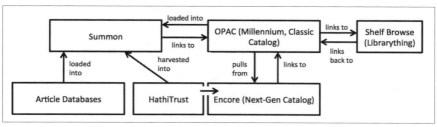

FIGURE 10.1
Discovery Environment at Penrose Library, University of Denver

169

author, title, subject, location within library, format of document, and language). The facets on the left and right margins enable users to restrict results by format, collection (*scoping* in III terminology), location, publication data, and other limits.

These two interfaces, however, cover only items in the traditional library catalog, not database and article content. For this reason, Penrose Library recently subscribed to the Summon web-scale discovery service from Serials Solutions. Summon enables discovery of nearly 80 percent of the library's subscribed article content, as well as records imported nightly from the online catalog. Millennium records are loaded nightly into Summon, and catalog records in Summon in turn link back to their counterparts in Millennium. Metadata representing a majority of article databases are also searchable in Summon. Penrose launched Summon at the end of March 2011, making it one of several search options on the library website. However, it was not prominently featured. Users had to stumble upon it or learn about it through instruction sessions. The keyword search under "Find Books and More" performs the search in Encore. From the pull-down menu, users can perform left-anchored searches in Millennium, such as author, title, and subject. The web page was retired just before the fall quarter, at the end of August 2011.

The new search interface features a tab with Summon as the default (see figure 10.2). The second tab, "Books and More," functions like the previous website, with Encore as the default search and other selections executing Millennium searches.

With the drastic changes to the physical library and the significant changes to the website, we wanted to see whether Google Analytics could show user behaviors in catalog searching and provide insights for possible new directions to consider. For example, should the library focus on the classic catalog and not emphasize

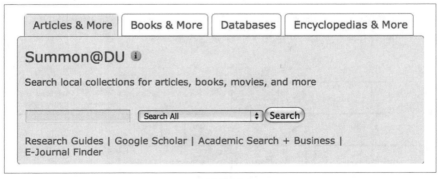

FIGURE 10.2
New Interface for the Penrose Library Website,
Fall Quarter 2011, University of Denver

the Encore next-generation catalog, or should we be doing the opposite? This case study focuses on how Google Analytics shows changing user behaviors and how this informs future library decision making in both the physical and the virtual library.

METHOD: PUTTING GOOGLE ANALYTICS TO WORK

The project period in 2011 can be split into three distinct periods, each representing phases in our physical and technological landscape. These are described in table 10.1.

Since these periods are uneven in terms of numbers of days, the percentages used throughout this study have greater meaning in interpreting the data, since they show the relative usage of each of the two catalog interfaces under consideration.

Google Analytics helped us answer four important questions:

1. Over the three periods, what percentage of users search the Millennium catalog and what percentage search the next-generation catalog?
2. How many users use the "Request It" feature in each of the two interfaces?
3. How many users refine their initial searches?
4. How much is the LibraryThing visual shelf-browse feature used in Millennium?

Many more questions could be posed and answered from the available data, but these questions were directly relevant to our renovation and access issues at Penrose Library.

Google Analytics code has been set up on most library-related servers, including the main library website (http://library.du.edu); the mobile library website

TABLE 10.1

Three time periods during the Penrose Library construction phase

Period	Time span	Description
1	January 1–March 31, 2011	Encore as default search, Millennium secondary with visual shelf browse; 29% of materials off-site by end
2	April 1–August 31, 2011	Same as above, but Summon active but buried; materials being moved off-site in stages; by July 1, 91% of materials off-site
3	September 1–October 31, 2011	Summon as default search tab; Encore and Millennium in secondary tab; all materials off-site

(http://m.library.du.edu); library research guides (http://libguides.du.edu); and each of our two catalog interfaces, Millennium (http://catalog.du.edu) and Encore (http://lib-lakshmi.cair.du.edu). Kilzer (2008) provides instructions for setting up Google Analytics in Millennium. Google Analytics in Encore must be set up with a call to the vendor's help desk. Summon had just initiated Google Analytics tracking as this chapter was being completed, so data analysis from it is unfortunately not possible at the time of this study.

Question 1

Although the first question—"Over the three periods, what percentage of users search the Millennium (classic) catalog and what percentage search Encore, the next-generation catalog?"—seems basic, it is actually quite important to our library. When we loaded our catalog records into Summon, we intentionally had Summon link out to the classic catalog rather than the Encore catalog so that the virtual shelf-browse feature would get used. In the future we may want to make adjustments to Summon so that catalog records in Summon link to the Encore records. We hope that Google Analytics data inform our future decisions.

Superficially, we could have answered this simply with the total page views from Google Analytics. However, this would not be a fair comparison; as previously mentioned, several user options from within Encore invoke Millennium features. We needed to examine only the search-related statistics, and not the patron access activities such as web authentication (in Google Analytics, "top content" page results containing "/validate"), account login ("top content" page results containing "/patroninfo"), and item requesting ("top content" page results containing "/request"), all of which register as Millennium statistics in Google Analytics. These criteria were excluded from the result set using a custom segment in Google Analytics.

To eliminate the non-search-related pages within Encore, we needed to exclude the numerous hits to the main landing page, which accounts for nearly 20 percent of the statistics, and the item-requesting function ("top content" page results excluding "doRequest=REGULAR"). Table 10.2 shows both the total page views for each of the three periods and the search-related pages. Because the three periods are unequal in terms of number of days, the percentage is the more significant statistic.

Google Analytics shows that Encore, the default search during period 1, was used more often. In period 2, as materials were disappearing from public view because of the renovation, Millennium gained in use because it was the default

TABLE 10.2
Statistics from two catalog interfaces, Penrose Library, University of Denver

	Period 1	Period 2	Period 3
Millennium searching			
Total page views	347,449	480,542	321,989
Total page views (only search-related pages)	222,713	302,034	221,890
Percentage of all searches (Millennium + Encore)	35.8%	52.4%	62.8%
Encore searching			
Total page views	507,567	529,348	171,638
Total page views (only search-related pages)	398,923	390,630	131,546
Percentage of all searches (Millennium + Encore)	64.2%	43.6%	37.2%

search. But when Summon was made the default tab in period 3, the fact that Summon drove users to Millennium significantly raised the statistics for the classic view. Overall, it was found that the default search for the catalog increased the usage of that catalog.

Question 2

For the second question—"How many users use the 'Request It' feature in each of the two interfaces?"—because all of our materials are in off-site storage, it was interesting to see how many times users request materials in each of the two systems for each of the three time periods. By examining the URLs underlying the links of the "Request It" button in both Millennium and Encore, we arrived at unique strings that would isolate all and only the requesting URLs. For Millennium the top-content page filter was "/request" and for Encore it was "doRequest-REGULAR." We see the effects of two factors in these statistics in table 10.3.

With materials increasingly off-site, users had to rely on the "Request It" feature with greater frequency. A dramatic increase in requests made can be seen from period 1 to period 2 in the Millennium interface. In addition, as Summon was set out as the default tab by period 3, users were searching and requesting an increasing number of materials from the Summon interface, which forced users into the Millennium interface over the Encore interface. The greater number of requests under the Millennium interface was driven upward by the fact that all requests initiated in Encore were driven over to Millennium.

TABLE 10.3
Usage of the "Request It" feature in the two catalog interfaces,
Penrose Library, University of Denver

Catalog interface	Period 1	Period 2	Period 3
Millennium			
Total page views (only search and request-related pages)	227,080	319,154	242,611
Requests made ("/request")	4,367	17,120	20,721
Percentage of request activity in Millennium	1.9%	5.4%	8.5%
Percentage of all request activity	36.9%	61.4%	75.0%
Encore			
Total page views (only search and request-related pages)	406,400	401,381	138,572
Requests made ("doRequest=REGULAR")	7,477	10,751	6,926
Percentage of request activity in Encore	1.8%	2.7%	5.0%
Percentage of all request activity	63.1%	38.6%	25.0%

Question 3

The third question was "How many users refine their initial searches?" The Millennium catalog really does not lend itself to postresult limiting. In the Millennium interface, limits by location, material type, language, year of publication, and words in title are possible but not readily apparent. A "Limit this Search" button is at the top of the search results page, but Google Analytics statistics show that this is used less than 1 percent of the time.

The next-generation Encore interface, however, lends itself to limiting by facets as previously defined. Google Analytics results show a stunning difference in user behaviors. Table 10.4 shows data for each of the periods by category of facet and the Google Analytics filter applied. In the case of Millennium, the filter "limit:relimit" was applied; in the case of Encore, the filter "ff:facet" was applied. Again, since the periods represent varied time spans, the most important numbers are the percentages. Assumedly because limiting results is not visually foregrounded in the Millennium interface, users rarely limit their search results.

By contrast, Encore users apply limits much more frequently (via filtering using facets). Over the three periods, the total number of Encore search-related

TABLE 10.4
Limiting within two interfaces, Penrose Library,
University of Denver

	Period 1	Period 2	Period 3
Millennium limiting			
Total page views (only search-related pages)	222,713	302,034	221,890
Used "Limit this Search": (limit:relimit)	264	247	135
Percentage refining by limits	<1%	<1%	<1%
Encore filtering			
Total page views (only search-related pages)	398,923	390,630	131,546
Used facets ("ff:facet*")	54,940	48,626	19,231
Percentage refining by facets (cumulative, deduplicated)	13.8%	12.4%	14.6%

page views was 921,099, whereas the total number of times facets were used was 122,797, for an overall percentage of 13.3 percent. This number is higher than Ballard and Blaine's (2011, 267) finding of 8.47 percent of Encore searches being refined by facets. Perhaps this can be explained by the University of Denver library users' need to isolate searches to electronic versions that are readily available over the physical collection stored remotely.

To further examine facet use in Encore, we can use Google Analytics to segment search results (table 10.5). Because Encore encourages multiple facet selections, the sum of all the facets will be greater than the total number in "used facets" below. The "overall %" is based on the sum of each individual search facet type across all three periods (148,747), rather than the sum of "used facets" (122,747).

From table 10.5, we see that the format facet is the most used across all three periods. Upon closer examination with Google Analytics, it is possible to discern that 40.7 percent of facet limits were for books and journals, but (rather surprisingly to our library) 37.2 percent of facet limits were for DVDs. This showed us that users do care about the format of the materials they use (e.g., print, online) and that, to the shock of several of our subject specialists, a high number of users are searching for DVDs.

TABLE 10.5
Facet use in Encore, Penrose Library, University of Denver

	Period 1	Period 2	Period 3	Overall (%)
Encore filtering by facets				
Total page views (only search-related pages)	398,923	390,630	131,546	
Used facets ("ff:facet*")	54,940	48,626	19,231	
Search found in ("ff:facetfields"); includes title, subject, author below	7,311	7,458	3,018	
Title ("ff:facetfields:title")	2,938	3,240	1,574	5.2%
Subject ("ff:facetfields:subject")	1,846	1,442	525	2.6%
Author ("ff:facetfields:author")	2,617	2,882	977	4.4%
Format ("ff:facetmediatype")	26,206	23,223	10,095	40.0%
Collection ("ff:facetcollections")	9,513	7,801	2,533	13.3%
Location ("ff:facetlocations")	8,512	7,106	2,574	12.2%
Language ("ff:facetlanguages")	2,781	2,016	1,282	4.1%
Publish date ("ff:facetpubdate")	5,511	3,294	1,121	6.7%
Place ("ff:facettopicplace")	969	772	532	1.5%
Cloud ("ff:facetcloud")	6,921	5,433	2,511	10.0%

Question 4

Of the questions examined in this case study, the question "How much is the LibraryThing visual shelf-browse feature used in Millennium?" was the most difficult issue to isolate with Google Analytics. The shelf-browse feature automatically appears as an embedded feature at the bottom of each classic catalog record (figure 10.3), and there is no unique "hook" in the URLs from within the LibraryThing shelf browse that is perceptible to Google Analytics and that isolates all and only clicks through to other books on the visual shelf. If the item in the virtual shelf has an ISBN number, an ISBN search is executed containing the string "search/i?SEARCH=". However, if no ISBN is present, a general keyword search is executed. We added the following segment to Google Analytics: for

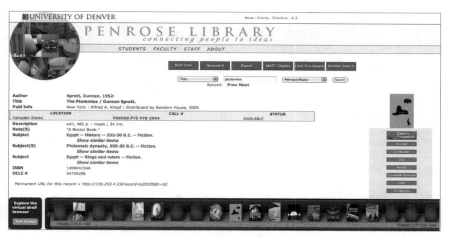

FIGURE 10.3
Virtual Shelf Browse in the Millennium Catalog,
Penrose Library, University of Denver

pages containing "i\?SEARCH" and pages excluding "/validate", pages excluding "/request", and pages excluding "/patroninfo". Note that the question mark in the first filter above had to be amended with a backslash to force this to be a literal expression rather than a regular expression.

The only hope of recovering any kind of statistics was to examine the relative increase of ISBN searches before and after the implementation of the visual shelf browse feature. This gave us some relative, but not absolute, statistical measures. Since LibraryThing was launched on October 15, 2010, we examined search strings in the Millennium interface containing "i\?SEARCH=" both before and after that time using Google Analytics. The easiest way to do this was to use the Google Analytics feature that allows you to compare data from different time spans. We compared the period January 1–October 15, 2011 with the same period in the year before (figure 10.4). The monthly summary view shows a stunning increase after the LibraryThing feature was launched, indicating that at least some users were using the virtual shelf browse. Although we might have used Google Analytics' event-tracking capability, we did not know about this feature at the time. Perhaps future research can explore this functionality.

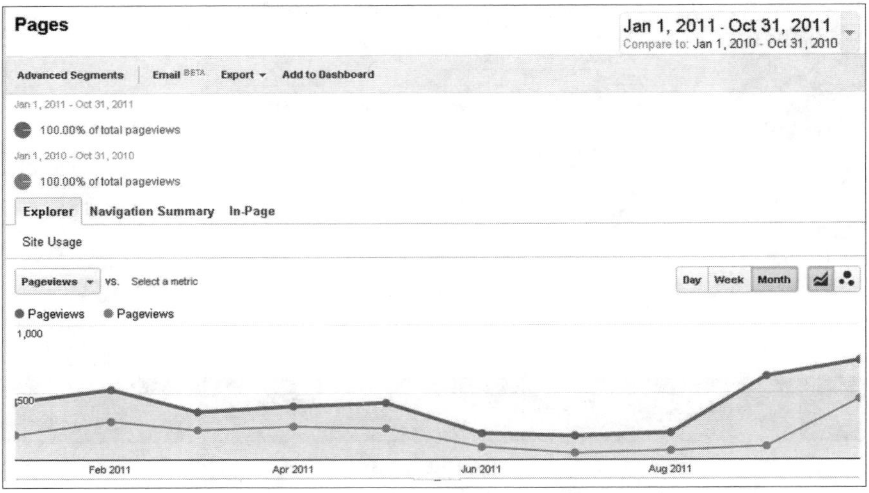

Pages   Jan 1, 2011 - Oct 31, 2011
Compare to: Jan 1, 2010 - Oct 31, 2010

Advanced Segments   Email ᴮᴱᵀᴬ   Export ▾   Add to Dashboard

Jan 1, 2011 - Oct 31, 2011
● 100.00% of total pageviews
Jan 1, 2010 - Oct 31, 2010
● 100.00% of total pageviews

Explorer   Navigation Summary   In-Page

Site Usage

Pageviews ▾ vs. Select a metric   Day   Week   **Month**

● Pageviews   ● Pageviews

1,000

500

Feb 2011   Apr 2011   Jun 2011   Aug 2011

FIGURE 10.4
Comparing Searches by ISBN in 2010 and 2011,
Google Analytics, Penrose Library, University of Denver

CHALLENGES WHEN USING GOOGLE ANALYTICS

As we have seen, Google Analytics provides many answers, and yet there are many things that are beyond its capabilities.

When we attempted to see whether users were using LibraryThing's shelf browse feature, our installation of Google Analytics let us down in this particular instance. This is merely a consequence of the technologies underlying the linking protocols.

With libraries increasingly adding links to external content in catalog records (856 fields), integrated library systems are generally not able to track these links. This is a great disappointment to library administrators who need statistics. We have circulation statistics for physical items, but we generally have no idea of whether users click those links in our catalog. It is true that vendors give us statistics, but these are not comparable to circulation statistics of physical items. Google Analytics in not a reliable source for this either.

At Penrose Library, we saw the need to track these statistics, and in 2003 we began tracking outbound links to online federal documents when users clicked links to website content from library catalog records (from 856 fields). Later we also began tracking outbound linking to nongovernmental freely available resources.

What Google Analytics Can (and Cannot) Do for Online Catalogs

Google Analytics can

- provide information on where users visit from (country, state, city)
- disclose what operating systems and browser versions are being used
- provide some information on accesses from mobile devices
- show catalog searches entered and sort by most popular searches
- show entrance and exit pages within a web interface
- distinguish new and returning users as well as frequency and recency of visits
- determine where catalog searches were initiated from (libraries may have a variety of possible entry pages)

Google Analytics cannot

- automatically provide click-through statistics to specific links in an 856 field in a catalog record—additional configurations are required to track outbound links
- give statistics analogous to print circulation statistics from the integrated library system
- give statistics similar to vendor-supplied e-book statistics
- track an individual user's clicking experience as user behavior-monitoring software can do (e.g., eye movements)

It would be helpful if Google Analytics could provide a similar kind of statistics. Although Google Analytics can be configured to manually track outbound links (http://support.google.com/analytics/bin/answer.py?hl=en&answer=1136920), doing so in an integrated library system where there may be multiple outbound URLs in 856 fields, is not feasible. Our click-through tracking process, which uses a library server to track the time and date of an outbound click, and afterward directs the user to the requested website, has proved a most reliable solution for us over the past nine years. These procedures and the statistical results are described in Brown (2011). This major oversight on the part of integrated library system vendors needs to be addressed.

BEST PRACTICES

Google Analytics has specific applications for a library undergoing renovation and redesign. As libraries experience change, there is a need for statistical support, either to study past decisions or to anticipate future ones. We suggest several best practices applicable to Google Analytics, or to any of the other web analytic tools, to enable libraries to present a more complete understanding of user's web behaviors.

> Place the Google Analytics code in every appropriate web page. This should include the main library website, the mobile site, catalog interfaces, web-scale discovery tools, and digital repositories. Even if you do not know what to do with the data immediately, Google Analytics will store data for your future analysis.
>
> Study URL strings to determine URL patterns. This is essential in databases that output dynamic links, as is the case with those from most integrated library system vendors. This will enable you to mine the data out of Google Analytics. This is a tedious task but one that is key to mining the depths of user behaviors.
>
> Examine Google Analytics for other features such as bounce rate, on-campus versus off-campus access (geographic location), time spent on each respective site, browser used, operating system used, mobile-device access, and searches by subject discipline. Depending on what is important to your library's goals, some of these topics will be in the foreground, and others may be of lesser importance.
>
> Do not give up on your native integrated library system statistics. The two sets of statistics are complementary. While Google Analytics gives a very visual and granular view of website statistics, it is not able to do everything. The native integrated library system statistics are still necessary for circulation statistics, record counts, collection development profiling, and other areas beyond the scope of Google Analytics.
>
> Anticipate how analytical statistics might affect change in your library. Google Analytics statistics can be used to complement user studies to make decisions as to default search boxes, user search patterns, and feature usage.

CONCLUSION

This case study focused on Google Analytics statistics particularly germane to the University of Denver's renovation situation and the accompanying website redesign. Google Analytics clearly showed that defaults do make a difference. When the default catalog interface was Encore, the statistics far overshadowed Millennium; however, when the default was changed to Summon as a search across all resources, the Millennium statistics overtook Encore. It is also apparent that next-generation interfaces are more conducive to information discovery than older interfaces, as evidenced by the increased usage of search limiters in Encore over Millennium. After the renovation is completed and resources return to the building, it is likely that we will reconsider linking to Encore from Summon rather than to Millennium on the basis of these data.

Although we rely on integrated library system statistics to track actual item requests and user status, Google Analytics tells us user discovery behaviors that we otherwise would not have known. With further configuration of Google Analytics' implementation in the library catalog, we have the opportunity to learn more about how users search and interact with it. These data will be invaluable in making informed decisions related to the catalog and overall improving the user's experience in searching for materials in the library.

REFERENCES

Ballard, Terry, and Anna Blaine. 2011. "User Search-Limiting Behavior in Online Catalogs." *New Library World* 112, nos. 5–6: 261–273.

Brown, Christopher C. 2011. "Knowing Where They Went: Six Years of Online Statistics via the OPAC for Federal Government Information." *College and Research Libraries* 72 (1): 43–61.

Forbes, Carrie, and Christopher C. Brown. 2012. "Analyzing the Past to Invest in the Future: Use Statistics for Research Guides from Multiple Data Sources." In *Leading the Reference Renaissance: Today's Ideas for Tomorrow's Cutting Edge Services,* edited by Marie L. Radford, 275–290. New York: Neal-Schuman.

Kilzer, Rebekah D. 2008. "Using Google Analytics for the Proprietary OPAC." *Knowledge Bank.* http://hdl.handle.net/1811/31951.

Chapter Eleven

Optimizing Open-Source Web Analytics Tools for Increased Security of WordPress and Drupal

Junior Tidal

L ibraries have traditionally used metrics to gauge their services. From the count of visitors to the circulation statistics of materials, data has been used as a quantitative measure of use. These measurements have been used to improve, alter, or completely remove services. Data and statistics from a library's website use can be utilized not only to better shape user-centered functionality but also to identify potential web security issues. For example, site administrators can use website statistics to determine whether unauthorized users are trying to access back-end pages.

This chapter examines the statistical capabilities of WordPress and Drupal, both out of the box and extended, and how they can be used to monitor website security and vulnerabilities. Spam bots, unauthorized attempts to access sensitive areas, and even creation of fake pages or users are concerns for both Drupal and WordPress sites. However, there are web analytics tools that work with these publishing platforms to combat these problems. This chapter introduces each of the tools and focuses on their ability to identify potential web page errors and website security risks.

BACKGROUND

This case study features the Ursula C. Schwerin Library, a medium-sized academic library that supports the community of the New York City College of Technology of the City University of New York (CUNY), and its strategy in monitoring its website and blog. The Drupal content management system (CMS) powers the library's main site (http://library.citytech.cuny.edu), whereas the WordPress blogging platform is used to maintain the library's blog, *LibraryBuzz* (http://library.citytech.cuny.edu/blog).

Although the website was first launched in 1999, collecting server statistics is a relatively new practice for the library. Before moving to its own web server in 2008, the library had a difficult time collecting website use data because of complications inherent in sharing a web server with other websites on campus. The library now has access to its own server, where it is able to use the internal statistic reporting tools in Drupal and WordPress. The native web analytics functions in these platforms are quickly and easily augmented with plug-ins and additional tools.

OPEN-SOURCE WEB ANALYTICS TOOLS

The web analytics tools discussed in this chapter are mostly open source, which gives them certain advantages over proprietary software. First, open-source software is typically free and available through a general public license (GPL). Under this license, developers may modify and redistribute software, free of financial compensation to the original developers, so long as they include the source code.

One particular advantage that open-source analytics tools have over commercial ones is privacy. Commercial web analytics tools, such as Google Analytics, are not hosted on the local site. This raises concerns over user privacy, since the data gathered through this tool are stored on separate web servers that libraries cannot necessarily access. However, open-source tools typically require installation directly on the local server, which may be problematic in some library environments. One significant benefit, though, is that the library retains full control over its own use data and does not have to concern itself about third-party party access to it. See chapter 1 for more information about user privacy concerns in web analytics practice.

WORDPRESS'S WEB ANALYTICS CAPABILITIES

WordPress is a popular, open-source blogging and web development platform built on PHP and driven by MySQL. That is, content is stored in a database (MySQL) and then is retrieved and presented to users using PHP/HTML. This system, which can be hosted externally or locally installed, uses templates to render web content, an integrated search system, tagging, RSS feeds, and additional site customization. Although the WordPress platform is commonly associated with blogging, its functionality extends well beyond blog support; there are numerous plug-ins that further augment its functionality, thus making it a versatile publishing platform.

WordPress's Internal Statistics

Site Stats is WordPress's internal statistics dashboard that reports visitor data. Site Stats provides blog usage data including the number of visitors to the blog, and those data can be segmented by days, weeks, and months. To install and set up Site Stats, administrators can install the plug-in found on the WordPress website (http://wordpress.org/extend/plugins/stats/). An API key is needed to activate the plug-in, which is available after registering an account at www.wordpress.com. If you have installed the Jetpack plug-in, the Site Stats link can be found under that section. This plug-in also notes site referrers, top posts and pages search terms, and total number of views, the "busiest day" of the blog, and the views of the current day. A summary table of blog stats shows the most heavily and least used days, months, and weeks. Although these data are useful in understanding how visitors access and use the blog, they reveal little about security risks or technical errors on the blog.

WordPress Extensions

There are numerous plug-ins that can enhance the functionality and capabilities of WordPress. These tools go beyond measuring site traffic, as they also log analytical information, such as real-time tracking, hardware configurations, and referral sites. Depending on your WordPress installation, you can add these plug-ins through the browser or can upload them to your WordPress site. This section focuses on the statistical plug-ins Akismet, WassUp, and FireStats. For general information about installing WordPress plug-ins, consult the documentation at http://codex.wordpress.org/Managing_Plugins.

Akismet

Akismet (http://wordpress.org/extend/plugins/akismet/) is an open-source (under a GPLv2 license) spam prevention plug-in that filters out false comments and trackback URL spam. Developed by Automattic, the creators of WordPress, this

FIGURE 11.1
Akismet Stats LibraryBuzz, Ursula C. Schwerin Library, New York City
College of Technology of the City University of New York

extension provides statistics to WordPress administrators. The plug-in processes comments by sending them to the Akismet server, where false comments are flagged. These results are then returned back to your blog.

Akismet flags spam comments and tracks these numbers in the WordPress dashboard. Monthly statistics on spam comments posted to the blog, legitimate comments ("ham"), and false positives (when spam comments are flagged as ham) are collected and reported with this plug-in (figure 11.1). It is important to recognize spam within your WordPress blog because of phishing attempts and/ or redirection URLs. Comment spam may include a phishing URL. These sites attempt to acquire sensitive information such as user names or passwords by masquerading as a trustworthy website. With this information, an unauthorized individual can infiltrate a site or impersonate a user's credentials and gain access to administrative pages.

It is necessary to update the Akismet plug-in regularly. Unfortunately, a good indicator that an update is necessary is a spike in spam comments. Upgrading the Akismet plug-in to the newest version enables the plug-in to have the most recent software to combat spam.

WassUp

WassUp (http://wordpress.org/extend/plugins/wassup/) is another open-source plug-in (under a GNU license) that tracks visitors. What sets it apart from similar extensions is its ability to track in real time. Administrators can view users navigating their site, click by click. Real-time statistics present visits, page views, pages per visit, and spam. WassUp also records Internet protocol (IP) addresses, host name, operating system, referrer data, and visitor type data. It also clearly identifies which visitors are bots or humans. This extension can monitor visitors by using both the "spy view," which displays the visitor's IP, the referral URL, and geographic location in real time, or the currently logged users view. This extension is useful for determining the volume of nonhuman visitors that the blog receives.

WassUp has numerous customizable options such as refreshing minutes, enabling (or disabling) the recording of bots and spiders, recording exploit attempts, and spam attempts. The setting variable of refreshing minutes allows administrators to adjust how long it takes for the data to update. For instance, if this is set at one minute, then the current list of visitors will refresh every minute. Enabling the recording of bots and spiders allows administrators to see whether human or nonhuman visitors are accessing the site. This is useful if you want to look at only human visitors and not crawlers. Last, WassUp records exploit and spam attempts, noting the IP address, pages accessed, and time stamp (figure 11.2). This important information helps in identifying security vulnerabilities, detailing where the exploit originated and which page was accessed and when.

FireStats

FireStats (http://firestats.cc/wiki/wordpress) is a stand-alone web analytics tool (figure 11.3). However, it also has a WordPress plug-in that provides use information on website visitors. Not only is it compatible with WordPress; it can be integrated with other CMS software such as Drupal, MediaWiki, Joomla!, and Django. Currently, FireStats is not open source, but it is still free to use.

This particular plug-in was selected because of some of its features, including support of user privacy and its ability to filter out crawlers and bots. In addition, FireStats reports a variety of statistics, including page views, visits, referrers, search terms, popular pages, browsers, operating systems, and visits by country. A "hits table" is also provided, which filters visitor IP address, time stamp, URL, referrer website, and operating system and browser combination. This is useful for providing basic web analytics data on visitors.

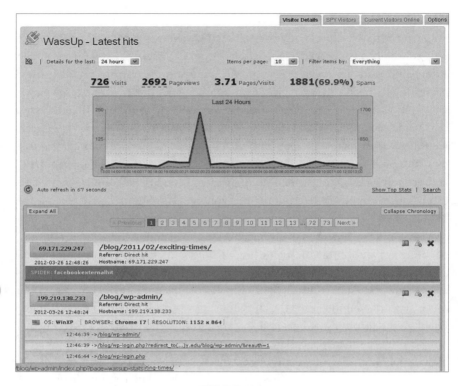

FIGURE 11.2
WassUp Stats, LibraryBuzz, Ursula C. Schwerin Library, New York City
College of Technology of the City University of New York

FireStats provides another source of web analytics data that supplements WordPress's Site Stats and the WassUp plug-in. Multiple analytics tools may provide different insights into how your site is being used. From a security standpoint, using these different plug-ins may help monitor intrusion or hack attempts because it may not necessarily be apparent when using just one tool.

DRUPAL'S WEB ANALYTICS CAPABILITIES

Drupal is a modular, web CMS that, like WordPress, is powered by PHP and MySQL. Developed by an open-source community, the system manages many aspects of a web development system such as content editing, user management, and site administration. The Ursula C. Schwerin Library's website migrated to

FIGURE 11.3
FireStats, LibraryBuzz, Ursula C. Schwerin Library, New York City
College of Technology of the City University of New York

Drupal 6 to facilitate librarian-created content, to develop online collaboration, to conduct easier maintenance, and to develop a more user-friendly site.

Drupal's Core "Statistics" Module

Drupal consists of core and custom modules. Core modules are the system base and are included in standard installations, whereas custom modules are extensions of core functionality developed by Drupal developers and users. These custom modules are available through the official Drupal site (http://drupal.org) and the project developers' web pages. The core statistics module provides some basic site reports and can be used to monitor site security. Data tracked include recent log entries, top access-denied errors, top page-not-found errors, top referrers, top search pages, top pages, and top visitors. These reports can be found in Drupal's administrative back end and can help identify problems within the site if viewed regularly. For this module to be used, Drupal administrators must enable the access log through the statistics module settings page with the appropriate permission levels. This may take some further configurations, such as having access to the statistics module for certain roles and users. More information about this module can be found on the official Drupal site (http://drupal.org/documentation/modules/statistics).

Recent Hits Report

The recent hits report outlines the most recent website visits. This includes registered users who are currently logged into the site, the title of the page visited, the URL of the page, and the time stamp of the event. More in-depth information, available through the "details" link, includes the user's IP address and referring URL. This page can be used to find erroneous links or to track logged-in users. Visitors without user names are logged as anonymous, or unregistered, users. This includes web crawlers and bots. It is important to track anonymous users and how they use the site, to make sure that your site is secure. For instance, anonymous users may try to access administrative pages or run maintenance scripts to enter the back end of your Drupal installation. Additionally, if an anonymous user successfully registers on your site, it will also be necessary to track this new user's interactions with the site and the security vulnerabilities that allowed the user to register in the first place. In essence, you can follow how unauthorized users have entered or have attempted to enter your Drupal site using this report.

Recent Log Entries

The recent log entries page displays server events, such as file downloads. By clicking individual events, more details including usage data, performance data, errors, warnings, and operational information are shown. This information, much like the recent hits report, can help administrators evaluate the different errors that visitors of the site have encountered. Errors such as 404 errors, 403 errors, redirects, and security errors, can be tracked on this page. This page also contains other useful information, such as search-term usage and the corresponding results pages. More important, these errors can point out intrusion attempts. If multiple users are unsuccessfully trying to load the user registration or user log-in page, it should be logged on this page. This page also allows you to filter events based on severity. That is, you can list events based on emergency status down to warnings, which will help find other problems with your site.

Top Access-Denied Error Report

This report (admin/reports/access-denied) displays pages that visitors have attempted to access and failed (figure 11.4). Typically, the server displays these errors (403 indicates an access-denied page, and 404 is a missing page) to the server log and the visitor's browser. This is useful for evaluating permissions for various Drupal roles and potential hacking attempts to the administrative back end, and for pinpointing broken links. In terms of permissions, administrators can use this page to determine whether newly installed modules are working for particular roles. For instance, if a certain Drupal module that has a link to a particular page has multiple 403 errors, then the permissions may not be correctly configured for that module. Hack attempts can be detected by examining specific URLs displayed on this page. This page will display the count of how many times a page has been

FIGURE 11.4
Top Access-Denied Errors, Drupal Statistics Module,
Ursula C. Schwerin Library, New York City College
of Technology of the City University of New York

accessed unsuccessfully. By blocking these URLs, or moving administrative pages, you can prevent unauthorized access (or attempted access) to these sections of the site. Last, since this page displays missing pages, you can determine which URLs are not linked and not functioning.

Top Page-Not-Found Error Report

This page (admin/reports/page-not-found) shows a list of pages that were not found within the site (figure 11.5). This is useful for identifying broken links and possible intrusions. These errors, along with the referring URLs, are recorded in the server log, which can be used to troubleshoot bad or missing links. You can determine between a missing page and an intrusion attempt by looking at the URLs listed on this page. If there is persistent access to administrative pages (/admin), files that

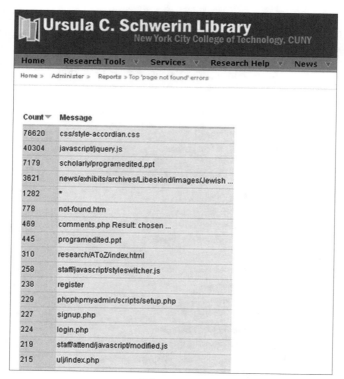

FIGURE 11.5
Top Page-Not-Found Errors, Drupal Statistics Module,
Ursula C. Schwerin Library, New York City College of
Technology of the City University of New York

contain sensitive data (i.e., settings.php) and the user login or registration screens (/user or /user/register), then those users could be unsuccessfully trying to access those pages.

Even though the page-not-found report is similar to the top access-denied report, and the URLs found here may be the same as in the other report, it is also important to monitor this page. Missing-pages errors are different from access-denied errors and it is better to use this information from this report than others.

Top Visitors

The top visitors report displays users who have most frequently visited the site and allows administrators to ban users. They are identified by IP address or user name and are ranked by the number of times the visitor has accessed the site. Page-generation time is also recorded for each user. This may be useful for monitoring highly accessed pages with registered users. If administrative pages or links to those pages are accessed by registered users who do not have the necessary permissions to conduct site operations, then those users may be a security risk.

193

Piwik: Drupal Module

Piwik is an open-source, PHP/MySQL-based analytics engine that is touted as an alternative to Google Analytics. It is initially installed on the web server hosting the site (the Piwik package can be retrieved at http://piwik.org), followed by an installation of its separate Drupal module (http://drupal.org/project/piwik). For general information about installing Drupal modules, consult the documentation found at http://drupal.org/documentation/install/modules-themes. After installation, this module generates the JavaScript tracking code to be embedded within Drupal pages, which is used to monitor and collect use data. This analytics software allows the use of alternate tracking methods either using web beacons or PHP-based code, which may be necessary to track mobile devices and/or browsers that have JavaScript turned off.

After installing the Drupal Piwik module, a few settings must be configured to get it up and running. In the site's Drupal administrator panel, go to the Piwik module (under "Site Configuration") and further customize it—for example, by selecting what types of users should be tracked. Additionally, specific file extensions can be tracked as well. This is useful if you want to track downloads or visits to PDF files, Microsoft Office documents (e.g., Word, PowerPoint, Excel), or other media files (e.g., MP3, AVI) on your site.

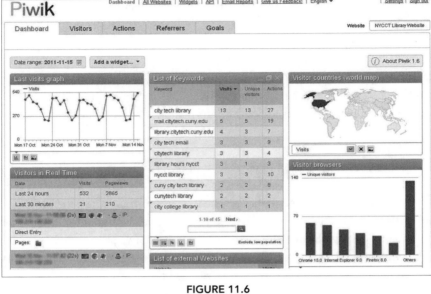

FIGURE 11.6
Piwik Dashboard, Ursula C. Schwerin Library, New York City
College of Technology of the City University of New York

Piwik Dashboard

Piwik uses a widget interface, which allows administrators to select what functions appear on the main dashboard (figure 11.6). The data can be filtered by day, week, year, or between two periods. This tool can also track multiple websites, and email reports. The dashboard displays the number of visits, search terms used to find the site, visitors' geographical data, browser types, referral websites (including keywords), search-engine usage, and lengths of visit. RSS feeds using the FeedBurner service can also be tracked; this displays the statistics of users who subscribe to your site or blog. Depending on your needs, it may be necessary to see the other points of entry, such as RSS feeds, into your site.

Piwik and Security

Piwik was installed at the Schwerin Library because of the lack of detailed information through Drupal reports. The analytics information collected by Piwik can help pinpoint potential security vulnerabilities. Hypothetically, if the server goes down because of an attack, you can use Piwik to examine IP addresses before the time of the system's shutdown. This can be done by looking at the visitor log under the "Visitor" tab. Even though you can also track IP addresses through the recent log entries report from Drupal, you can use the records found on Piwik to compare and contrast the two. Additionally, you can compare the number of visitors between given dates to determine whether there is a security risk. This may also be helpful in revealing the IP addresses of a denial-of-service, or DOS, attack (a DOS attack is when there are multiple requests for a connection to a web server, to the point that it paralyzes the system by overloading it). Administrators can use Piwik to track IP addresses after such an occurrence.

FINDINGS

This case study analyzed the usage data in identifying potential security risks. This includes the data collected by each of the tools described here. These reports examine statistics from July 2011 through September 2011.

WordPress Usage

The WordPress internal statistics dashboard provides a basic report on visitors. This was not particularly useful for this case study since it focuses on security data, but it does provide insightful, general use data that showed how users accessed the blog and which blog posts were the most viewed. A major limitation of internal statistics is that it cannot filter the data by custom periods; rather, each individual month had to be reported separately. Additionally, WordPress site statistics do not count bots or logged-in users, which account for a portion of the blog's traffic—this is further discussed here.

WordPress's internal statistics were also less than helpful for identifying security risks, so it was important to analyze the use data captured in Akismet, WassUp, and FireStats. Since different web analytics tools track and report data differently, this section focuses more on the features and findings of the tools than on a direct data comparison.

Spam Comments

One particular type of interaction that can be used to gauge security on a blog is user comments. The number of actual, human comments the blog receives averages about 8 comments a month, but the blog received many more spam comments. Akismet's strength is its ability to track and filter those spam comments. During the case study, Akismet reported 6,702 spam comments posted on the blog—nearly 78 spam comments a day! On closer examination, 24 spam comments caught by

Akismet turned out to be real comments, and it missed 4 spam comments. While Akismet mistakenly identified a comment less than .05 percent in its reporting, it is still crucial for blog owners to monitor Akismet to ensure actual comments do not get filtered, and vice versa.

Interestingly, WassUp only reported 1,074 comments or track-back links as spam during the same period. According to WassUp, the blog receives about 11 spam comments or track-back links a day. Despite the large discrepancy between Akismet and WassUp, this still implies a high amount of spam comments that the blog attracts. Spam comments are a significant security risk for a few reasons. First, these types of comments usually contain embedded URLs. These URLs may lead to phishing sites, where unsuspecting users could unknowingly disclose confidential information, such as user names or passwords. Second, these URLs take advantage of a search-engine optimization (SEO) technique that place sites with many links at the top of search results. The more links to a site, the higher its place in page rankings.

To combat spam, one strategy is to regularly update spam detector plug-ins to avoid spam. Another strategy is to employ Completely Automated Public Turing Test to Tell Computers and Humans Apart (CAPTCHA), which are forms used to filter out spam bots. This information could be used to justify the moderation of comments. That is, comments will not be posted on the blog unless there is prior approval from a blog administrator.

Nonhuman (Robot) Visitors

WassUp also reported that a majority of visitors to the blog are bots (spiders and crawlers) indexing the site for search engines. We learned that a large portion—more than 70 percent—of our visitors are not human. Generally, crawlers from search engines do not pose a security threat. This type of software is used to index all of the pages on a website. However, this same technology can be used to test security vulnerabilities. The information that crawlers retrieve—URLs, email addresses, file names and types—can be used to discover weaknesses in a WordPress installation. One method to prevent the use of crawlers to index your site is to use a robot.txt file. If this file does not exist, crawlers and spiders are free to index the contents of your site. This includes sensitive areas such as the /wp-content directory. You can create a file called robot.txt and insert the following code to prevent search engine indexing. This file can be placed within the /wp-content directory or copied to other directories that you do not wish to be indexed.

```
Robots.txt
#
User-agent: *
Disallow: /cgi-bin
Disallow: /wp-admin
Disallow: /wp-includes
Disallow: /wp-content/plugins/
Disallow: /wp-content/cache/
Disallow: /wp-content/themes/
Disallow: */trackback/
Disallow: */feed/
Disallow: /*/feed/rss/$
Disallow: /category/*
```

This will still allow the content and information on your site to be used by search engines.

Referring Websites and Spam Trackbacks

FireStats found that the top ten (out of ten) referrers were spam track-back URLs. Administrators can browse through the "hits table" and identify the referrer URLs with the landing pages of the blog. Of the traffic to our blog, 52 percent originated from track-back links. These URLs, like comment spam links, are used for SEO optimization and can lead back to malicious phishing sites. Plug-ins, like Akismet, prevent track-back URLs from being posted on a site.

A more extreme option is to manually rename the wp-comments.php file (and the reference to it in comments.php) to something else. Since this filename is provided in all WordPress installations, bots are specifically programmed to search and find this file. The previous robots.txt solution, which counters site indexing, is also another way to prevent track-back spam.

Analyzing Drupal

Drupal's core statistics module revealed mostly security issues rather than information about the website's users. On the basis of the library's results, it can be argued that the statistics module is more suited for error tracking, whereas Piwik provided more comprehensive use data about website users. However, both were useful in this case study.

Bot Problems

This study found that a majority of missing pages and access-denied pages exist and were triggered by bots. From a security perspective, crawlers and bots can cause havoc by exploiting vulnerable and unsecured sites. As previously mentioned, there are several solutions that can counter web crawlers while still accommodating beneficial ones.

Referring Spam Websites

For the Schwerin Library, the top referring websites in Drupal includes the college website (New York City College of Technology of the City University of New York) and several spam advertising sites. The spam links pose a potential security problem because they may point to malicious or phishing websites. These websites may attempt to gather user names, passwords, and other sensitive information to unsuspecting users. On our Drupal installation, we have disabled the commenting of all pages to prevent track-back spam. Although there are other sections of the site that require user interaction, such as email forms and the comments page, we have employed CAPTCHA to control bots from posting on our site. Additionally, we have restricted user registration to only librarians to better regulate the content on our site.

Error Pages in the Top Content Reports

According to Piwik, our custom 404 page was one of the top pages reached on our site. This is a problem because it may indicate intrusion attempts to the Drupal back end, such as malicious users attempting to reach the administrative sections of the site. However, this may also indicate a broken link or a typo. To be sure, administrators can view the report on recent log entries to pinpoint specific URLs and users. Simple solutions to plugging a possible 404 error exploit include repairing broken and missing links. Additionally, web administrators using Apache web server software may also turn off directory indexing to prevent intruders from exploring the site by updating Apache configuration files.

CHALLENGES

During the case study, there were several challenges in collecting and comparing the data. These challenges were not specific to the case study—all libraries should be aware of these potential pitfalls in using multiple web analytics tools to gain a better perspective of website use.

Comparing Data in Different Web Analytics Tools

The accuracy of the data between multiple analytics tools should be scrutinized when analyzing potential security threats on either a Drupal or WordPress installation. Each tool collects data in different ways, so it is not recommended to compare similar data between the different types of tools. With this in mind, it is best to understand how each tool collects and reports data. This will allow administrators to better analyze the data and thus make better decisions on securing their sites. As noted earlier, one shortcoming in the native WordPress and Drupal statistics reporting features is that neither allows statistics filtering by specific date. This made it difficult to pinpoint certain time frames for data comparisons. For instance, WordPress can generate a report for a certain day, week, month, or year, but statistics cannot be segmented between two specific dates. Drupal's error reports and top pages report do not allow date filtering.

Tracking Users

Piwik uses the JavaScript tagging method to collect data, which means that users who have JavaScript turned off or certain older mobile browsers that do not use JavaScript may not be recorded. This presents a problem. There are several hardware and software combinations that may interfere with accurate page visits. The number of bots may also skew the true number of visitors, as neither Piwik nor Drupal reports actively track crawlers and spiders. JavaScript-based analytics tools do not include them in data collection.

BEST PRACTICES

When evaluating website security, web analytics should not be the only measurements that librarians and library web developers investigate. Web metrics have limitations and should be used as supplementary information. The official Drupal site has some tips on keeping your installation secure. More information can be found at http://drupal.org/security/secure-configuration. Some of these tips include topics discussed earlier, such as Drupal permissions and securing administrative areas.

Keeping separate sets of metrics, such as one for the main site and blog, will point out the strengths and weaknesses of each installation's security. The behaviors of visitors utilizing a library's blog will be drastically different from those using the main library site; a blog is used for publicity, whereas the library website facilitates information seeking and access to resources. For libraries and librarians who are in a similar situation, it is best to focus on the specifics of having a separate blog and website. At City Tech, our blog is mostly read by full-time faculty, which we know because of the large number of faculty members creating comments. With this in mind, blog posts are written to a faculty audience more than a student one. Content, including new e-resources, library events, and professional development workshops, caters to that audience. Since the library's main site may contain more sensitive information, such as unique institutional links to e-resources or information about library staff, the Drupal installation should be more secure to protect this content. The blog, in contrast, has the potential to lead users away to malicious websites, so measures should be taken to disallow the posting of URLs and redirecting sites. Different security techniques should be tailored for each installation.

Analytical tools can help recognize potential cyberattacks and spam. As such, using multiple tools can help identify cyberattacks. The built-in reports of both Drupal and WordPress indicate attempts to circumvent website security, and the extended functionality of FireStats and WassUp found several referral spam requests within their respective visitor logs. Akismet was used to evaluate whether the blog is genuinely viewed or is being indexed by bots. In this regard, these analytical tools can help pinpoint vulnerabilities in a website; however, libraries need to take the extra step to prevent security breaches. As mentioned, limiting registered users and installing CAPTCHA plug-ins or modules can aid in repelling potential attacks. The simplest best development and maintenance practices, such as keeping your core web CMS software and any extended functionality up to date, go a long way toward keeping your site secure. The server environment—where Apache, MySQL, and PHP are installed—must be kept up to date as well.

CONCLUSION

Statistics derived from open-source tools can be just as powerful as their commercial counterparts. By adding plug-ins and custom modules to the basic installations of Drupal or WordPress, you get a more comprehensive use data that can help recognize potential cyberattacks and spam. The built-in reports of both Drupal (statistics module) and WordPress (Site Stats) can reveal attempts to circumvent website security. The WordPress extensions FireStats and WassUp are useful for finding referral spam requests on the library's blog, and the WordPress extension Akismet was used to evaluate whether the blog is viewed by "real" humans or is being indexed by bots. For the library's website, Drupal's Piwik module helps provide views of website use data not available in Drupal's statistics module—it is now possible to track unexpected spikes in usage that may indicate a DOS attack and identify the offending IP address that caused the attack.

In this regard, these web analytics tools can help pinpoint vulnerabilities in a website, but libraries need to take the extra step to follow through on actionable data to prevent security breaches. Limiting registered users, moderating comments, and installing CAPTCHA modules can repel potential attacks in WordPress and Drupal. Additionally, it is recommended that libraries keep any software, including WordPress, Drupal, and their extensions or modules, up to date with the software's security updates. All web servers and their programs, such as PHP and MySQL, should also be current. Although these are all steps to prevent security breaches to your websites, keep in mind that libraries should also be vigilant to these attacks. Use the freely available open-source tools described in this chapter to help monitor and notify the library of potential risks.

Glossary of Web Analytics Terms and Concepts

action-oriented analytics—The process of using web analytics data to inform a decision-making process.

benchmark—A standard to compare or measure change.

bounce—When a visitor enters a website and automatically navigates away from it. Basically, visitors who view only one page or are on the site less than a few seconds.

bounce rate—The number of bounces divided by the number of visits to a website.

click-density report—A visual report that shows where visitors click on a web page. Heat maps and site overlay reports are examples of common click-density reports.

competitive benchmarking—The process of comparing website statistics with similar institutions. May also be referred to as external benchmarking.

conversion—When a visitor performs a desired result or outcome on a website.

conversion rate—The total number of conversions divided by the total visits or unique visitors. This reveals the percentage of how many times that conversion occurs on the site.

custom report—A reporting feature that lets an individual decide which metrics to select and analyze in a report.

depth of visit—This metric totals the number of web pages a visitor views before exiting the site.

direct traffic—Visitors who enter the site via a bookmark in their browser, type in the URL address in their browser, or have the site set as the browser's default home page.

duration of visit—Sometimes referred to as time on site, this metric records the amount of time a visitor is on a website or an on individual web page.

entry page—Also referred to as a landing page, an entry page is any web page through which a visitor enters the site.

event—An action that does not generate a Page View. Also referred to as a pageless experience.

event tracking—Monitoring of actions that do not trigger a page view, such as a file download.

exit page—The last web page a visitor views before leaving or navigating away from the website.

external benchmarking—See *competitive benchmarking*.

filter—Removes unwanted use data before it is collected in the profile of a web analytics tool.

funnel—Tracks the desired pathway to a goal page in the URL destination goal report.

goal tracking—Monitoring and reporting of identified conversions.

goal—Another term for conversion; not to be mistaken for website goals, which involve strategic planning for a website.

heat map—A click-density report that shows areas of high and low traffic using color; the warmer the color (yellows, oranges, or reds), the greater the usage.

hit—A request to a web server. Hits can be triggered by a person's web browser downloading a web page and related files and by nonhuman robots or spiders indexing a website.

internal benchmarking—See *self-benchmarking*.

IP address–Also known as Internet protocol address, this is a unique number assigned by an Internet service provider that can identify an individual computer on a network.

key performance indicator—Abbreviated to KPI, this custom metric is designed to measure the desired actions on a website. A KPI could be a conversion or a standard metric—whatever it takes to measure a website's goals.

macro conversion—The main desired outcome for a website translated into a measurable conversion.

metric–A unit of measurement in web analytics. Page view is an example of a simple metric, whereas bounce rate is a complex metric because it is the total number of bounces divided by total visits to the web page.

micro conversion—Secondary desired outcome for a website translated into a measurable conversion.

mobile analytics—A subset of web analytics that focuses on mobile device users or analyzing mobile websites and applications.

mobile user—A visitor who accesses a website using a mobile device, such as a tablet or smart phone.

new visitor—A visitor who has not been previously tracked on the website. While not perfect, this metric implies that this is the first time the user visited the site.

outbound link—A link that navigates users away from the current site to a different site on a separate domain.

page depth–See *pages per visit*.

page view—The accessing of a single web page or online document by a visitor.

pages per visit—Sometimes noted as page depth, this metric averages the number of web pages visitors view before exiting the site.

path analysis—Also called navigation summary, path analysis demonstrates how visitors navigate a website by listing the web page by web page path a visitor uses to guide him- or herself through the site.

referral traffic—Visitors who are directed to a website from links on other, outside websites.

referring sources—Also called referrers, this metric identifies how a visitor found a website. There are three referring sources: direct traffic, referral traffic, and search traffic.

report—A combination of metrics in a single document that is designed to analyze a selected aspect of the data.

regex—An abbreviation for "regular expression," a syntax that allows you to match a string of text.

returning visitor—A visitor who has previously visited the website and is currently being tracked in the web analytics tool.

search traffic—Visitors who enter a website from a web search engine like Google or Bing.

segment—A metric used to create a subset of data in a report.

segmentation—The process of temporarily removing unnecessary data from a report to create a subset of data to analyze.

self-benchmarking—The process of comparing previous data to current data to monitor changes in use.

semicustom report—Standard report that allows for some customization either through the applying of segments or the visualization of data for improved data analysis.

session—Also referred to as a visit, which is a set of interactions on a website from an individual browser that is initiated when a visitor enters the site and ends when that visitor exits or the session times out.

site overlay—A click-density report that displays click data for links or tracked objects over a snapshot or live version of a web page.

standard report—A report generated in a web analytics tool out of the box.

tracking code—A snippet of code (typically in JavaScript) that must be added to every single web page you want a web analytics tool to track. Also known as page tagging.

Time on site—See *duration of visit*.

top content report—A standard report that reveals the most popular web pages on a site by either page views or visits.

unique visitor—A visitor who is counted only once regardless of how many times the visitor accesses a website within a specific period.

205

visit—Also referred to as a session, which is a set of interactions on a website from an individual browser that is initiated when a visitor enters the site and ends when that visitor exits or the session times out.

visitor—An Internet browser on a computer or device that accesses a website.

web analytics—The process of collecting and analyzing website use data.

web analytics strategy—The structured process of identifying and evaluating your key performance indicators on the basis of the website's goals.

web analytics tool—Software or technology that tracks and measures website use data.

web beacon—A small, transparent image that is used to track web pages or other online objects such as email. Web beacons are a type of page tagging method for web analytics tools.

web server log—A text file that records the requests to the web server.

Web Analytics Tool Profiles

Information about any type of software becomes out of date and/or incomplete as soon as it is collected, much less published. However, this section aims to provide a shopping list of potential analytics products for you to explore. We feature the products mentioned in the preceding chapters and note a few honorable mentions of products that we have not discussed but that have established themselves as players in the web analytics market. This is by no means an exhaustive list, and new players enter—and leave—the field regularly. For a more complete and up-to-date listing of analytics tools on the market, see the website AboutAnalytics (www.aboutanalytics.com).

Alexa

Vendor: Alexa
URL: www.alexa.com
Pricing: Intro account (free), basic subscription (small monthly fee), advanced subscription (moderate monthly fee)
Hosting: Remote
Support: FAQs and help desk (ticketing)
Open source: No
Tracking type: Not applicable
Features and suggested uses for libraries: Useful for benchmarking and competitive analytics; provides a global perspective of site performance
See chapter(s): 5

AWStats

Vendor: Not applicable
URL: http://awstats.sourceforge.net/
Pricing: Free
Hosting: Local only
Support: Documentation and user forums
Open source: Yes
Type: Log file analyzer
Features and suggested uses for libraries: Works well on large legacy sites that are not contained in a web content management system (CMS) or on which it would otherwise be difficult to implement tagging solutions (e.g., JavaScript, web beacons)
See chapter(s): 1, 2, 3, 8

Bango Analytics

Vendor: Bango

URL: http://bango.com/mobileanalytics/

Pricing: Standard (moderate monthly cost), advanced (high monthly cost), and service-level options

Hosting: Remote and/or vendor only

Support: Depends on service level; knowledge base for lower, 24/7 email and phone support for higher

Open source: No

Type: Web beacon

Features and suggested uses for libraries: General tracking and reporting use of mobile library sites

See chapter(s): 7

ClickHeat

Vendor: LabsMedia

URL: www.labsmedia.com/clickheat/index.html

Pricing: Free

Hosting: Local only

Support: Bug tracking system (open to all)

Open source: Yes

Type: JavaScript tagging

Features and suggested uses for libraries: Features heat maps, including "hot" and "cold" zones, which show where users are and are not clicking on a web page—this can be particularly helpful during a website redesign

See chapter(s): 4

ClickTale

Vendor: ClickTale

URL: www.clicktale.com

Pricing: Limited free plan, bronze (moderate monthly fee), silver (moderate monthly fee) and gold (high monthly fee) plans

Hosting: Remote and/or vendor only

Support: FAQs, tutorials, wiki, forums

Open source: No

Type: JavaScript tagging

Features and suggested uses for libraries: Includes mouse tracking, heat map, and conversion suites; records mouse movements of entire visitor sessions; useful for seeing exactly how users move through the site; expensive but provides a great deal of information about user behavior, but is probably too expensive for most library environments to fully implement (most features can be found in other free or low-cost solutions)

See chapter(s): 1

Crazy Egg

Vendor: Crazy Egg

URL: www.crazyegg.com

Pricing: Free trials are available for thirty days, after which monthly subscription is required; basic, standard, plus, and pro plans available, all under $100 per month.

Hosting: Remote and/or vendor only

Support: Help center, FAQ, email and phone

Open source: No

Type: JavaScript tagging

Features and suggested uses for libraries: Heat map, scroll map, overlay, and "confetti" reports, all highly useful for observing user behavior during the redesign process and beyond

See chapter(s): 3, 4, 6

FireStats

Vendor: Not applicable
URL: http://firestats.cc/
Pricing: Free for noncommercial use
Hosting: Remote and local
Support: Bug tracking and ticketing, blog, FAQ, discussion groups (Google groups)
Open source: No
Type: Log file analyzer
Features and suggested uses for libraries: Integrates into WordPress, Drupal, Joomla!, and MediaWiki; security features; API for more extensive customization
See chapter(s): 11

Flurry

Vendor: Not applicable
URL: www.flurry.com
Pricing: Free
Hosting: Remote
Support: FAQ, blog, support center, email
Open source: No
Type: Tagging for different mobile platforms
Features and suggested uses for libraries: Tracking code automatically generated for the most popular mobile platforms (iOS, Android, Blackberry, Windows Phone, JavaME, and HTML 5) and can be added after the mobile application is already finished; robust web analytics capabilities, including goal funnels, segmentation, and conversions
See chapter(s): 7

Google Analytics

Vendor: Google Inc.
URL: www.google.com/analytics
Pricing: standard: free; premium: flat annual fee
Hosting: Remote and/or vendor only
Support: Standard: help center, forums, blogs; premium: 24/7 support
Open source: No
Type of tracking: JavaScript tagging
Features and suggested uses for libraries: An analytics industry leader; excellent for general statistics collection in most library web environments; has extensive data segmentation, filtering, and reporting capabilities, and integrates well with web content management systems and other library products
See chapter(s): All

Open Web Analytics

Vendor: Not applicable
URL: www.openwebanalytics.com
Pricing: Free
Hosting: Local only
Support: Documentation wiki, forums, bug tracking, mailing list
Open source: Yes
Type: JavaScript tagging (but requires local download for data storage)
Features and suggested uses for libraries: Integrates easily into WordPress, Drupal, and MediaWiki; unlimited tracking; includes reporting on heat maps and mouse movement
See chapter(s): 3

209

Piwik

Vendor: OpenX
URL: http://piwik.org/
Pricing: Free
Hosting: Local only
Support: Documentation, FAQs, blog, forum
Open source: Yes
Type: JavaScript tagging (but requires local download for data storage)
Features and suggested uses for libraries: Touted as an open-source response to Google Analytics; provides general-purpose website data tracking and reporting; mobile app available
See chapter(s): 1, 3, 4, 11

StatCounter

Vendor: StatCounter
URL: http://statcounter.com/
Pricing: Free, paid account (small monthly fee)
Hosting: Remote and/or vendor only
Support: Knowledge base and forums
Open source: No
Type: JavaScript tagging
Features and suggested uses for libraries: Built-in exit link reporting; supports real-time monitoring; good for general-purpose tracking and reporting; stores a summary of stats with a deeper analysis of the data from the previous 500 page views, but not ideal for sites with more than 250,000 page views a month
See chapter(s): 9

Webalizer

Vendor: Not applicable
URL: www.webalizer.org
Pricing: Free
Hosting: Local only
Support: FAQ and "Simpleton's Guide to Web Server Analysis"
Open source: Yes
Type: Log file analyzer
Features and suggested uses for libraries: Extensive language support; fast; command line report configuration; perhaps not user-friendly to those who are not system administrators
See chapter(s): Not applicable

Yahoo! Web Analytics

Vendor: Yahoo!
URL: http://web.analytics.yahoo.com
Pricing: Free but currently only available to Yahoo! small business merchants and those supported by a Yahoo! account manager
Hosting: Remote only
Support: Help center, blog, forum, FAQs, glossary
Open source: No
Type: JavaScript tagging
Features and suggested uses for libraries: Yahoo!'s answer to Google Analytics—good for general all-purpose reporting; includes real-time data tracking; most libraries cannot use because it is tied to merchant and commercial Yahoo! accounts
See chapter(s): Not applicable

Bibliography and Suggested Resources

General Web Analytics Resources

Clifton, Brian. 2010. *Advanced Web Metrics with Google Analytics*. 2nd ed. Indianapolis, IN: Wiley.

Kaushik, Avinash. 2007. *Web Analytics: An Hour a Day*. Indianapolis, IN: Sybex.

———. 2010. *Web Analytics 2.0: The Art of Online Accountability and Science of Customer Centricity*. Indianapolis, IN: Wiley.

Marek, Kate. 2011. *Using Web Analytics in the Library*. Chicago: ALA TechSource.

Blogs

Cutroni, Justin. *Analytics Talk: Untangling the World of Web Analytics*. http://cutroni.com/blog/.

Kaushik, Avinash. *Occam's Razor*. www.kaushik.net/avinash/.

Peterson, Eric T., Adam Greco, John Lovett, and Brian Hawkins. *Web Analytics Demystified*. www.webanalyticsdemystified.com/wad-weblogs.asp.

Web Analytics and Usability

Arendt, Julie, and Cassie Wagner. 2010. "Beyond Description: Converting Web Site Usage Statistics into Concrete Site Improvement Ideas." *Journal of Web Librarianship* 4, no. 1: 37–54.

Asunka, Stephen, Chae Hui Soo, Brian Hughes, and Gary Natriello. 2009. "Understanding Academic Information Seeking Habits through Analysis of Web Server Log Files: The Case of the Teachers College Library Website." *Journal of Academic Librarianship* 35, no. 1: 33–45.

Breeding, Marshall. 2008. "An Analytical Approach to Assessing the Effectiveness of Web-Based Resources." *Computers in Libraries* 28, no. 1: 20–22.

Cohen, Laura B. 2003. "A Two-Tiered Model for Analyzing Library Website Usage Statistics, Part 1: Web Server Logs." *portal: Libraries and the Academy* 3, no. 2: 315–326.

Cohen, Laura B. 2003. "A Two-Tiered Model for Analyzing Library Website Usage Statistics, Part 2: Log File Analysis." *portal: Libraries and the Academy* 3, no. 3: 517–526.

Farney, Tabatha A. 2011. "Click Analytics: Visualizing Web Site Use Data." *Information Technology and Libraries* 30, no. 3: 141–148.

Lehman, Tom, and Terry Nikkel. 2008. *Making Library Web Sites Usable: A LITA Guide.* New York: Neal-Schuman.

Jung, Seikyung, Jonathan L. Herlocker, and Janet Webster. 2007. "Click Data as Implicit Relevance Feedback in Web Search." *Information Processing and Management* 43, no. 3: 791–807.

Turner, Steven J. 2010. "Website Statistics 2.0: Using Google Analytics to Measure Library Website Effectiveness." *Technical Services Quarterly* 27, no. 3: 261–278.

Whang, Michael. 2007. "Measuring the Success of the Academic Library Website Using Banner Advertisements and Web Conversion Rates: A Case Study." *Journal of Web Librarianship* 1, no. 1: 93–108.

Library Specific Uses of Web Analytics

Black, Elizabeth L. 2009. "Web Analytics: A Picture of the Academic Library Web Site User." *Journal of Web Librarianship* 3, no. 1: 3–14.

Archives or Special Collections

Herold, Irene M. H. 2010. "Digital Archival Image Collections: Who Are the Users?" *Behavioral and Social Sciences Librarian* 29, no. 4: 267–282.

Prom, Christopher J. 2011. "Using Web Analytics to Improve Online Access to Archival Resources." *American Archivist* 74, no. 1: 158–184.

Library Catalogs

Brown, Christopher C. 2011. "Knowing Where They Went: Six Years of Online Statistics via the OPAC for Federal Government Information." *College and Research Libraries* 72, no. 1: 43–61.

Kilzer, Rebekah D. 2008. "Using Google Analytics for the Proprietary OPAC." *Knowledge Bank.* http://hdl.handle.net/1811/31951.

Wei, Fang, and Marjorie E. Crawford. 2008. "Measuring Law Library Catalog Web Site Usability: A Web Analytic Approach." *Journal of Web Librarianship* 2, nos. 2–3: 287–306.

Public Services

Welch, Jeane M. 2005. "Who Says We're Not Busy? Library Web Page Usage as a Measure of Public Service Activity." *Reference Services Review* 33, no. 4: 371–379.

About the Authors and Chapter Contributors

AUTHORS

Tabatha Farney

Tabatha Farney (tfarney@uccs.edu) is the web services librarian for the Kraemer Family Library at the University of Colorado Colorado Springs, where she actively explores and implements various web analytics tools in her library's web presences. She has presented sessions related to web analytics at several national conferences and looks forward to continuing her research in website data analysis. Tabatha earned an MS in library and information science from the University of Illinois at Urbana-Champaign and was named a 2011 ALA Emerging Leader.

Nina McHale

Nina McHale (nmchale@ald.lib.co.us, ninermac.net) is assistant systems administrator at the Arapahoe Library District, which is located in metropolitan Denver, Colorado. In addition to web analytics, her research interests include open-source web development, user experience design (UXD), web accessibility (Section 508 and Web Content Accessibility Guidelines), knowledge management in libraries, and emerging technologies in libraries. She has presented nationally on these and other topics and was named a 2012 Library Journal Mover & Shaker.

CONTRIBUTORS

CHRISTOPHER C. BROWN (christopher.brown@du.edu), associate professor, is reference technology integration librarian at the University of Denver, Penrose

Library. He is also coordinator for government documents and currently serves on the Depository Library Council to the U.S. Public Printer. His research interests include tracking online usage of government publications, integration of discovery tools into library services, and the future of reference services. He has been an adjunct professor at the University of Denver's Library and Information Science program for more than thirteen years.

TARA L. COLEMAN (tcole2@k-state.edu) is the web services librarian and associate professor at Kansas State University Libraries in Manhattan, Kansas. She is responsible for the oversight of a well-managed web presence and is the lead in design, usability, content, and function of the libraries' websites. Tara cochairs the K-State Book Network (KSBN), the university's common reading program, and she serves on K-State First, the university's first-year experience program. She received a BA in English at Kansas State University and an MLIS from the University of Oklahoma.

HARRIETT E. GREEN (green19@illinois.edu) is the English and digital humanities librarian and assistant professor of library administration at the University of Illinois at Urbana-Champaign. Her research interests include use and users of digital humanities tools, research workflows of humanities scholars with digital resources, and humanities data curation. She earned her MSLIS from the University of Illinois, and she holds an MA in humanities from the University of Chicago.

JOELLE PITTS (jopitts@ksu.edu) is the instructional design librarian and assistant professor at Kansas State University Libraries. She is responsible for the creation and maintenance of web-based learning objects and environments aimed at improving the information literacy of the Kansas State University community. Joelle's research interests include distance education and the role of libraries in e-learning, as well as the development of learning analytics for personalized instruction. She holds degrees in agricultural business and library science.

JORDAN RUUD (jordan.ruud@gmail.com) earned his MS in library and information science in 2012 from the Graduate School of Library and Information Science at the University of Illinois at Urbana-Champaign. He also holds a BA and an MA in English literature from the University of Tulsa.

JUNIOR TIDAL (jtidal@citytech.cuny.edu) is the multimedia and web services librarian and assistant professor for the Ursula C. Schwerin Library at the New York City College of Technology of the City University of New York. His research interests include usability, web metrics, and information architecture. Originally from Whitesburg, Kentucky, he has earned a master's degree in Information science and library science from Indiana University.

ANDREW WALSH (walshandj@gmail.com) earned his MSLIS in 2012 from the Graduate School of Library and Information Science at the University of Illinois at Urbana-Champaign. He also holds a BA in Spanish from Grinnell College.

Index

A

access-denied errors, 190–191
action, event tracking and, 65
action-oriented analytics, 79–93, 203
administrators
    data and, 104–106
    as decision makers, 96–98
Advanced Web Metrics (Clifton), 159, 164
Akismet (plug-in), 185–186, 196
Alexa (website), 84, 207
Analytics Data API, 75
Apache Lucene, 168–170
Apache SOLR, 168–170
API keys, 185
application programming interfaces (APIs),
    111–113
Association of Research Librarians, 7
audit of content, 138–140
auto-oriented analytics
    benchmarking, 79–84, 203
    data and, 87–90
    redesign process, 90–92
    strategy, 84–87
Automatic (developer), 185
AWStats
    Kansas State University, 132–134
    new versus returning visitors, 20
    overview, 207
    redesign and, 132–134
    reports, 139
    robots and spider visitors, 38
    tracking methods, 33

B

Ballard, Terry, 175
Bango (mobile tool), 121, 208
behavior data, decision makers and,
    104
benchmarking, 79–84, 203
best-practices, 180
    Drupal and WordPress, 199–200
    Google Analytics and, 180
    highlights, 165
Blackboard (management tool), 25
Blaine, Anna, 175
board, reports and, 105
bounce rate
    about, 27
    board and, 105
    core standard metrics and, 52
    defined, 203
    key performance indicators, 91
    tracking mobile use, 126–127
    University of Illinois, 164
branding, defined, 119
Brockman, William, 148, 164
browsers
    hits on, 5
    LibraryThing's Shelf Browse, 169,
        178
    mobile types, 115–116
    reports for, 4
    types of, 21
    virtual shelf, 177
Bryne, Tony, 34

C

"came from" reports, 162
CAPTCHA, 196
case studies
    City University of New York, 183–201
    Kansas State University, 131–145
    University of Denver, 167–181
    University of Illinois, 147–166
categories, event tracking and, 65
chaining, 164
Chuang, Ta-Tao, 32
City University of New York (CUNY),
    183–201
Clarke, Arthur C., 7
click-density analysis reports, 59–61,
    101, 203
ClickHeat, 59, 208
ClickTale (analytic tool), 6, 208
ClickTale Mobile (mobile tool), 121
Clifton, Brian, 159, 164
coders, 96–100
codes, 65, 157
Cohen, Laura B., 98
communicating website usage
    about, 95–96
    best practices in, 106–109
    data access, 96–98
    decisions regarding, 141–142
    identifying needs, 98–106
    technology of, 109–114
comparisons, 107
Compete (website), 84
competitive benchmarking, 79–84, 203
comprehensive versus specialized tools,
    40–42
concepts and terms, 203–206
content
    audit of, 138–140
    board and, 105
    changing contributors, 95
    contributor data and, 100–102
    defined, 205
    reports for, 8–9, 16–17, 124–125
    segmenting, 57
content management systems (CMS), 6,
    95–96, 120
contributors, 96–97, 101

conversions
    adding value, 73–74
    defined, 203
    goals and, 28
    poorly performing, 92
    reports, 68–69
    tracking mobile use, 126–127
    web analytic tools and, 70–73
cookies
    mobile browsers and, 116
    new versus returning visitors and, 20
    tracking codes, 5–7
core modules, Drupal, 189–193
core reporting API, 35, 111–113
core standard metrics, 52
cost, analytic tools and, 32
COUNTER initiative, 167
Crazy Egg (website), 41, 59, 61, 101, 208
custom reports, 74–77
    about, 74–75
    conversion reporting and, 76–78
    creating, 75–76
    defined, 203

D

dashboard, Piwik, 194
data
    accessibility and simplicity, 106–108
    accuracy of, 9–11
    administrators and, 104–106
    coders and managers, 99–100
    comparisons, 81–82, 199
    comprehensive versus specialized tools,
        40–42
    content contributors, 100–102
    decay of, 82
    decision makers and, 102–104
    keyword, 161–162
    outbound links, 38–39
    real-time and delayed, 35–36
    redesigning incomplete, 143–144
    reporting data, 39–40
    review of, 45
    robots as visitors, 37–38
    storage of, 5
    support for, 40
    tracking, 32–34, 37

data comparison, 81
data storage, 34–35
dead links, 89
deans, as administrators, 98
Deep Log Analyzer, 33
delayed reporting, 35–36
DeNardis, Nick, 139
department heads, as administrators, 98
design
    AWStats, 132–134
    challenges and solutions, 143–144
    communicating decisions, 141–142
    Google Analytics, 134
    LibQual Lite, 134–136
    LibStats, 136–137
    organizational politics and, 144
    redesign toolbox, 132
    using analytics in, 131–132
device, defined, 118
Digital Analytics Association, 15, 26
direct traffic, 25, 203
directors, as administrators, 98
Django, 187
downloading files, 64
Drupal
    best practices, 199–200
    City University of New York, 183–201
    content management systems, 6, 95–96,
        120
duration of visits, 17–18, 52
Dynamic Host Configuration Protocol
        (DHCP), 20
dynamic scripts, 64

E
email reports, automatic, 111–112
embedded objects, 64
Encore interface, 168–170
entry and exit pages
    about, 24
    entry defined, 203
    exit defined, 204
    University of Illinois, 158–161
error pages, 198
error reporting, 89
evaluation
    analytics and, 151

exporting reports, 111
tool access, 110
event tracking, 65–66
    codes for, 65
    defined, 203
    types of, 64–68
Excellent Analytics (plug-in), 112–113
exporting reports, 110–111
extensions, WordPress, 185
external benchmarking, 79–84, 203

F
Facebook Insights (website), 41
facet use, 176
features, tools and, 37–42
FeedBurner, 41
files
    downloading, 64
    requests for, 5
filters
    creating, 23
    defined, 204
    process of, 58
FireStats (tool), 187–188, 209
Flash support, 22
Flurry, 209
footnote chasing, 164
403 errors, 191
404 errors, 36, 89, 99, 190
functionality of websites, 99–100
funnels
    defined, 204
    goals and, 71–72
    visualization of, 73

G
garbage data, 37
general public license (GPL), 184
geographic location
    IP addresses and, 22–24
    privacy and, 12–13
    segmenting and, 56
    tracking and, 10–11
    University of Illinois, 153
goals
    conversion reporting and, 28,
        70–73

goals (cont.)
    defined, 204
    web analytics and, 27–28
Greco, Adam, 37
groups, tracking, 10–11

H
heat maps, 59, 61, 204
help pages, 26
hits, Internet browsers and, 5, 204
Hitwise, 83
home page revisions, 140–141
HTTP cookies, 116

I
In-Page reports, 60
individuals, tracking, 11
inflated page view, 134
Innovative Interfaces Inc. (III), 168–170
input selector, defined, 119
internal statistics, 185
Internet browser hits, 5
Internet protocol (IP), 10–11
Internet Service Provider (ISP), 12, 23–24
inventory of web presence, 44
IP addresses
    defined, 204
    geographic locations and, 22–24
    handling of, 13
    new versus returning visitors, 19–21
    segmenting and, 56
IP Location Finder, 12–13

J
Java support, 22
JavaScript, 5–6, 22, 33, 116
job responsibilities, analytics and, 8
Joomla!, 187
jQuery, 66–67

K
Kansas State University, 131–145
Kaushik, Avinash
    best practices, 106
    codes, 6
    event tracking, 64
    metrics and reports, 16

multiple tools, 42
Occam's Razor blog, 26, 28
testing tools, 46
tracking mobile data, 116–117
key performance indicators
    about, 28
    defined, 204
    University of Colorado Colorado
        Springs, 85–86
keywords report, 26
Kilzer, Rebekah D., 172
KissMetrics (mobile tool), 121

L
labels, event tracking and, 65
landing pages, 54, 62
Lehman, Thomas, 11, 22
LibGuides, 97, 120
LibNotes, 38
LibQual Lite, 134–136
LibraryBuzz (blog), 184
LibraryThing's Shelf Browse, 169, 178
LibStats, 136–137
limitations, web analytics, 9–11
links, outbound, 38–39, 61
Literatures and Languages Library, 148
location, segmenting and, 56
log entries, 190
log files, 5
Lovett, John, 87

M
macro and micro conversions, 69–70, 204
Making Library Websites Usable (Lehman and
    Nikkel), 11, 22
management API, 111–113
map overlay report, 23
Marek, Kate, 13
marketing campaign testing, 90
Massey-Burzio, Virginia, 165
measurements in web analytics, 9–10
MediaWiki, 187
metrics
    bounce rate, 27
    core standard, 52
    defined, 15–16, 204
    mobile analytics and, 117–121

mobile browsers and, 115
path analysis reports, 62–63
referrers and, 24–26
reports and, 15–16
reports to board, 105
simple and accessible, 106–108
micro and macro conversions, 69–70, 204
Millennium, 168–170
mobile analytics
about, 115
challenges in tracking, 116–117
defined, 204
metrics, reports, and tools, 117–121
overview reports, 117
tracking use, 126–127
web analytics in, 121–126
mobile devices
communicating to board, 105
development projects, 122
and nonmobile segmenting, 56–57
nonmobile tracking versus, 34
overview report, 117
reports for, 118
tracking use, 126–127
users defined, 204
mobile versus nonmobile tracking, 34
Mouseflow, 60
multiple tool usage, 149
MySQL, 184

N

Nakatani, Kazuo, 32
navigation
improving, 141
summaries, 62–63
Neumann, Laura, 148, 165
new visitors
board and, 105
defined, 204
new versus returning visitors, 19–21, 52,
152–153
Nikkel, Terry, 11, 22
nonbounced visits, 57
nonmobile versus mobile tracking, 34

O

OAuth 2.0, 113

Occam's Razor (website), 26, 28
Omniture (analytic tool), 6
online catalog usage, 167–181
online public access catalog (OPAC), 136
open source tools, 132–134
open web analytics, 35, 59, 67, 209
OpenID, 113
operating systems
data tracking and, 10–11
defined, 119
visitor technology and, 21
opt-out procedures, 13
OS technology report, 4
outbound links
analytics and, 39
click density and, 61
defined, 204
event tracking and, 64
University of Colorado Colorado
Springs, 38–39
OverDrive, 25
overview, 209

P

page-level reports, 100
page-not-found errors, 192–193
pages
individual, 57
per visit, 71, 205
reports, 16
tagging, 33
views and visits, 16–24, 52, 204
Pages Report, 16
Palmer, Carole, 148, 165
path analysis
defined, 205
reports, 62–64
pattern-matching tools, 76
percent mobile, 119–120
performance indicators, 27–28
pie charts, 107
Piwik (analytic tool)
about, 34
Analytics Data API, 75
Drupal module, 193–195
heat maps and, 59
mobile analytics and, 121

Piwik (analytic tool) (cont.)
overview, 210
tracking outbound links, 39
platform considerations, 123–124
poor performing goals or reports, 92
portal model, 18
print-based referrals, 90
privacy in web analytics
about, 13–14
geographic location and, 22–24
new versus returning visitors, 20–21
project implementation questions, 171–178

Q
Quick Response code (QR), 90

R
real-time reporting, 35–36
redesign decisions, 138–141, 144
referral sources, 52, 55, 153–156, 205
referral traffic, 25, 205
referrers, 24–26
referring websites, 197–198
Regex, 76, 205
reports
access-denied, 190–191
applying segments, 53–54
automatic email types, 111–112
AWStats, 139
"came from," 162
by city, 23
click-density, 101
communicating data, 108–109, 141–142
comparing, 37–42
contents of, 8–9
conversion types, 68–69
custom types, 74–77
customizing, 51–52
data comparison, 81
defined, 205
event-tracking, 66
exporting, 110–111
goal types, 70–73
keywords, 26
landing page report, 54
LibStats, 137
metrics and, 15–16

mobile analytics and, 117–121
page-level, 100
page-not-found errors, 192–193
poor performing, 92
real-time and delayed, 35–36
recent hits, 190
robots and spider visitors, 38
segmentation and, 53–58
segmented goal types, 86
semicustom, 59–68
standard content, 16
top content, 17, 124–125
traffic sources, 25
resources, 211–212
returning visitors, 205
returning versus new visitors, 19–21, 52
revising humanities websites, 147–166
robots as visitors, 37–38, 196–197
rolling migration, redesign and, 138
RSS feeds, adding to conversions, 73–74

S
screen capture tool, 143
screen resolution
defined, 119
visitor technology and, 21–22
Screencast-O-Matic, 143
search engine optimization (SEO), 196
search traffic, 25, 205
searches, comparing, 178
seasonal patterns, adjusting for, 151
security, Piwik, 194–195
segmenting
custom reports, 77–78
defined, 205
filters versus segments, 57–58
useful ideas, 54–57
self-benchmarking, 79–84, 205
semicustom report, 205
Serials Solutions, 170
servers, data storage and, 5
service providers, 56, 119
session defined, 205
site navigation, 141
site overlay defined, 205
Site Stats, 185
spam

prevention filters, 185–186
trackbacks, 197
WordPress, 195–196
specialized versus comprehensive tools,
40–42
spider visitors, 37–38
standard content reports, 16, 205
Standardized Usage Statistics Harvesting
Initiative, 167
StatCounter, 149, 210
storage, 5, 34–35
strategy example, 85–86
Summon discovery tool, 168–170
support, data collection and, 40

T
tables as comparison charts, 107
tacking code, 6–7
tagging, 33
terms and concepts, 203–206
testing
process of, 89–90
questions during, 46–47
Text on 9 Keys (T9), 120
time length of visits, 17–18, 52, 70–71
tips for user analysis, 151
tools
accuracy in data, 9–11
AWStats, 132–134
comparing data, reports, and features,
37–42
cost options, 32
data and storage, 32–35
library needs and, 42–45
mobile analytics and, 117–121
mobile types, 121
new versus returning visitors, 19–21
pattern matching, 76
profiles of, 207–210
real-time and delayed reporting,
35–36
screen capture, 143
segmenting and, 56
testing, 46–48
using multiples, 149
top content
board and, 105

defined, 205
set up, 124–125
tracking
analytics and, 34, 126–127
codes defined, 205
codes for, 5–7
groups, 10–11
IP addresses, 12–13
methods of, 33
mobile sites and, 116–117
online marketing, 90
outbound links, 38–39
scripts, 66
users, 199
traffic
mobile considerations, 132–133
types of, 25
volume of, 101
Twitter feeds, 144

U
unique visitors, 19, 28, 69, 152, 205
University of Denver
about, 167
best practices at, 180
Google Analytics and, 171–179
project background, 168–171
University of Illinois at Urbana-Champaign,
147–166
about, 147–149
adding tools, 162–163
best practices, 164–165
bounce rates, 164
identification and analyzing data,
150–151
identifying targets, 163
multiple tool use, 149
user information, 161–162
user profiling and demographics,
151–157
website structure and organization,
157–161
University of Kansas
about, 131–132
AWStats and, 132–134
communicating decisions, 141–142
content audits, 138–140

University of Kansas (cont.)
    data based decisions, 143–144
    Google Analytics and, 134
    home page revisions, 140–141
    LibQual Lite, 134–136
    LibStats, 136–137
    managing politics, 144
    site navigation, 141
URL destination, 71–72
usability, mobile considerations, 126
user analysis tips, 151
user-friendly sites, redesign and, 138
user groups, 55
user technology, 21–22
users
    administrators and, 105
    behaviors, 91
    privacy and, 12–13
    redesign and, 91
    segmenting behavior, 57
    synthesizing data, 154–157
    tracking groups, 10–11, 199

V
value, event tracking and, 65–66
virtual page view, 134
virtual private network (VPN), 102
virtual shelf browse, 177
visitor technology
    browser type, 21
    coders and managers and, 100
visitors
    defined, 11, 206
    flow analysis, 63
    geographic location, 22–24
    new versus returning, 19–21, 52
    robots as, 37–38
    technology for, 21–22
visits
    defined, 203, 206
    duration of, 52, 57
    page views and, 16–24
Visual IP Locater, 12

Visual Website Optimizer (website), 41
Voyager, 136

W
Warwick, Claire, 148
WassUp (plug-in), 187, 196
web analytics
    action-oriented, 79–93, 203
    communicating website usage, 95–114
    creating customized reports, 51–78
    defined, 206
    driving design, 131–145
    libraries and, 3–29
    mobile analytics and, 115–128
    online catalog usage, 167–181
    optimizing open-source, 183–201
    revising humanities websites,
        147–166
    tool selection, 31–49
Web Analytics Association, 3
web beacons
    challenges with tracking, 116
    defined, 206
    mobile analytics and, 120
    tracking, 33
web log parser, 121
web managers and coders, 96–98
web pages, low-use, 92
web server logs
    about, 33
    analysis and, 5–6
    defined, 206
Webalizer, 210
websites
    data from other libraries, 83–84
    errors and code, 96
    segmenting, 53–58
Webtrends (analytic tool), 6
Webucator (blog, 75
WordPress, 6, 120, 183–201

Y
Yahoo! Web Analytics, 210